MODELS OF CONTEXTUAL THEOLOGY

FAITH AND CULTURES SERIES

An Orbis Series on Contextualizing Gospel and Church
General Editor: Robert J. Schreiter, C.PP.S.

The *Faith and Cultures Series* deals with questions that arise as Christian faith attempts to respond to its new global reality. For centuries Christianity and the church were identified with European cultures.Although the roots of Christian tradition lie deep in Semitic cultures and Africa, and although Asian influences on it are well documented, that original diversity was widely forgotten as the church took shape in the West.

Today, as the churches of the Americas, Asia, and Africa take their place alongside older churches of Mediterranean and North Atlantic cultures, they claim the right to express Christian faith in their own idioms, thought patterns, and cultures.To provide a forum for better understanding this process, the Orbis *Faith and Cultures Series* publishes books that illuminate the range of questions that arise from this global challenge.

Orbis and the *Faith and Cultures Series* General Editor invite the submission of manuscripts on relevant topics.

Also in the Series
Faces of Jesus in Africa, Robert J. Schreiter, C.PP.S., Editor
Hispanic Devotional Piety, C. Gilbert Romero
African Theology in Its Social Context, Bénézet Bujo
Models of Contextual Theology, first edition, Stephen B. Bevans, S.V.D.
Asian Faces of Jesus, R. S. Sugirtharajah, Editor
Evangelizing the Culture of Modernity, Hervé Carrier, S.J.
St. Martín de Porres: "The Little Stories" and the Semiotics of Culture, Alex García-Rivera
The Indian Face of God in Latin America, Manuel M. Marzal, S.J., Eugenio Maurer, S.J., Xavierio Albó, S.J., and Bartomeu Melià, S.J.
Towards an African Narrative Theology, Joseph Healey, M.M., and Donald Sybertz, M.M.
The New Catholicity, Robert Schreiter, C.PP.S
The Earth Is God's: A Theology of American Culture, William A. Dyrness
Mission & Catechesis: Alexandre de Rhodes and Inculturation in Seventeenth-Century Vietnam, Peter C. Phan
Celebrating Jesus Christ in Africa, François Kabasele Lumbala
Popular Catholicism in a World Church: Seven Case Studies in Inculturation, Thomas Bamat and Jean-Paul Wiest, Editors
Inculturation: The New Face of the Church in Latin America, Diego Irarrázaval, C.S.C.
The Bible on Culture: Belonging or Dissenting? Lucien Legrand, M.E.P.

FAITH AND CULTURES SERIES

Models of Contextual Theology

Revised and Expanded Edition

Stephen B. Bevans, SVD

ORBIS BOOKS

Maryknoll, New York 10545

Fifth Printing, September 2005

Founded in 1970, Orbis Books endeavors to publish works that enlighten the mind, nourish the spirit, and challenge the conscience.The publishing arm of the Maryknoll Fathers and Brothers, Orbis seeks to explore the global dimensions of the Christian faith and mission, to invite dialogue with diverse cultures and religious traditions, and to serve the cause of reconciliation and peace.The books published reflect the opinions of their authors and are not meant to represent the official position of the Maryknoll Society.To obtain more information about Maryknoll and Orbis Books, please visit our website at www.maryknoll.org.

Manufactured in the United States of America.

Library of Congress Cataloging-in-Publication Data

Bevans, Stephen B., 1944-
    Models of contextual theology / Stephen B. Bevans.— Rev. and expanded ed.
        p. cm. — (Faith and cultures series)
    Includes bibliographical references and index.
    ISBN 1-57075-438-1 (pbk.)
        1. Theology—Methodology. 2. Christianity and culture.
I. Title.   II. Series.
BR118.B44   2002
230'.01—dc21   2002004748

TO

my mother and father

BERNADETTE O'GRADY BEVANS
(1921-1993)

and

BERT BENNETT BEVANS
(1920-1993)

models of faith and courage

my first context

Contents

Foreword to the Revised and Expanded Edition

ROBERT J. SCHREITER, C.PP.S.

Since the early 1970s, interest in how diverse cultural contexts shape theology has continued to grow. That interest was whetted initially by a number of different factors: the coming to voice of so many Christian communities, the dissatisfaction with some inherited ways of doing theology, the need to find theological expressions more attuned to changing realities. Since that time, the attempts to create theologies critically attuned to culture have multiplied at near exponential rates.

To be sure, not all of these attempts have been immediately successful. Some have been merely calls that such contextual theologies be developed. Others were halting, first steps. Still others found the pervasiveness of imported theologies almost impossible to escape. But contextual theologies have continued to develop, growing out of the reflections of small communities, encounters between cultures, in the praxis of those trying to understand how the Gospel is taking root in local circumstances amid shifting realities. And this proliferation of theologies more sensitive to culture can be found at all levels of Christian life—from small communities where the theologies remain largely oral in form, to more programmatic attempts by the leadership in church bodies to articulate theologies for whole regions and even continents.

After a quarter century of such efforts, reflection on the shape and method of these theologies is very much in order. There are concerns that one sees again and again in the midst of these theologies: Are there patterns discernible in how contextual theologies develop and are brought about? Are there convergences of opinion around the vexing issues of how to ascertain fidelity to the scriptures and church traditions in theologies of markedly different form from what we have known in the past? Are the roles culture can and does play in the shaping of theologies clearer? Are we able to interpret the cultural configurations of past theologies more appropriately because of what we see happening today? While no one would expect definitive answers to any of these questions, one would hope that we have made some headway toward clarifying these vital matters.

Stephen Bevans has done us a great service in proposing a way to think more clearly about the interaction of the gospel message and culture, and about honoring tradition while responding to social change. Using a "model" approach (something now familiar in theology as well as in the social sciences), he provides us a map through the sometimes bewildering array of contextual theologies today—both those that are consciously contextual and those that are best understood from their contexts. He initially proposed five such models, and in this second edition now suggests six: translation, anthropological, praxis, synthetic, transcendental, and countercultural. In so doing, he provides a clear yet flexible way of sorting out some of the ways in which contextual theologies are being constructed. Like any good use of a models approach, each model Bevans presents helps clarify the internal structure of a theology, and his use of a similar structure for the explanation of each model helps us relate models to one another. He notes that these models are not exclusive of one another. Rather they are to be understood heuristically, as a means for understanding contextual theologies better—not just descriptively, but critically as well.

This book is more than a handy map, however. By showing how these models operate in the concrete theological work of a variety of men and women, coming from very different circumstances and responding to very different challenges, Bevans invites us to reflect on our own work in the theological enterprise—be it in small communities, in the wider church, or in the academy. To what elements of a situation does each of the models best respond? How does the interaction of gospel message and culture illumine part of that gospel message most insightfully? And how might each of these models function in my own situation?

Bevans provides us also with something else in his proposal of these six models. In the plurality of theologies and theological methods today, he reminds us that context is part of developing and understanding all theologies. By focusing upon culture in the way he does (recognizing at the same time that even concepts of culture have been shifting), he does provide something of a common ground where different theologies might meet and explore their respective ways of operating. In the conclusion to his book, he does not attempt to rank or otherwise categorize the six models he has presented. He reminds us, rather, that different models will be more or less appropriate to and effective at communicating the gospel in different contexts. To say that the choice of model "depends upon the context" (his closing words) is not a retreat into relativism, but an acknowledgment that now—as in the past—some ways of doing theology have been more compelling for the church than others. Moreover, by calling us back to context, he provides us with an opportunity to understand ever more fully how context—in all its dimensions—may shape our thinking in ways we do not realize.

The first edition of this book appeared ten years ago. In the intervening period, it has shown itself to be an excellent resource and guide for introducing people to the array of contextual theologies. Its clear style and generous use of examples have helped beginning students of theology, as well as those more schooled in theological traditions, understand contextual theologies. In the course of a decade it has gone through nine printings, a clear indication of its widespread use. This new edition not only introduces a sixth model but also makes significant revisions to reflect the developments in thinking about contextual theologies. And readers will find especially helpful the updating and expansion of bibliographic references to work published during the last decade. All of this makes this book an even greater resource for understanding contextual theologies today. We are grateful to Stephen Bevans for this new edition of what has been a pioneering work in contextual theologies. In so doing, he keeps us at the growing edge of one of the most important developments in theology in the contemporary period.

Acknowledgments

I can hardly begin to credit by name all the people who have contributed to the development of this book, but I must name a few. Lenny Mercado has been a friend these past twenty years and has always encouraged me in my work. My students over the years—both in the Philippines and here in Chicago—have been both a challenge and an inspiration to me. I want to mention in particular two students and good friends, Pio Pitawen and Eddie Balicao: Pio died all too young a few years ago, and Eddie became a member of the New Peoples Army, a guerrilla group in the mountains of Luzon. I also want to single out Bob Schreiter, my colleague at Catholic Theological Union and the editor of the Faith and Cultures series of Orbis Books, in which this volume appears. His encouragement and help over the last years have been most generous, and I value him deeply as a friend. Bill Burrows, Managing Editor of Orbis Books, has been best friend and theological-dialogue partner for forty years, and I want to thank him here especially for his patience and confidence in the preparation of this work. I also want to thank my colleagues at Catholic Theological Union at Chicago for their friendship and inspiration over the past six years, especially Barbara Bowe (who read part of the manuscript), Mark Francis, Ana María Pineda, and Barbara Reid. Special thanks goes to Dianne Bergant, Professor of Old Testament here at CTU, whose questions helped me form the idea of the praxis model, and to Phil Gibbs, who read the manuscript while it was in process and who offered a number of useful comments. My SVD brothers Stan Uroda, Roger Schroeder, Gary Riebe-Estrella, Mark Schramm, Ed Peklo, Roger Arnold, Sam Cunningham, Peter De Ta Vo, and Mark Weber continue to be wonderful supports, as have my friends George Reisch, Judy Borchers, Judy Logue, Priscilla and Jack Pope-Levison, and Gene and Nancy Ahner. To the number of students and colleagues who have given me feedback in the ten years that the first edition has been in print, I am extremely grateful. Among literally hundreds who have shown their appreciation for this work, let me mention only Clemens Sedmak, Darrell Whiteman, Peter Phan, Roger Haight, and Eleanor Doidge.

I am dedicating these pages to my mother and father; they were my first context, and they were strong models of courage and faith. They both died from cancer in 1993, soon after the first edition of this book was published. I miss them greatly. To them both go my undying thanks and love.

Preface to the Revised and Expanded Edition

There is a cartoon that I have on the bulletin board in my office that depicts a man bent at the waist with his hand in front of his mouth. On the ground is a book, and in the background one person is telling another: "Everybody's got at least one book in him." In many ways, that is the way I feel about *Models of Contextual Theology*. Since its publication in 1992 I have not been able to find the time to write another monograph. Although I have written a number of articles, have a number of book projects on the way, and have done a fair bit of editing—some six books and work on several periodicals—it has been "the Models book," as I call it, that has provided me some small recognition in the academic world. That so many people over the past ten years have found this little book helpful in their pastoral work and academic scholarship has been truly gratifying, and quite humbling. I have received letters and e-mails about the book from all parts of the world, and I am grateful to students and scholars alike in Britain, Denmark, New Zealand, Irian Jaya, Korea, and Wilmore, Kentucky, for their appreciation and helpful critiques. A number of scholars have even used the five models in the 1992 version of the book as a basis for doctoral dissertations, for example, Eduardo Fernández's dissertation at the Gregorian University, published as *La Cosecha: Harvesting Contemporary United States Hispanic Theology [1972-1998]* (Collegeville, MN: The Liturgical Press, 2000). My friend Gideon Goosen mentions the models prominently in his *Australian Theologies* (Strathfield, Australia: St. Pauls, 2000). And I have been especially honored by the fact that students in the Doctor of Ministry program at Catholic Theological Union, where I have taught theology since 1986, have used the book as a regular text in their "Core Colloquium II," a course that focuses on various methods employed in practical theology.

About a year ago, with the possibility of a Spanish translation (and, subsequently, with additional possibilities of translations into Indonesian and Korean), my friend Bill Burrows at Orbis Books broached the possibility of a new edition. Although I had some hesitations at first (another delay for a book that I am co-authoring with a colleague!), I began to think that Bill's suggestion was a good one. In a number of talks around the United States and abroad, I had learned a good deal more about contextual theology; there were opportunities to make a few corrections of factual errors in the text (for example, regarding polygamy, as pointed out in a letter from Eugene Hillman); and footnotes and bibliographical references needed to be updated. More importantly, I needed to add a new model to the five that I had presented in the first edition. Even as I was working on the original version of the book I began to suspect that there was another way of doing contextual theology that took culture seriously, thoroughly engaged it, but also was thoroughly suspicious of it. I began to conceive of it as a kind of counter-cultural model. But as I worked on the book I realized that the book was already more than a year overdue at Orbis, and that working out another entire model would take a good deal of time. So I sent the book off for publication with only five models.

Less than a year after the book was published I drafted a presentation at a Gospel and Our Culture conference entitled "Doing Theology in North America: A Counter-Cultural Model?" The paper was well received at the conference, and I was grateful for the criticism given, especially by Mike Goheen, who called me to task for a too-negative reading of Lesslie Newbigin. Over the years I floated the model in several other publications and workshops, but I never found the time nor the energy to work it out more fully. This second, revised edition of *Models of Contextual Theology* has at last given me the opportunity. I thank Mike Goheen, George Hunsberger, Mike Baxter, Roxanne Morin, and Joel Shorn for reading the chapter in the form of a first draft, and I am grateful for their critique and corrections (although, as it is customary to say, any errors are my own!). After reading the draft, George Hunsberger still insists that the perspective of the Gospel and Our Culture Network should not be seen as countercultural. We disagree on this, and I have stubbornly held on to my own opinion in this regard.

Besides a few style changes, updating bibliography and biographical information, I have changed very little in most of the text. Had I had more time I would have liked to propose some other examples for the models; but that simply was not possible. There is one significant change, however, that might need more explanation. In the first version of the book I spoke of contextual theology as the process of doing theology that takes seriously (1) the spirit and message of the gospel, (2) the tradition of the Christian people, (3) the culture in which one is theologizing, and (4) social change within that culture. In this second edition I have tried to nuance that definition somewhat. I speak now of contextual theology as taking *two* things seriously: the experience of the *past* (recorded in scripture and preserved and defended in tradition) and the experience of the *present*, that is, *context* (individual and social experience, secular or religious culture, social location, and social change). What I have realized as I have engaged with colleagues and students is, first, we can never divorce ourselves from experience; scripture and tradition, rather than given data, are themselves products of particular, contextual experiences. This does not mean that as data they are not normative, but it does mean that they need to be interpreted. Secondly, rather than simply to speak of *culture* (and only of what Robert Schreiter calls an "integrated" concept of culture), I would prefer to speak of *context*. In the first edition of the book the concept of "culture" was broadened somewhat by the notion of "social change within culture," but I have tried to be even broader in my understanding now. In other words, to use the shorthand expression, we should not speak of "gospel and *culture*," but "gospel and *context*." Contextual theology is done when the experience of the past engages the present context.

I have thanked a number of friends and colleagues on the "Acknowledgement" page. I want to offer special thanks here, however, to Bob and Pat Wheeler for the use of their wonderful cabin on Plantinground Lake in Three Lakes, Wisconsin, during October and November of 2001. The beauty of the Wisconsin autumn, the brilliant lake, the virtually tame deer and the rich solitude that Bob and Pat's generosity provided have shaped a context for writing and rewriting that has also nourished and renewed my soul. I don't think that there is any way to express my gratitude adequately.

Three Lakes, Wisconsin
November 10, 2001

Introduction

In the late 1960s, when I was a theology student in Rome, I remember preparing an Advent liturgy around the theme of the sun. The central idea of the liturgy was based on the song by the Beatles' George Harrison, "Here Comes the Sun" (those were the days of "theme liturgies"), and after playing a recording of the song at the beginning of the homily, I remember saying how it captured the spirit of the liturgy of Advent. Christ was the sun, bringing light to our darkness and warmth to our cold, God-less world—"little darlin', its been a long, cold, lonely winter; little darlin', it seems like years since it's been here; here comes the sun . . . its all right." As a twenty-something child of the sixties, I was very enthusiastic about what I said, and I thought I had really done a good job of interpreting a traditional Christian symbol in contemporary terms.

One of the participants in that liturgy, however—an Indian—was not very impressed. For someone from India, he said, the sun is not a very striking symbol for the coming of Christ into our world. In India, the sun is an enemy. It is not something that brings refreshment; it is something that brings unbearable heat that is to be escaped by staying in the shade. The sun's heat makes men and women thirsty, and too much exposure to the sun causes sunstroke. He could not really relate to a God who comes into the world like the sun, despite the fact that the image is found very frequently in the Advent liturgical texts.

This incident was my first encounter with the fact that some of our predominantly western and northern liturgical and theological images are meaningless in other cultural contexts. I had read about this fact in books. I had heard other people talk about it in student conversations, but this was the first time that I had ever met someone who simply had no use for an idea that really meant something to me and that was deeply nourishing both theologically and spiritually. This incident, in retrospect, marks the beginning of a continuing interest in the possibilities of what theologians have called contextual theology. In a certain sense, this book began to be written that Saturday evening in Rome.

When I arrived as a missionary to the Philippines several years later, one of the first people I talked to was Lenny Mercado. Lenny was just finishing his doctoral dissertation on Filipino philosophy, and in our conversation he challenged me to teach my students *Filipino*, not western, theology. My response was to offer a seminar on Filipino theology in my first semester of teaching at the Immaculate Conception Major Seminary in the small town of Vigan in northern Luzon. The seminar went quite well, and in the several times I offered the seminar subsequently, my ideas about the importance of developing a truly Filipino theology began to take shape.[1] What also began to be clear was that there was no *one* way to construct a Filipino theology. My friend Lenny was convinced that one had to start from the culture of the ordinary Filipino; others, such as Catalino Arévalo and Carlos Abesamis, talked about the "signs of the times" and the oppressed situation of the Filipino people as the proper point of departure. Still others talked about the importance of translating our traditional biblical and doctrinal formulae into Filipino language and thought patterns. I began to see that various approaches or models were not only possible but were actually operative in theologians' various efforts. I wrote a preliminary article about this in 1976.[2] When I returned to the United States, I taught a course entitled Models of Contextual Theology here at Catholic Theological Union in 1984, and published a short article on the topic in the journal *Missiology: An International Review*.[3] The ideas in this book are the result of an expansion and revision of these articles.

Part One

Methodological Issues and Concerns

1

Contextual Theology
as a Theological Imperative

There is no such thing as "theology"; there is only *contextual* theology: *feminist* theology, *black* theology, *liberation* theology, *Filipino* theology, *Asian-American* theology, *African* theology, and so forth. Doing theology contextually is not an option, nor is it something that should only interest people from the Third World, missionaries who work there, or ethnic communities within dominant cultures.[1] The contextualization of theology—the attempt to understand Christian faith in terms of a particular context—is really a theological imperative. As we have come to understand theology today, it is a process that is part of the very nature of theology itself.

In this first chapter I will explore this thesis by first pointing to the discontinuity and continuity of a contextual approach to theology in comparison with traditional or classical theology. Then I will reflect on several factors, both external and internal, that make the contextualization of theology necessary in today's world and in today's understanding of Christian faith.

CONTEXTUAL THEOLOGY AS BOTH NEW AND TRADITIONAL

A contextual approach to theology is in many ways a radical departure from the notion of traditional theology, but at the same time it is very much in continuity with it. To understand theology as contextual is to assert something both new and traditional.[2]

CONTEXTUAL THEOLOGY AS RADICALLY NEW

First of all, contextual theology understands the nature of theology in a new way. Classical theology conceived theology as a kind of objective science of faith. It was understood as a reflection in faith on the two *loci theologici*[3] (theological sources) of scripture and tradition, the content of which has not and never will be changed, and is above culture and historically conditioned expression. But what makes contextual theology precisely *contextual* is the recognition of the validity of another *locus theologicus*: present human experience. Theology that is contextual realizes that culture, history, contemporary thought forms, and so forth are to be considered, along with scripture and tradition, as valid sources for theological expression. And so today we speak of theology as having *three* sources or *loci theologici*: scripture, tradition, and present human experience—or context.

The reason we add experience/context to the traditional theological sources is the revolution in thinking and understanding the world that is characterized as the "turn to the subjective at the beginning of modern times."[4] While classical theology understood theology as something objective, contextual theology understands theology as something unabashedly subjective. By *subjective*, however, I do not mean relative or private or anything like that but the fact that the human person or human society, culturally and historically bound as it is, is the source of reality, not a supposed value- and culture-free objectivity "already out there now real."[5]

As Charles Kraft puts it:

> there is always a difference between reality and human culturally conditioned understandings (models) of that reality. We assume that there is a reality "out there" but it is the mental constructs (models) of that reality inside our heads that are the most real to us. God, the author of reality, exists outside any culture. Human beings, on the other hand, are always bound by cultural, subcultural (including disciplinary), and psychological conditioning to perceive and interpret what they see of reality in ways appropriate to these conditionings. Neither the absolute God nor the reality [God] created is perceived absolutely by culture-bound human beings.[6]

Reality is not just "out there"; reality is "mediated by meaning,"[7] a meaning that we give it in the context of our culture or our historical period, interpreted from our own particular horizon and in our own particular thought forms. United States Americans, for example, see "rice," whether it is just about to be harvested, drying in the sun, or cooked on the table; Filipinos have particular names for each of these forms of rice: *sinaing* (plain steamed rice), *sinangag* (fried rice), *tutong* (fire-burnt rice at the bottom of the cooking pot), *bahaw* (left-over rice), *tugaw* (rice porridge), *suman* (sticky rice), and *am* (rice broth usually given to babies).[8] Anthony Gittins says that "many Pacific languages contain a whole repertoire of words for kinds of water—words that mark flow and eddy, drift, current, waveheight, and numerous shades of meaning."[9] And Asian languages reflect a view of the world that is strongly hierarchical and reflective of the respect that Asians hold for people in authority. Our world is not just *there*; we are involved in its construction. We do not simply see, Ian Barbour points out; we only "see as."[10]

As our cultural and historical context plays a part in the construction of the reality in which we live, so our context influences the understanding of God and the expression of our faith. The time is past when we can speak of one, right, unchanging theology, a *theologia perennis*. We can only speak about a theology that makes sense at a certain place and in a certain time. We can certainly learn from others (synchronically from other cultures and diachronically from history), but the theology of others can never be our own. Henri Bouillard once said that a theology that is not up-to-date (French: *actuelle*) is a false theology. I think we can paraphrase Bouillard by saying that a theology that is not somehow reflective of our times, our culture, and our current concerns—and so contextual—is also a false theology. Charles Kraft says practically the same thing when he says that theology, when it is perceived as irrelevant, *is in fact* irrelevant.[11]

Not until our own time (as we have reaped the positive benefits of the Enlightenment's discovery of subjectivity and the nineteenth century's discovery of historical consciousness)[12] have theologians been so aware of the importance of context in constructing human thought and—at least in the minds of some—of the sacredness of context in terms of God's revelation. Indeed, when we say that there are three sources for theology, we are not just adding context as a third element; *we are changing the whole equation.*

When we recognize the importance of context for theology, we are also ac-knowledging the absolute importance of context for the development of both scrip-ture and tradition. The writings of scripture and the content, practices, and feel of tradition did not simply fall from the sky. They themselves are products of human beings and *their* contexts. They have been developed by human beings, written and conceived in human terms, and conditioned by human personality and human circumstances. As we study scripture and tradition, we not only have to be aware of their inevitable contextual nature; we have to read and interpret them within *our own* context as well.

We can say, then, that doing theology contextually means doing theology in a way that takes into account two things. First, it takes into account the faith experi-ence of the *past* that is recorded in scriptures and kept alive, preserved, defended—and perhaps even neglected or suppressed[13]—in tradition. A major part of the theological process, insists Douglas John Hall, "is simply *finding out* about the Christian theological past."[14] Second, contextual theology takes into account the experience of the present, the *context*. While theology needs to be faithful to the full experience and contexts of the past, it is authentic theology only "when what has been received is appropriated, made our own. For that to happen, the received tradition must of course pass through the sieve of our own individual and contemporary-collective experience: we cannot give it, profess it as ours, unless such a process occurs."[15]

This "individual and contemporary-collective experience," or context, is rather complex and represents a combination of several realities. First, context includes the experiences of a person's or group's personal life: the experiences of success, failure, births, deaths, relationships, and so forth, that allow persons to, or prevent persons from, experiencing God in their lives. There are also experiences of life—personal or communal—in our contemporary world: moments of tragedy such as the genocide and explosion of refugees in Rwanda and Burundi in the 1990s and the September 11, 2001, terrorist attacks on New York City and Washington, D. C., in the United States; or moments of wonderment such as the 1986 "People Power" revolution in the Philippines, the heady times in Europe at the end of 1989, and the televised marvel of the millennium dawning in Kiribati, Paris, London, and New York.

Second, personal or communal experience is possible only within the context of culture, that "system of inherited conceptions expressed in symbolic forms by means of which people communicate, perpetuate, and develop their knowledge about and attitudes toward life."[16] Such culture, it seems to me, can be either "secular" or "religious." A "secular" culture might be a culture such as that of Europe, North America, New Zealand, or Australia and would comprise the values and customs of a particular group of people. A "religious" culture might be a culture such as that of India, where values and customs are permeated with the symbols and myths of a religious system such as Hinduism. Not only the values and customs of a people need to be engaged, therefore, in contextual theology; often the religion of peoples needs to be understood and appreciated. The Asian bishops have spoken eloquently of a threefold dialogue, with Asian poverty (about which we will reflect below), Asian cultures, and Asian religions. It is to these last two aspects that this understanding of context as "culture" refers.[17]

Third, we can speak of context in terms of a person's or a community's "social location." It makes a difference, both feminist and liberation theologians have insisted,[18] whether one is male or female, rich or poor, from North America or Latin America, at the center or at the margins of power. Social location can be a limiting factor in some ways, but it can also be a position from which one can detect flaws or riches in the tradition. It can be a position from which one can ask questions never before asked or entertained in theological reflection. As theologians do theology, their social location needs to be acknowledged and even embraced. We can certainly move beyond our social locations, and our "etic" insights can be important in particular situations (see my discussion of this in Chapter 2). However, we disregard who we are only at the risk of doing poor theology.

Finally, the notion of present experience in our context involves the reality of social change. No context is static, and even the most traditional culture is one that is growing, improving, or declining. In today's globalized world of compressed time and space,[19] two factors in particular are having an impact on social change within cultures. First, there is the cultural impact of modernity, with the revolutions brought about by electronic media and the contemporary expansion of global connectedness. Benjamin R. Barber names this "McWorld" and describes it as a "product of popular culture driven by expansionist commerce. Its template is American, its form style. Its goods are as much images as matériel, an aesthetic as well as a product line."[20] Over against this so-called global culture there have arisen various protests. On the one hand, peoples' inherited ethnicity takes on new meaning and purpose to assert identity over against the leveling power of "McDonaldization"; on the other hand, various constructed and hybridized identities have emerged as well, such as U. S. Hispanic/Latino culture born of *mestizaje* and Asian-American cultures that see themselves as "in-beyond" a dominant culture.[21]

Second, the idealist side of modernity has had a worldwide impact as well.

Many societies that have been ruled by oppressive forces now recognize the rights and dignity of oppressed peoples who are struggling for their liberation. This is the case politically in societies in Latin America or Asia, or in situations of marginality such as among women, people of color, or homosexuals.

Theology today, therefore, needs to take into account all of these aspects of context. It needs to realize that many of these aspects were already at work in the development of both the witness of scripture and the witness of tradition. It needs to realize even more that context in all its dimensions is the inevitable starting point of theological reflection today. Figure 1 illustrates the centrality of experience/context (past and present) in any kind of theological endeavor.

Figure 1
Contextual Theology

Experience of the Past   Experience of the Present
                                                           (Context)

→ ←

—Recorded in scripture   —Personal/communal experience
—Preserved, defended in tradition   —Culture
                                                          —Social location
                                                          —Social change

CONTEXTUALIZATION AS TRADITIONAL

The enterprise of contextualization is a departure from the traditional way of doing theology; it is something new. But at the same time, contextualization is also something that is very traditional. While we can say that the doing of theology by taking culture and social change in culture into account is a departure from the traditional or classical way of doing theology, a study of the history of theology will reveal that every authentic theology has been very much rooted in a particular context in some implicit or real way. "Contextualization . . . is the sine qua non of all genuine theological thought, and always has been."[22]

Contemporary scripture studies, for example, have revealed that there is no one theology of the Hebrew or Christian Scriptures, and much less of the Bible as a whole. The Bible literally means "books" (Greek: *biblia*), and if the Bible is anything, it is a library, a collection of books and consequently of theologies. The Hebrew scriptures are made up of the Yahwist theology, the Elohist theology, Priestly theology, Deuteronomic theology, and Wisdom theologies—to name but a few. These theologies are all different and sometimes even contradictory of each other; they reflect different times, different concerns, and even different cultures as Israel moved from an agrarian society to a monarchy, from an independent state to a vassal of powers such as Assyria, Greece, and Rome. And in the Christian scriptures we know that every gospel is different because of the different circumstances in which they were written, each reflecting the concerns of quite different communities. Paul is different from James, and the deutero-Pauline pastoral epistles reflect quite different concerns from the genuine Pauline letters. Indeed, British theologian (now bishop) Stephen Sykes has argued that the Christian message itself contains a basic ambiguity that makes pluralism and controversy part of the identity or essence of Christianity itself.[23]

If we turn to the church's early theologians after the New Testament era, we see theologians who were trying to make sense out of the faith in terms of the dominant and all-pervasive Hellenistic culture. Clement of Alexandria, for instance, made use of the insights of the Stoics; Origen made use of Plato, and Augustine was strongly influenced both by Plato and by the neo-Platonists of his time.[24] The whole structure of the post-Constantinian church reflected imperial structures. Bishops were treated like members of the imperial court, wore vestments that rivaled those of the emperor, and presided over imperial political divisions called dioceses. The early councils of the church made use of Greek words (albeit stretching their meanings sometimes) to express points of Christian doctrine. One of the most significant moments in theology was when, at Nicea, a philosophical term (*homoousios*, or "consubstantial") was used to express what was meant by the scriptures regarding the identity of the *Logos*, or incarnate Word.[25] As Virginia Fabella points out, the true significance of Nicea, and later of Chalcedon, is "the underlying challenge they pose to us to have our own contemporary culturally-based christological formulations."[26]

It is also well known that Thomas Aquinas used the newly discovered works of Aristotle as a vehicle for a new synthesis of Christian doctrine. Aquinas now is regarded as the paragon of orthodoxy, but he was perhaps as controversial in his day as Hans Küng or Charles Curran is in ours—his books were even burnt by the bishop of Paris soon after his death!

In his important study *Corpus Mysticum*, Henri de Lubac presents additional evidence of the contextuality of medieval theological thinking. Within the more symbolic mentality of the patristic era, de Lubac points out that the Eucharist was referred to clearly as the *corpus mysticum*, or mystical body of Christ; the church, on the other hand, was referred to as the *corpus verum*, or real body of Christ. However, as Christian thinking began to be dominated by a more Teutonic realistic mentality, the two terms began to be used in exactly the opposite way to refer to exactly the opposite realities. And so by the time of Berengarius, who spoke of the symbolic presence of Christ in the Eucharist, the Eucharist was spoken of as the *real* body of Christ (*Ave, Verum Corpus, natum ex Maria Virgine!*), and the church began to be spoken of as Christ's *mystical* body.[27]

One of the aspects of Martin Luther's greatness as a theologian is that he articulated the whole new consciousness of the individual as it emerged in the West at the dawn of modernity. His struggle to find a personal relationship with God was very much in tune with the tenor of the times and was a major reason his call for the reformation of the church was heard by so many people. And the theology of the Catholic Counter-Reformation was forged in the context of opposition to the Protestant challenge. Theology of the sixteenth and seventeenth centuries, both Protestant and Catholic, was nothing if it was not contextual![28]

Many more examples from the history of theology could be given—for instance, Schleiermacher's monumental attempt to root theology in experience in response to the romanticism of his age, and the Catholic Tübingen school's efforts to align Catholic theology with post-Kantian philosophy (particularly that of Schelling).[29] We could mention as well Paul Tillich's conviction that theology needs to be done as a correlation of human "existential questions and theological answers in mutual interdependence,"[30] and Karl Barth's highly contextual theology of the Word of God.[31] What becomes clear, in any case, is that even a cursory glance at the history of theology reveals that there has never been a genuine theology that was articulated in an ivory tower, with no reference to or dependence on the events, the thought forms, or the culture of its particular place and time.[32]

WHY THEOLOGY MUST BE CONTEXTUAL TODAY

There seem to be two sets of factors that point to why theology today must take into more serious account the context in which a particular theological effort is articulated. The first set of factors might be called external: historical events, intellectual currents, cultural shifts, and political forces. These external factors in turn bring to light certain internal factors within Christian faith itself that point to not only the possibility but also the necessity of doing theology in context. These internal factors are ultimately much more important than the external ones, since they point to a contextual imperative within Christianity itself. They are factors that have not always been recognized as important, but in our day, due in large part to the historical circumstances expressed in the external factors, they have emerged in a new way as essential to Christian faith and Christian theologizing.

EXTERNAL FACTORS

The first of these external factors[33] is a general dissatisfaction, in both the First and Third Worlds, with classical approaches to theology. In the First World, the various classical philosophies that have served as the bases of theology in the past do not seem to resonate with contemporary experience. There is a move to base theology on so-called process thought, in an attempt to do theology more in tune with the insights of contemporary science. Other theologians use the insights and framework of existentialist, personalist, or linguistic philosophies.[34] Still others, in a move that is even less traditional, have abandoned philosophy as a basis for their theologizing and have tried to construct theologies based on narrative, autobiography, or biography or on social sciences such as anthropology.[35] The point is that any kind of understanding of theology as an unchanging, already finished *theologia perennis* is being challenged in the First World in the name of relevance.

In Asia, Africa, Latin America, and Oceania, Christians are becoming increasingly convinced that traditional approaches to theology do not really make sense within their own cultural patterns and thought forms. Indian philosopher-theologian Raimon Panikkar, for example, maintains that Indians cannot really accept the principle that might be called the backbone of western philosophical thinking, the principle of contradiction. For Indians, Panikkar insists, things can indeed be and not be at the same time.[36] This seems to be close to the more Taoist idea of Yang and Yin, which points to the fact that all things participate in the reality of their opposites: light and darkness, male and female, good and evil, flesh and spirit, and so forth.[37]

On a more practical level, some traditional theological positions don't seem to jibe very well with aspects of nonwestern cultures. My late colleague Carroll Stuhlmueller spoke often about his dismay that wine had to be imported into the Philippines for the celebration of the Eucharist. What better symbol can we have, he would muse, that Christianity is also something imported, basically western, basically non-Filipino? How can the important symbol of baptism express cleansing and inclusion when, in the Masai culture in Africa, pouring water over a woman's head is a ritual that curses her to barrenness?[38] And modern western Christianity's strong influence from the Enlightenment often tries to explain away beliefs such as witchcraft, miraculous healings, and the existence of spirits—beliefs that are central to the religious life of many peoples in Africa, Asia, the Caribbean, and Latin America.[39] These are just a few examples of how traditional theology has been a cause of unease and dissatisfaction.

A second external reason theology is being understood today as necessarily contextual is the oppressive nature of older approaches. United States black theologian James Cone has pointed out repeatedly in his works how traditional theology ignores the black experience and makes blacks invisible and inaudible.[40] Similarly, Latin American theologians have discovered that the traditional theology, rather than speaking a word of hope to the marginalized masses of Latin America's poor, has often been used ideologically to justify the status quo of the continued domination by the rich and powerful. Classical western theology with its emphasis on individual salvation and morality was often disruptive of cultures that only recognize the individual within the context of the group. Older approaches to theology were filled with assumptions of male superiority, and produced consequent distortions regarding the notion of God, liturgical language, and the role of women in ministry. The neo-Thomist theology that dominated Roman Catholic theology from the 1870s through the 1960s insisted on loyalty to Rome often to the detriment of pastoral relevance: the continued insistence, for example, on celibacy for African clergy despite the fact that in many African societies one's place as a man in society is determined by one's proven ability to have children. Such culturally insensitive and oppressive attitudes have in the last several decades been unmasked as having little to do with the real meaning of Christianity, and so there have been movements and pressures to make theology and church practice more consonant with what is positive and good in various cultures, and more critical of what is really destructive in them.

In the third place, the growing identity of local churches is demanding development of truly contextual theologies. Filipino patriot and national hero José Rizal wrote in his novel *El Filibusterismo* that "there are no tyrants where there are no slaves."[41] What Rizal meant was that when a person or nation or culture comes to a clear realization of its identity, no other person, nation, or culture can use it, oppress it, or foist any unwanted or destructive thing upon it. Colonialism fostered a feeling among those who were colonized that anything that was really good and worthwhile was something that originated in the colonizing country and that what was in the colony was sketchy, of poor quality, only an imitation of the real thing. Toward the end of the era of colonialism and after it was finished, nations and cultures in former colonies began to wake up to the fact that the "colonial mentality" did not necessarily convey the full truth. What African and Asian countries began to realize was that there are values in their cultures that are just as good as, if not better than, those of their colonizers, and once this had been realized, former colonies and churches in these nations began to have the confidence to work things out for themselves, on their own terms and in their own way. In the area of religious practice and theology, the need to express this new consciousness of independence and self-worth is particularly important, and although they are often still tentative, efforts at contextual theologizing are being made and *need* to be made.

Underlying all three of these external factors is a fourth, and that is the understanding of culture that is provided by the contemporary social sciences. Bernard Lonergan distinguishes between a classicist notion of culture and one that is empirical. For the classicist notion of culture, there really is only one culture, and that culture is both universal and permanent. Within this understanding of culture, one became "cultured" and so listened to Bach and Beethoven, read Homer and Dickens and Flaubert, and appreciated van Dyck, Renoir, and Picasso. The person of culture, in other words, was one who nourished oneself on the great human achievements of the West. The empiricist notion of culture, however, defines culture as a set of meanings and values that informs a way of life—and there are obviously many such "sets" throughout the world. Within the parameters of this understanding of culture, one is already "cultured" by being socialized within a particular society. Culture is not something "out there," but something that everyone participates in already.[42]

If one works out of a classicist conception of culture, there can be only one theology—one that is valid for all times, all places, in all cultures. However, if one works out of an empirical notion of culture, there not only *can* be a theology for every culture and period of history; there *must* be. Theology, according to Lonergan, is what mediates between a cultural matrix and the significance and role of religion in that matrix.[43] Theology, in other words, functions precisely as the way that religion makes sense within a particular culture.

INTERNAL FACTORS

The various external factors that contribute to the possibility and necessity of the contexualization of theology bring out some internal factors that also point to contextualization as a theological imperative. These internal factors, brought to light by the forces of history and the movements of the times, are really dynamics within Christianity itself, and these, much more than the external factors, are particularly strong arguments for a theology that takes culture and cultural change seriously as it attempts to understand Christian faith.

The first of these internal factors is the incarnational nature of Christianity.[44] God so loved the world (Jn 3:16) that God wanted to share God's very self with men and women and invite them into a life-giving relationship with the Godhead. If God was going to do this, the means of communication would have to be in a way that human beings could fully grasp, a way that expressed the reality of what this invitation into friendship and relationship was all about. And so God became *flesh* (Jn 1:14), and not generally, but particularly. God became flesh, a human being, in the person of Jesus, a Jew, son of Mary, a male. God became flesh in a human person of such and such a height, with a particular color hair, with particular personality traits, etc. Incarnation is a process of becoming particular, and in and through the particular the divinity could become visible and in some way (not fully but in some way) become graspable and intelligible.

It follows quite naturally that if that message, through our agency, is to continue to touch people, we have somehow ourselves to continue the incarnation process. Through us God must become Asian or African, black or brown, poor or sophisticated. Christians must be able to speak to inhabitants of twenty-first-century secular suburban Lima, Peru, or to the Tondo slum dweller in Manila, or to the ill-gotten affluence of a Brazilian rancher. Christianity, if it is to be faithful to its deepest roots and to its most basic insight, must continue God's incarnation in Jesus by becoming contextual. As René Padilla says:

> The incarnation makes clear God's approach to the revelation of himself and of his purposes: God does not shout his message from the heavens; God becomes present as a man among men. The climax of God's revelation is Emmanuel. And Emmanuel is Jesus, a first-century Jew! The incarnation unmistakably demonstrates God's intention to make himself known from within the human situation. Because of the very nature of the Gospel, we know this Gospel only as a message contextualized in culture.[45]

A second internal factor is the sacramental nature of reality. The doctrine of the incarnation proclaims that God is revealed not primarily in *ideas* but rather in concrete reality. It is in the flesh of Jesus that we encounter God most fully. Jesus may not be the exclusive way by which men and women can encounter God, but Jesus is, to use the famous phrase of Edward Schillebeeckx, "the sacrament of the encounter with God."[46] Encounters with God in Jesus continue to take place in our world through concrete things. Thus, God is encountered in the poured water of baptism, in the remembering of the Christian community gathered around the table on which are bread and wine, in oil given for healing or as a sign of vocation, in gestures of forgiveness or commissioning. But these sacraments are only concentrated ritual moments that point beyond themselves to the whole of life. They are moments that proclaim a deep faith in the fact that the world and its inhabitants and their deeds and events are holy and that, at any time and in any place and through any person, these persons and things can become transparent and reveal their creator as actively and lovingly present to creation.[47] Luther speaks of the world as a mask of God and as God's word; and the British poet Gerard Manley Hopkins speaks of the world as "charged with the grandeur of God."

If the ordinary things of life are so transparent of God's presence, one can speak of culture, human experience, and events in history—of contexts—as truly sacramental and so revelatory. Culture, human experience, and history, if we are true to a real dynamic in Christianity's self-understanding, must be "unpacked" of its sacredness. Carroll Stuhlmueller and Donald Senior show clearly that the sacramental nature of a particular context is not something radically new. The whole movement of the Bible is one of interpreting the ordinary, the secular, in terms of religious symbolism.[48] This is the continuing task of theology: to reveal God's presence in a truly sacramental world.

In the third place, we can speak of a shift in the understanding of the nature of divine revelation as being an internal factor determining the contextual nature of theology. In theology written before the Second Vatican Council, revelation was conceived largely in terms of propositional truth. As José de Mesa and Lode Wostyn describe it, revelation was presented "in form of eternal truths handed down to us from Christ and the Apostles. Faith was understood to be the intellectual assent to those truths. All these were systematically arranged and presented as the Catholic Faith."[49] God's revealing action, in this understanding, was viewed as letting people know certain pieces of arcane information about God, the world, and themselves that they could not otherwise get through the use of their own reason, and acceptance of these "truths" was necessary for salvation. God's revelation of these truths had ceased with the "death of the last apostle," and so nothing was to be done but to communicate these truths from generation to generation and constantly try to penetrate their meaning.

Theological thought leading up to Vatican II, however, began to shift its emphasis from such an understanding and spoke of revelation in more interpersonal terms. In this "newer" understanding—always present in theology implicitly but seldom explicitly and systematically appropriated—revelation was conceived as the offer of God's very self to men and women by means of concrete actions and symbols in history and in individuals' daily life. In interpersonal terms, revelation was understood as God's self-communication to men and women: the giver as such is the gift, and the person to whom the gift is given is thus called to his or her personal fulfillment.[50] Consequently, faith was understood as a personal response as well—a self-gift of a person to God. In Vatican II's Decree on Divine Revelation, 2, therefore, we read that, in revelation, "the invisible God (cf. Col. 1:15; 1 Tim. 1:17), out of the abundance of love, speaks to men and women as friends (cf. Ex. 33:11; Jn. 15:14-15) and dwells among them (cf. Bar. 3:38), so that God may invite and receive them into communion with Godself." Although revelation was still understood as being complete in an objective sense—as Karl Rahner said, in Christ God has expressed Godself completely—God's revealing action was also seen as something that was ongoing as God continues to offer Godself to men and women in their daily lives.[51]

When Revelation was understood in terms of eternal truths framed in unchanging and unchangeable divinely given language, theology could only be conceived as being itself unchanging and as having little or nothing to do with the realities of culture and social change. But as revelation has come to be conceived in terms of a personal self-offer of God's very self to men and women, an offer of friendship and loving relationship, the question must inevitably be asked whether such an offer could be made in any way except in terms that men and women could understand. Revelation to Israel, for example, had to be God's offer of relationship in terms that made sense to men and women who shared Israel's culture. And revelation to first-century Hellenists had to be expressed in quite different language and categories. In the same way, God's revelation to the men and women of Africa in the first part of the twenty-first century has to be in terms of categories, language, and forms that really speak to twenty-first-century Africans. God's offer of love and friendship to contemporary Latin Americans has to be expressed in quite different ways.

A gift that cannot be recognized as such can hardly be a thoughtful or valuable gift; God, in offering God's self, would certainly take the time and effort to make that offer relevant. And we as church, who represent and continue God's work in the world, can do no less than God if we are to be faithful to our basic vocation. This new, interpersonal notion of revelation, in other words, points to the necessity of a theology that takes seriously the actual contexts in which men and women experience God.

A fourth dynamic internal to Christianity that calls for a contextual approach to doing theology is the catholicity of the church. First used to refer to the church in the early second century, catholicity reflects the essence of what the church of Christ should try to be. *Catholic* comes from the two Greek words *kata* and *holos* ("according to the whole") and points to the all-embracing, all-inclusive, all-accepting nature of the Christian community. As Avery Dulles has written, catholicity implies that "narrowness and particularism have no place in the true church of Christ. . . . To be qualitatively catholic the church must be receptive to the sound achievements of every race and culture. Catholicism pays respect not to the mind alone, nor only to the will and the emotions, but to all levels and aspects of human existence."[52]

A truly catholic church embraces the human because it sees the human as good and holy. Rather than regarding human culture and human events as unimportant or unhelpful in expressing life's deepest experiences and yearnings, catholicity actively enlists these things for help. A catholic church is a church that believes passionately in God's revelation in the incarnation and has a heightened sense of creation's sacramentality.

Catholicity is often translated as "universality," but this doesn't quite capture the richness of the word. Catholicity is certainly that "mark" or "dimension" of the church that insures that the church perseveres in the whole gospel and strives to live and flourish in every part of the world and in every cultural context. At the same time, however, catholicity is the dimension of the church that champions and preserves the local, the particular. Rather than a bland uniformity, Christianity is endowed with a dynamic that moves toward unity through a rich diversity, through conversation and even argument among people of particular personal, cultural, and historical experience. Only if every group in the church—Vietnamese, Laotian, Filipino, Salvadoran, European, North American, Ghanaian, and so forth—is included in its particularity will the church be able to be truly *the church*. Only as the church enters into serious dialogue with every culture can it be a witness to the "Pleroma" that is Jesus Christ. As Andrew Walls writes: "The full-grown humanity of Christ requires all the Christian generations, just as it embodies all the cultural variety that six continents can bring."[53] For such a dialogue to take place, all persons and cultural groups have to dig deep into their own social situation, personal experience, and cultural existence to see how these interact with God's offer of friendship and relationship in Jesus Christ. Thus the dynamic of catholicity calls for a contextual approach to theology by its very nature.[54]

A final dynamic in Christianity that calls for contextualization is found in the doctrine that is at the heart of Christianity: the Trinity. Contemporary theology has seen a renewal and revitalization of trinitarian thought and has placed it once more at the center and source of Christian theologizing.[55] Contemporary understandings of God as Trinity speak of God as a dynamic, relational community of persons, whose very nature it is to be present and active in the world, calling it and persuading it toward the fullness of relationship that Christian tradition calls salvation. Through the presence of the Spirit and the concrete flesh and humanity of the *Logos*, God works for salvation in the midst of human context, its cultures, its events, its sufferings, its joys. God's dialogical nature is the source for the church's catholicity and theology's need to embrace and wrestle with the concrete. As David Cunningham points out, Christian faith in God as Trinity opens up a vista of God's "marks" (what Augustine called *vestigia*) in the world's events, in people's experience and cultures, in the natural world. Christian theologians need to do theology contextually because God is present and acts contextually.[56]

CONCLUSION

Theology today, we can conclude, must be a contextual theology. Several important movements and currents of our times point out aspects in Christianity that make imperative a theology that takes seriously human experience, social location, particular cultures, and social change in those cultures. Pluralism in theology, as well as on every level of Christian life, must not only be tolerated; it must be positively encouraged and cultivated. In *Evangelii Nuntiandi*, Paul VI sums all of this up when he says that evangelization is something that must speak to every aspect of human life. Evangelization must be aimed at illuminating and transforming men and women as they are: "what matters is to evangelize human culture and cultures . . . , always taking the person as one's starting-point and always coming back to the relationships of people among themselves and with God."[57] Contextualization, therefore, is not something on the fringes of the theological enterprise. It is at the very center of what it means to do theology in today's world. Contextualization, in other words, is a theological imperative.

2

Issues in Contextual Theology

Because contextualization is a new way of doing theology, at least on the conscious, reflexive level, the contextual theologian faces a number of issues and questions that were seldom dealt with in classical theology. With the turn to the subjective and the new attending to experience, social location, culture, and social change that is involved in the contextual enterprise, it is as if the equilibrium established in more traditional ways of doing theology has been shaken and new ways of theologizing and of being a theologian are being discovered, along with new questions and problems. In this chapter, therefore, I would like to summarize and reflect on some of these issues.

Several authors have reflected long and hard on many of the points that I will make.[1] Nevertheless, I think it will be useful, before we begin to survey the various models of contextual theology, to review some of the legitimate concerns and questions that emerge when theology begins to take both culture and cultural change seriously in a conscious way. The issues that surround contextual theology might be said to cluster into four basic groups: issues of theological method; issues of basic theological orientation; issues of criteria for orthodoxy; issues of cultural identity over against theologies already in place in a culture (e.g., popular religiosity) and social change. This chapter will examine each of these clusters of issues. In a final section I will reflect briefly on the issue of terminology—is *contextualization* a more appropriate term than *indigenization* or *inculturation*?

ISSUES OF THEOLOGICAL METHOD

Contextual theology's addition of culture and social change to the traditional *loci* of scripture and tradition already marks a revolution in theological method over against traditional ways of doing theology. As José de Mesa and Lode Wostyn point out, no longer do we speak of culture and world events as areas to which theology is adapted and applied; culture and world events become the very sources of the theological enterprise, along with and equal to scripture and tradition. Both poles—human experience and the Christian tradition—are to be read together dialectically.[2]

In addition to this basic shift in theological method, a number of other methodological issues have emerged. When human experience, world events, culture, and cultural change are taken as *loci theologici*, one can ask whether theology is always to be done formally or discursively. What, in other words, is the *form* that theology should take? As theology becomes more of a reflection on ordinary human life in the light of the Christian tradition, one might ask whether ordinary men and women might not, after all, be the best people to theologize. And finally, as theology moves away from a *theologia perennis* to a reflection-in-faith on God's revelation in particular situations, the question naturally arises regarding the legitimacy of doing theology by a person who does not participate in a particular context. These are the three questions on which I will focus here.

WHAT FORM SHOULD THEOLOGY TAKE?

Since the Middle Ages and the beginning of scholasticism, theology has been regarded as a scholarly, academic discipline. Its main location has been in the university or seminary, and its main form has been discursive, whether in the classroom lecture or in the scholarly article or monograph. What contextual theology has realized, however, is that theology has not always been done discursively, nor need it be done so today. The discursive form, for one thing, is something typically western and a normal fruit of a visual, literate culture.[3] In addition, we can recognize that great theology was also written in the form of a hymn or a poem (witness the hymns of Ephrem and the stunning poetry of Aquinas) and theology has also been done in the form of the sermon or homily (e.g., Augustine's sermons on St. John or Newman's University Sermons). Theology does not even have to be verbal. Theology has always been embodied in ritual, as the rule *lex orandi, lex credendi* points out, and some of the most eloquent faith-seeking-understanding the world has ever known is expressed in art works ranging from paintings on catacomb walls, through the *figure* of Joachim of Fiore, to the sculpture of Michelangelo.[4]

When we begin to take culture and cultural change seriously, theological content is not the only thing affected. The form of theology comes under the influence of such *loci* as well. In an African culture, for example, the best form of theologizing might be collecting, creating, or reflecting on proverbs.[5] In U. S. African American culture, the sermon or homily might be the best vehicle for theologizing.[6] In India, faith might best be expressed by dance.[7] The point here, in any case, is to realize that theology is a wider activity than just scholarship and that various cultures have other preferred ways of articulating their faith. Works of art, hymns, stories, dramas, comic books, cinema—all these media can become valid forms for theology in particular cultures.[8]

WHO DOES THEOLOGY?

In the same way that classical theology understood the form of theology to be discursive and academic, it understood the theologian to be a scholar, an academic, a highly trained specialist with a wide knowledge of Christian tradition and the history of doctrine and with a number of linguistic and hermeneutical skills. Such a picture of theology and the theologian made sense as long as theology was conceived as being a reflection on documents that needed considerable background skill to understand. But when theology is conceived in terms of expressing one's present experience in terms of one's faith, the question arises whether ordinary people, people who are in touch with everyday life, who suffer under the burden of anxiety and oppression and understand the joys of work and married love, are not the real theologians—with the trained professionals serving in an auxiliary role.

A number of contextual theologians insist that theology is not really done by experts (such as Rahner or Lonergan or Gutiérrez) and then "trickled down" to the people for their consumption. If theology is truly to take culture and cultural change seriously, it must be understood as being done most fully by the subjects and agents of culture and cultural change. The process of contextualization, says Peter Schineller, is too complex and important to be left only to professional theologians.[9] The role of the trained theologian (the minister, the theology teacher) is that of articulating more clearly what the people are expressing more generally or vaguely, deepening their ideas by providing them with the wealth of the Christian tradition, and challenging them to broaden their horizons by presenting them with the whole of Christian theological expression. As Filipino theologian Leonardo Mercado puts it, "the people are the best contextualizers"; and the role of the theologian is to function as a midwife to the people as they give birth to a theology that is truly rooted in a culture and moment of history.[10] Krikor Haleblian says much the same thing when he says that "the believing community in each culture must take ultimate responsibility for contextualizing the gospel, but there is a place and a need for professionals who can act as 'brokers' in this difficult and ongoing task."[11]

What seems important is to conceive theology in terms of a constant dialogue between the people—who are the subjects of culture and cultural change and so have a preeminent place in the enterprise of seeking to understand Christian faith in a particular context—and the professional theologian who articulates, deepens, and broadens the people's faith expression with his or her wider knowledge of the Christian tradition and, perhaps, the articulation of faith in other contexts. What becomes clear as the context is taken seriously in theology is that, on the one hand, theology can never be understood to be a finished product, produced by experts, that is merely delivered to a Christian community for its consumption. On the other hand, theology cannot be the mere recording of what "the people think." Theology must rather be an activity of dialogue, emerging out of a mutual respect between "faith-ful" but not technically trained people and "faith-ful" and listening professionals.[12]

CAN A NONPARTICIPANT IN A CONTEXT DO CONTEXTUAL THEOLOGY?

In his famous essay "Self Reliance," Ralph Waldo Emerson wrote the following provocative sentence: "If, therefore, a man claims to know and speak of God and carries you backward to the phraseology of some old mouldered nation in another country, in another world, believe him not."[13] Emerson, of course, could not have been thinking explicitly about the contextualization of theology, but his words certainly are relevant in terms of the contextualization enterprise, and they express an important issue that has arisen within that enterprise: whether a person who does not share the full experience of another can actually do authentic theology within that culture or context.

We can state the issue of the nonparticipant's ability to do authentic theology in even more concrete terms: Can a non-Ghanaian do Ghanaian theology? Can a white U. S. American do black theology? Can a North American contribute to Latin American theological reflection on God's liberating action in history? Can a male do feminist theology?

We must answer, from one point of view, with a firm no. As Emerson seems to imply, a person who does not fully share one's experience is not to be fully trusted to speak of God in that person's context. Non-Africans do not know how Africans feel or perceive reality; whites cannot begin to understand the subtle ways in which blacks experience not only overt prejudice but also the more subtle oppression of invisibility and inaudibility.[14] North Americans can never, for all their solidarity and compassion, share the frustration, pain, and dehumanization of a Brazilian *favela* dweller. Even feminist men cannot fully appreciate the evils of patriarchy, and the most cross-culturally sensitive U. S. American may still be a beneficiary of his country's global economic power. Try as they might, nonparticipants ultimately bring their own feelings, perceptions, experiences, and privilege into a situation, and however slightly, this foreignness works to distort theology in the other context.

On another level, to a certain extent and in limited ways, people who do not fully share the experience of the other can contribute to the development of a contextual theology.

In the first place, a person can participate in another context to some degree. In some cases, an outsider may be more in tune with a particular culture than many of those who were born within it. If a person approaches a culture or context openly, is willing to learn the necessary language or languages, and is willing to read and appropriate sociological and anthropological literature about a particular culture, he or she can understand much of what a particular culture is about. On the other hand, for example, it is possible that younger "strangers" to the culture can be more in tune with the culture than older indigenous persons who were formed in their Christianity and theology in an era when culture and cultural expression was taken little into consideration. It often happens, for example, that the first generation of indigenous religious superiors or bishops might be more westernized than many of their younger western missionaries or more Roman than Rome. Or it may be that a feminist man might be more sensitive to women's issues than many women who have not yet been exposed to the subtleties of patriarchy. In this case, the nonparticipant in a context can point out many things that the participants have never seen or have never attended to. In a limited but never complete way, the nonparticipant can help in developing a theology that is culturally and socially sensitive to the context by sharing his or her insights as a stranger into the culture.[15]

Second, the nonparticipant in a context can provide a kind of counterpoint by his or her critique of a particular culture or situation. In the same way that the outsider can gain insights into the positive aspects of a context and can serve it by pointing these aspects out, so also the outsider can be more aware than those who share in a context what its weak, negative, or inconsistent aspects might be. Cultures, for example, are never completely good; they are always ambiguous in terms of their values and worldview. A person who has no stake in a culture can often more easily and effectively bring out the "shadow side" of culture than one who lives within it; in this way, the nonparticipant can help spot areas in a culture that are dehumanizing and ideological. Foreign students and visitors to the United States can highlight, more than native-born U. S. Americans, the negative features of U. S. individualism and its success ethic. A European or U. S. American missionary can remind family-centered cultures such as the Philippines that families can sometimes demand too much of an individual and that Christian values of justice and honesty might have a greater claim than blind family loyalty. If participants in a culture or situation are honest and open, they can learn a lot from the stranger in their midst, and in this way the stranger can do a great service both to the local culture and the local church.

In the third place, by his or her own honesty in presenting his or her theological position, the nonparticipant can stimulate people from the culture or situation to do their own theological thinking. I base this idea on my own experience of trying to adapt to Italian culture as a student in Rome, trying to adapt to Filipino culture as a missionary, and trying to do theology in a multicultural classroom as a white, middle-class, U. S. American male. While I found that it was and is quite possible to adapt myself to these contexts and grow in and through them, I think my greatest lesson in my contact with other cultures has been learning what it means to be a U. S. American. In other words, I have found that one very important way to learn who you are is to learn, in an encounter with another, who you are not.[16] One way a nonparticipant can help in the construction of a local contextual theology is simply to do theology in a way that makes the most sense to him or her as a particular cultural subject. Inevitably, if this is done, one's students or congregation or readers will be struck by the difference from the way they think—some things will seem irrelevant, others challenging, still others will perhaps be found to be offensive. If participants in a particular context could take the further step of asking why a particular idea or theological approach is irrelevant or challenging or offensive, they are well on their way to actually doing theology as subjects in that context (having a certain experience, belonging to a particular culture, living in a particular social location or in a particular situation of social change). As they are confronted with what they are not, they might more easily discover who they are and how they might express their faith as who they are.[17] As black theologian James Cone puts it, "creative theological thinking is born out of conflict, the recognition that what *is* is *not* true, even though untruth has established itself as truth."[18] The nonparticipant, the westerner, the white, the North American, the male, can provide the stuff of such a conflict that will stimulate Asians, blacks, Latin Americans, women to think theologically on their own terms.

A person can in several significant but limited ways contribute to the contextualization of theology in a context that is not his or her own. But when a person does this, he or she must approach the host culture with both humility and honesty. He or she must have humility because he or she will always be on the margins of the society in which he or she has chosen to work; he or she can never be a real part of it or a direct contributor to it. And he or she must have honesty because only through honest sharing of himself or herself can he or she hope to contribute anything at all to people's understanding of their faith in terms of their cultural and social context. A genuine contextual theology, in other words, can indeed grow out of genuine dialogue between the participants in a particular culture and the stranger, the guest, the other. This is not easy and demands, I believe, a real spirituality. On the part of the nonparticipant, it demands a spirituality of "letting go"; on the part of the participants in a context, it demands the spirituality of "speaking out."[19]

ISSUES OF BASIC THEOLOGICAL ORIENTATION

Among several possible basic theological orientations in theology, two seem to have particular relevance for contextual theology. One can work out of a theology that is basically creation-centered, or one can do theology from a fundamentally redemption-centered perspective.

A creation-centered orientation to theology is characterized by the conviction that human experience, and so context, is generally good. Its perspective is that grace builds on nature, but only because nature is *capable* of being built on, of being perfected in a supernatural relationship with God.[20]

A creation-centered orientation sees the world, creation, as sacramental: the world is the place where God reveals Godself; revelation does not happen in set-apart, particularly holy places, in strange, unworldly circumstances, or in words that are spoken in a stilted voice; it comes in daily life, in ordinary words, through ordinary people.[21] It is within such a creation-oriented theology that we can best speak of "anonymous Christianity" (Rahner)[22] or of the Christ who is to be discovered in a culture (Raimon Panikkar's "unknown Christ of Hinduism").[23] Creation-centered theology approaches life with an analogical, not a dialectical, spirit or imagination and sees a continuity between human existence and divine reality.[24]

It is not that the world is perfect and sinless. Creation-centered theology certainly acknowledges the reality and ugliness of sin. But sin is sin precisely because it is an aberration in such a beautiful world, an attempt to "get out of life what God has not put into it."[25] And the only way that sin can adequately be exterminated is by confrontation with the power of good.

A redemption-centered theology, in contrast, is characterized by the conviction that culture and human experience are either in need of a radical transformation or in need of total replacement. In this perspective, grace cannot build on or perfect nature because nature is something that is corrupt. In a real sense, therefore, grace replaces nature. Rather than being a vehicle for God's presence, the world distorts God's reality and rebels against it. Rather than a culture being already holy with the presence of God, Christ must be brought to a culture for that culture to have any saving meaning whatsoever. In the famous phrase of Kierkegaard, there exists an "infinitely qualitative difference between God and humanity,"[26] and because of this difference, God's Word can only reach men and women by breaking into the world and calling men and women to say no to the world and yes to God. There can be no moving from created things to God; there can be no *analogia entis*.[27] Reality is approached, therefore, with suspicion—with a "dialectical imagination."[28]

This basic orientation will have many ramifications in terms of the contextualization of theology. If one were to opt for a more creation-centered approach, one would approach the context more positively. In a creation-centered approach, human experience, current events, and culture would be areas of God's activity and therefore sources of theology. If, on the other hand, one believes in a world that is first and foremost in need of redemption by the Word of God from outside the world, context would be seen more negatively. The Word of God might have to be adapted to differing and changing circumstances, but those circumstances could never be interpreted *as* Word of God. While context may be taken with utmost seriousness, it will be seen as what God's Word needs always to challenge. As we will see in later chapters, the choice of a basic theological orientation will play a large part in determining the kind of model or method one chooses for doing contextual theology.

ISSUES OF CRITERIA FOR ORTHODOXY

A real danger in contextualization is that one could mix Christianity and culture in a way that does not enhance but compromises and betrays Christianity. The fact is that a theology that takes culture seriously can easily become a "culture theology" along the lines of what nineteenth-century liberal theology was accused of. Harvie Conn reports that in evangelical circles a fear of "syncretism" has been evident almost from the beginning of discussions of the possibility of contextualizing theology, and he gives several examples of the expression of that fear at various theological conferences in the last decades.[29]

Such fear, however, is not confined to evangelical circles, although it is most urgently discussed there. Roman Catholic papal documents such as *Evangelii Nuntiandi* encourage "theological expression which takes account of differing cultural, social and even racial milieux," but they still caution that the content of the faith "must be neither impaired nor mutilated."[30] Joseph Cardinal Ratzinger's Congregation for the Doctrine of the Faith has issued stern warnings about mixing Latin American liberation theology with Marxist ideology.[31] In Roman Catholic theology, pluralism is a fact,[32] but it is also a fact that pluralism is often viewed with suspicion and caution.

Because of the contemporary pluralism in theology, to which the contextualization of theology is an important contributing factor, contextual theologians have been challenged to search for criteria of orthodoxy. De Mesa and Wostyn pose the question this way:

> If there are so many divergent, and sometimes apparently conflicting inter-
> pretations, how can we be sure that our understanding of our faith is correct,
> that is, faithful to the Judaeo-Christian Tradition? Is it possible to recognize
> the one faith in the different interpretations? Does pluralism not become an
> ideology of adaptation when what is adapted or inculturated is considered to
> be correct? Should we not, perhaps, re-introduce at least some basic and
> universal truths, conceptually expressed and accepted as such?[33]

De Mesa and Wostyn themselves present three criteria for orthodoxy. First, a new, contextual formulation of faith or of a doctrine should be oriented in the same direction as other "successful" or approved formulations. The point here is that the Christian message has a basic intentionality that can be expressed in a "basic religious proposal."[34] For Christians, this basic proposal is "God is Love,"[35] and anything that would run in a contrary direction could not at all be an appropriate Christian theological expression. Second, de Mesa and Wostyn propose a criterion of Christian orthopraxis. A theological expression that would lead to actions that are clearly un-Christian (e.g., hatred of the oppressor or the taking of innocent life) could never be considered orthodox, no matter how meaningful it might be in a culture. On the other hand, an expression that seems at first unorthodox might be justified in that it leads a group to truly Christian behavior. Such is the argument, for example, behind the legitimization of polygamy or of ancestor veneration. Third, there is the criterion of acceptance by the people of God, or proper reception. Theology is the creation of the whole church, and when the church as a whole seems to accept a particular theological teaching, one can trust that the *sensus fidelium* is in operation and that this expression is a genuine one.

In his book *Constructing Local Theologies*, Robert Schreiter names five criteria for deciding the genuineness of a particular local theological expression.[36] These are similar as well as complementary to de Mesa and Wostyn's three criteria. First, says Schreiter, an expression of theology should have an inner consistency. This is similar to de Mesa and Wostyn's first criterion of basic direction. Schreiter gives the example of the reaction of the church to the Arian heresy. While the thought of Arius was extremely subtle, convincing, and rooted in contemporary Hellenistic culture, what the church began to realize (of course, with the help of Athanasius) was that Arius's doctrine was not in the same direction with the basic movement of Christianity. If Jesus wasn't truly God in some decisive sense, then we were not saved—for only God can save. Therefore, Arius was wrong and Athanasius was right.

A second criterion is that a true expression of contextual theology must be able to be translated into worship. The basic principle called into operation here is *lex orandi, lex credendi*—that the way we pray points to the way we believe and vice versa. "What happens," asks Schreiter, "when the developing theology is brought into the worshipping context? How does it develop in the communal prayer of the Church? What happens to a community which includes such in its prayer?"[37] To refer again to the Arian heresy, another reason Arianism was judged to be wrong was liturgical practice: Christians prayed to Christ as God, not as a creature. The liturgical practice of Christianity forbade the innovation that Arius tried to effect. Third, Schreiter proposes the criterion of orthopraxis, much along the lines of de Mesa and Wostyn. A feminism that would be as exclusive as patriarchy could not be judged as genuine, nor could a theology of ministry which excludes the active participation at all levels by women. A theology that justifies an oppressive status quo would be as wrong as a theology of liberation that calls for violent action against oppressors. If the watchword of Schreiter's second criterion is *lex orandi, lex credendi*, the watchword for his third might be, "by their fruits you will know them" (Mt 7:16).

Fourth, a developing local theology or theological expression should be open to criticism from other churches. If a particular theory is open enough to allow critiques from other contextualized theologies, if it is willing to learn from others and grow from dialogue with them, there is every indication that what that theology proposes is genuine. On the other hand, if a theology is defensive and closed in upon itself, not willing to be corrected, one can wonder whether such a theology can be an authentic expression of Christianity even within its own context. As Michael Taylor points out, "If the theological task is a 'do-it-yourself' job, it is not a 'do-it-by-yourself' job. If it is local it must never be parochial. What we believe and decide to do must be exposed to what others believe and decide to do. Real heresy is not getting it wrong but getting it wrong in isolation."[38]

It is in connection with this criterion that we can mention the role of the official magisterium within the Roman Catholic tradition, whether on the local or the universal level. The magisterium exists as that service in the church which guards against any wrong doctrinal or moral expression. If the possibility of magisterial supervision is denied, it would hardly be a sign that a contextual theologian or a local church has expressed Christianity in a way that is valid. Theology, even contextual theology, is always a dialogical process.

In the fifth place, Schreiter proposes the criterion of the strength of a theology to challenge other theologies. If a theology is able to contribute positively to a dialogue among various contextual theologians, such vitality is a sign that it is a genuine expression of faith. One of the signs of the truth of the theology of liberation is how radically it has challenged not only other Latin American theologies but also theologies from various parts of the world. Similarly, one of the signs of the authenticity of feminist and black liberation theology is that it speaks significantly to other theologies and uncovers hitherto unthought-of areas for theological reflection.

There is no doubt that when a theologian takes context seriously, he or she can fall into the danger of taking these realities more seriously than the Judaeo-Christian tradition as expressed in scripture and church tradition. But even more dangerous is a theology that speaks to no one, that has no power because it has no real audience. Contextual theology will continue to seek for criteria, always mindful that the gospel can only really be faithful to the past if it is in touch with the present.[39]

ISSUES OF CULTURAL IDENTITY, POPULAR RELIGIOSITY, AND SOCIAL CHANGE

Because of the subtle or not-so-subtle mentality of colonialism and the narrowness of theology and missionary vision in the past, much of the richness of many local cultures has been ignored or suppressed. Today, however, with the national identity of the former colonies coming into sharper focus and a broader understanding of the cultural conditionedness of all theology emerging more clearly, cultural identity seems to be a prime *locus* for the construction of truly contextual theologies.[40]

This basic "appreciative awareness"[41] of the importance of culture as a theological source is an eminently true and valid way of doing theology in a particular context. However, it does have its drawbacks. One drawback in seeking cultural identity as a theological source is the danger of falling into a kind of a cultural romanticism—of basing one's theology not upon culture as it is today but on what African theologian John Pobee calls a "fossil culture," a culture that did exist before colonization but that after colonization and contact with the western world does not exist except in some people's romantic fantasies.[42] One of the primary facts about cultures is that they are not static. As ways of perceiving, organizing, and dealing with reality, cultures are realities that are always in flux, always adapting, always changing. Just the fact that a traditional culture has come into contact with the West means that the culture is changed irrevocably. Colonization and westernization brought with them aspects that have transformed cultures in incredibly radical ways: the fact that the remotest village in India or the Andes includes a number of people who own and listen to radios means that one can no more simply speak of a purely Indian or Peruvian culture; these cultures are their own, but they are now changed through their contact with the wider world.

If theology is really to be in context, therefore, it cannot simply deal with a culture that no longer really exists. Culture remains as a factor, but it is not the only factor to be taken into consideration. In an article about the inculturation of Korean theology, Sean Dwan cites a report by a Korean nun who was trying to make a Christmas crib relevant to the Korean context. At first, the sister said, she designed a crib with Mary, Joseph, and the child in a traditional thatched Korean hut. But this seemed too comfortable, too romantic, too irrelevant to contemporary Korean life. The final design was a small cardboard shack against the background of tall hotels, apartment complexes, and office buildings, complete with signs advertising cabarets, health clubs, and bars. This scene was much more faithful to the contemporary Korean context, while being faithful as well to the original scene described in the gospels. Romanticism was avoided, and the real Korean culture was depicted. Many people did not much like it, the sister said, but she felt that this just proved her point![43]

Another danger for a theology that places too much emphasis on cultural identity is a possible conflict with what has been called "popular religiosity." In the Philippines, for instance, religious customs and practices that were brought by the colonizing Spaniards have entered into the fabric not only of Philippine religious life but of Philippine culture as well. Customs such as the rosary, devotion to Mary, and processions in honor of Santo Niño are thoroughly Filipino and should not come into conflict with "newer" approaches that stress original Filipino customs. It might be more genuinely Filipino, for instance, to substitute palm wine and rice cakes for bread and wine at the Eucharist, but whether the people will actually feel comfortable with such a substitution might be very much in doubt.

From another angle, the reality of social change should not totally eclipse traditional culture as a source for contextualizing theology. Despite the growing reality of a "world culture" of predominantly western color, the rationalization and secularization of culture will almost certainly not be as strong in Asia and Africa as it might in Europe, North America, and perhaps Latin America.[44] A strong but realistic cultural identity is necessary for a theology that really does speak to a context in its particularity. And as valuable as popular religiosity is, it often needs to be purified of many subtly damaging dimensions. Despite the love of Filipinos, for instance, for *Santo Entierro* (the dead Christ) and *Santo Niño* (the baby Jesus), these images of Christ might need to be balanced with a strong image of Jesus the worker, Jesus the human being, or with an image of the risen Christ who has successfully faced the terrors of evil, injustice, and death.

INDIGENIZATION, CONTEXTUALIZATION, OR INCULTURATION?

All three aspects—cultural identity, popular religiosity, and social change— have to be taken into consideration when one develops a truly contextual theology. This need to include and balance each of these elements—along with the elements of scripture and tradition, and other aspects of context such as social location and particular experience—is why the word *contextualization* might be considered the best way of describing the process, which has also been called inculturation, indigenization, or incarnation of the gospel. As the members of the Theological Education Fund wrote when the term was introduced in 1972, the term *contextualization* includes all that is implied in the older terms *indigenization* and *inculturation*, but seeks also to include the realities of contemporary secularity, technology, and the struggle for human justice.[45] One could also say that it includes the need to respect and deal with previous forms of theology and Christian practice that, while not native to a particular context, have over the years become part of it. Although not all theologians have accepted the terminology of contextualization,[46] the term does seem to have several advantages over the several other terms that have been used in the past. As the Asian bishops pointed out in 1979, *contextualization* both extends and corrects the older terminology.[47] As the Asian Bishops express it, *indigenization* focused on the purely cultural dimension of human experience, while *contextualization* broadens the understanding of culture to include social, political, and economic questions. In this way, culture is understood in more dynamic, flexible ways and is seen to be not closed and self-contained, but more open and able to be enriched with an encounter with other cultures and movements. And while *indigenization* "tended to see both the home culture and the culture 'out there' as good," *contextualization* "tends to be more critical of both cultures."[48] One final reason to use the term *contextualization* is that the term avoids exclusive attention to what Robert Schreiter terms "integrated" understandings of culture, and can include what he terms "globalized" understandings of it. *Contextualization* points to the fact that theology needs to interact and dialogue not only with traditional cultural value, but with social change, new ethnic identities, and the conflicts that are present as the contemporary phenomenon of globalization encounters the various peoples of the world.

Contextualization, then, as the preferred term to describe the theology that takes human experience, social location, culture, and cultural change seriously, must try to keep a balance. It is not enough to focus exclusively on cultural identity, but it is also too much to lose that identity by selling out to western modern thought. One must take popular religiosity into account as well, but the old ways must never get in the way of making the gospel the challenging and good news that it really is.

Now that we have surveyed the reasons for contextual theology and the several issues that commitment to contextual theologizing raises, we can move on to consider various ways in which men and women today are actually doing contextual theology. Before we do that, however, a few remarks on our method of procedure are in order. These remarks will be the topic of our next chapter.

3

The Notion and Use of Models

In the last three decades, a large number of theological books and articles have made use of the term *model*, either in their titles or in their method of approaching a particular theological subject. In 1976, Peter Schineller published a landmark article that proposed four systematic models[1] of Christology and ecclesiology. In 1978, Thomas F. O'Meara traced several models of philosophical thought which might found in approaches to understanding the Christian church.[2] Besides other works that have employed the "models approach" in order to understand religious life, ministry, pastoral activity, or styles of liturgical celebration, David Tracy's five models of theological reflection might be mentioned, as well as Sallie McFague's three models of speaking of God.[3]

At least for Catholics, using models to approach an understanding of a complex or difficult theological issue can be traced back to the appearance of Avery Dulles's *Models of the Church*, a book that has already become somewhat of a classic in post-Vatican II Roman Catholic theology.[4] In this book, Dulles showed quite convincingly the power of using models to sort out questions in theology. He proposed five models—the church as institution, as mystical communion, as sacrament, as herald, and as servant—each of which discloses a distinct way of understanding the mystery of the church. Then Dulles drew out the implications of each model for eschatology, ecumenism, ministry, and revelation and ended with an evaluation of the models in which he pointed to aspects of the models that needed to be preserved or needed to be discarded in any ecclesiology. Almost three decades later, readers of the book are still impressed with its ability to clarify paradigmatic ecclesiological positions and to draw out their implications in areas as diverse as ministerial skill and spirituality.

While Dulles's book on the church and a subsequent one on revelation[5] provide the immediate inspiration for the spate of theological works that employed a similar approach, Dulles himself acknowledges that his inspiration for using models comes from H. Richard Niebuhr's *Christ and Culture*, originally published in 1951. Niebuhr himself claimed to be influenced in developing his famous five types by works as diverse as Augustine's *City of God*, Ernst Troeltsch's *The So-*

cial Teachings of the Christian Churches, and C. G. Jung's *Psychological Types*.[6] In addition, Dulles developed his notion of model from a study of the work of Ian G. Barbour, Ian T. Ramsey, and Max Black, who, in the face of the challenge to theological language from logical positivism, pointed to the use of models in the fields of natural science as appropriate also for theological discourse.[7] Particularly in terms of what Ramsey calls disclosure models and what Dulles names heuristic models, complex theological realities such as the church or God's grace or human redemption can be opened up to expression, reflection, and critique.[8] These kinds of models suggest, disclose, or, as Paul Ricoeur says, "give rise to thought."[9] No one model is able to capture the Reality under consideration; each, however, can help a person enter into the Reality's mystery in a kind of suprarational way.

In this chapter we will present an understanding of the nature of models in general; then we see how models will be employed as descriptive of the various options available to theologians who are committed to doing theology in terms of a particular cultural, historical, and social context.

THE NOTION OF MODEL

There are many senses in which the word *model* is used in contemporary thought. Ian G. Barbour distinguishes four uses of the term—experimental, logical, mathematical, and theoretical—and states that, for his purposes of comparing the use of models in science and theology, the theoretical model is his main concern.[10] Barbour defines this kind of model as "a symbolic representation of selected aspects of the behaviour of a complex system for particular purposes,"[11] but perhaps more useful is the definition proposed by Avery Dulles in the beginning of his book *Models of Revelation*. As Dulles describes it, a model is "a relatively simple, artificially constructed case which is found to be useful and illuminating for dealing with realities that are more complex and differentiated."[12]

It is of utmost importance to understand that models are constructions. Models are not mirrors of a reality "out there"; they are "ideal types," either logically constructed theoretical positions ("You could do this, and then things would look so") or abstractions formed from concrete positions ("So and so does it this way; someone else proceeds this way"). As constructions or ideal types, it is important, as Barbour says (reminiscent of Reinhold Niebuhr), that models be taken "seriously but not literally."[13] Nothing in real life is quite like a model; the atom doesn't really resemble a solar system. People don't just think of the church, for instance, as an institution, or as a servant or mystical community. The most institutionally minded cardinal still can thrill to the church being called the body of Christ, and to speak of God as Father does not mean that God literally has primary and secondary male sex characteristics. A model, as Sallie McFague points out, partakes in the metaphorical nature of all language, and so, while it certainly affirms something real, it never really captures that reality, and so one can say that "the key to the proper use of models is . . . to remember always the metaphorical tensions—the 'is and is not'—in all our thinking and interpreting."[14]

Nevertheless, Barbour insists that models are not simply "useful fictions."[15] Models can and do disclose actual features in the matter under investigation; they are disclosive of reality. Using models is a way of dealing with a complex, highly differentiated reality. Even though models are not, so to speak, the axe, they can function as a kind of wedge; even though they cannot bring the whole picture into focus, they can provide an angle of vision. Understanding models in this way requires that one subscribe to a philosophy of critical realism. While the critical realist recognizes that one can never fully know a reality as it is in itself, at the same time she or he realizes that what is known is *truly* known. Models, in the same way as images and symbols, provide ways through which one knows reality in all its richness and complexity. Models provide a knowledge that is always partial and inadequate but never false or merely subjective. Bohr's model of the atom really, though not fully, explains atomic structure; the model of church as institution manifests the essential way that the cardinal thinks about the church; the model of God as Father provides an adequate though not exclusive understanding of God's Mystery.

A further distinction is necessary. Theoretical models can be either exclusive or complementary, or, as Schineller says, either systematic or descriptive.[16] Schineller's own "spectrum of views" in regard to Christology and ecclesiology are examples of exclusive or systematic models. If one has an exclusive Christology and ecclesiology, it would be illogical to think positively of ways of salvation other than Christianity. If one is persuaded that Jesus is one of many saviors, it would be illogical to speak in terms of a normative Christology or an exclusive ecclesiology. Niebuhr's five ways in which Christ is understood in relation to culture are another example of this exclusive type of model: one has to settle on Christ above culture, Christ transforming culture, Christ in paradox with culture, and so forth. This kind of model might be called a paradigm. Although this word is a disputed one and rather difficult to define, we might say that a paradigm is a worldview, a way of seeing the world, involving a set of commitments or positions that cannot easily be related to others, if they can be at all. While Thomas Kuhn may have exaggerated in saying that a change in paradigm involves nothing less than conversion, paradigms nevertheless do represent very distinct ways of understanding reality and give rise to particular sets of questions that are only possible within their scope.[17]

A complementary or descriptive model expresses a more tentative position. Barbour speaks of a model as an organizing image that gives a particular emphasis and enables one to notice and interpret certain aspects of experience.[18] What this indicates, it seems to me, is that if one model points to certain aspects of experience, another model or other words can be employed to bring other aspects of experience to light. Because of the complexity of the reality one is trying to express in terms of models, such a variety of models might even be imperative. Since models are not pictures of reality "out there," an exclusive use of one model might distort the very reality one is trying to understand.[19]

Physicists employ this complementarity of models when they try to understand the nature of light. Is light composed of waves or particles? As is well known, the answer to this question is that light in a certain sense is composed of both—and neither. "A complete elucidation of one and the same object," writes physicist Niels Bohr, "may require diverse points of view which defy a unique description."[20] While neither particle nor wave models should be regarded as literally picturing reality, when they are taken together and understood as interpretations, they do give real knowledge of the real world.[21]

In a similar way, Dulles says, "in order to offset the defects of individual models, the theologian, like the physicist, employs a combination of irreducibly distinct models. Phenomena not intelligible in terms of one model may be readily explicable when another model is used."[22] All models, in the inclusive sense, are really inadequate and need to be supplemented by others. One might settle on one model as the model that most accurately conveys the reality under consideration, "but this will not require one to deny the validity of what other theologians may affirm with the help of other models. A good theological system will generally recognize the limitations of its own root metaphors and will therefore be open to criticism from other points of view."[23] No one model can account for all the data of a particular area or for the complexity of a theological doctrine or position. That is why, says scientist Francis Crick, if one tries to squeeze everything into one model or theory, the result will be "a teetering architecture that is bound to fall."[24]

To summarize, a model—in the sense that it is most often used in theology—is what is called a theoretical model. It is a "case" that is useful in simplifying a complex reality, and although such simplification does not fully capture that reality, it does yield true knowledge of it. Theoretical models can either be exclusive or paradigmatic or be inclusive, descriptive, or complementary.

THE USE OF MODELS IN THIS BOOK

When we propose the various models of contextual theology in this book, we will be speaking of theoretical models of the inclusive or descriptive type. The models here, however, differ in one small but perhaps significant degree from those envisioned by Barbour, Dulles, and McFague. The difference lies in the fact that instead of symbolic images, such as "Mother" for God or "sacrament" for the church, we will be speaking about models of operation, models of theological method. Each model, therefore, presents a different way of theologizing that takes a particular context seriously, and so each represents a distinct theological starting point and distinct theological presuppositions.

The various models emerge out of the various ways that theologians combine the elements, described in the first chapter, that make a theology contextual. The most conservative of the six models, the countercultural model, recognizes the importance of context but radically distrusts its sanctity and revelational power. The translation model is one that, while certainly taking account of experience, culture, social location, and social change, puts much more emphasis on fidelity to what it considers the essential content of scripture and tradition. The most radical of the six models, the anthropological model, will emphasize cultural identity and its relevance for theology more than scripture or tradition, which it considers important but a product of contextually relative theologies that have been hammered out in very particular contexts. The practitioner of the praxis model will zero in on the importance or need of social change as she or he articulates her or his faith; the one who prefers the synthetic model will attempt the extremely difficult task of keeping all of the elements in perfect balance. Finally, the view of the transcendental model focuses not on a content to be articulated but on the subject who is articulating. The hope here is that if one is personally authentic in one's faith and in one's being-in-the-world, one will be able to express one's faith in an authentically contextual manner. If we were to draw a map of the models as we have described them here, it might look like the diagram in Figure 2.[25] The anthropological model, since it is the model that departs most from traditional theological content, is found on the farthest left. The countercultural model, since its concern is to challenge the context with the content of scripture and tradition, is located on the extreme right. The other models fall in between, even though the transcendental model floats above all, since it is more concerned with the theologizing subject than with theological content.

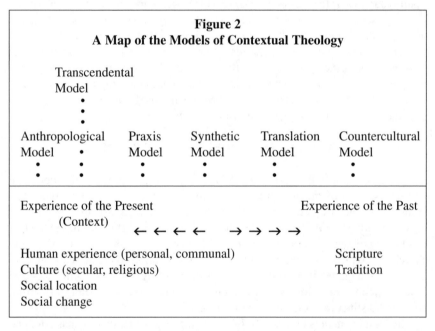

Figure 2
A Map of the Models of Contextual Theology

Though each model is distinct, each can be used in conjunction with others. A particular use of the translation model may have several aspects of the praxis model within it; or a version of what is basically an anthropological model may be much more cognizant of the importance of the traditional content of Christian message than another version. In the same way, it is my contention that no one model can be used exclusively and an exclusive use will distort the theological enterprise. While every one of these models is in some sense a translation of a message, an adequate theology cannot be reduced to a mere application or adaptation of a changeless body of truths. Even the biblical message was developed in a dialogue with human experience, culture, and cultural and social change, and a theology that neither issues forth in action nor takes account of the way one lives one's life can hardly be theology that is worth very much. At the same time, any theology that is not in some sense countercultural cannot be a truly Christian theology. As Darrell Whiteman astutely points out, "when the Gospel is presented . . . along appropriate cultural patterns, then people will more likely be confronted with the offense of the Gospel, exposing their own sinfulness and the tendency toward evil, oppressive structures and behavior patterns within their culture."[26] Finally, a theology that is not the activity of a faithful and integrated subject cannot claim to be an adequate expression of Christian faith.[27]

There is no one completely adequate way of doing theology. The various models discussed in this book point to various approaches that are actually being used in constructing contextual theology today, but no model is exhaustive or applicable to all situations of faith. Certain circumstances might call for the theologian to be more protective of the received tradition and of the language and worldview within which it comes. Other circumstances will call the theologian to be attentive to Christian life and action, drawing on the rich experience that such life and action can reveal. At still other times the theologian must point to the richness of the culture and the wealth of spiritual values that it contains and expresses inchoately. One may choose a particular model in a particular context, but one must also be aware that other models may be equally valid in other contexts.

PROCEDURE OF THE FOLLOWING CHAPTERS

Bearing in mind, then, how we will be understanding and employing models throughout the rest of this book, let me now outline how these models will be described and analyzed in the chapters that follow.

The first part of every chapter will consist of a description and critique of the model under investigation. In each case some reflection will be done on the title of the particular model, and then the presuppositions on which the model is based will be spelled out in some detail. The model will then be illustrated by a diagram, and this will be followed by a discussion of the model's advantages and disadvantages.

In the second part of each chapter, the work of two theologians who employ the particular model will be reviewed. The only exceptions to this are in Chapter 6, in which the second example draws from a book published by a number of Asian feminist theologians, and in Chapter 9, in which the first example used is that of a number of theologians who make up the Gospel and Our Culture Network. After a general description of the content of the theologian's work and a description of a particular book or article, the theologian will be critiqued in terms of his or her faithfulness to the model and the effectiveness of the model to articulate an adequate theology.

After the book's conclusion is a chart (see pages 141-43) that summarizes the main features of each model. The appropriate section of the chart will be placed after the presentation of each model.

Part Two

Six Models
of Contextual Theology

4

The Translation Model

Of the six models we will be considering in this book, the translation model of contextual theology is probably the most commonly employed and usually the one that most people think of when they think of doing theology in context. Robert Schreiter points out that much of the renewal of the Roman Catholic liturgical texts has been guided by a translation approach, keeping only what is essential to the rites while adapting customs deemed inessential to local culture and practice.[1] Indeed, an article in an important dictionary of liturgical theology speaks of the appropriateness of the term *adaptation* to describe the way that liturgy needs to be related to particular cultures.[2]

Practitioners of the translation model also point out that it is possibly the oldest way to take the context of theologizing seriously and that it is found within the Bible itself. Pope John Paul II writes that Paul's speeches at Lystra and Athens (Acts 14:15-17 and 17:22-31) "are speeches which offer an example of the inculturation of the Gospel."[3] For Daniel von Allmen, St. Paul's efforts to speak of Christians' union with Christ are a prime example of how our own theologizing should be carried out today.[4] Charles Kraft maintains that this way of doing theology—with an eye to translating the Christian message into ever-changing and always particular contexts—is no more than a recovery of the original spirit of Christian theologizing. The message that was originally so adaptable soon became captive of Greek categories, but every true theology must liberate that message from those categories and restore it to its original flexibility.[5]

In many ways, every model of contextual theology is a model of translation. There is always a content to be adapted or accommodated to a particular culture. What makes this particular model specifically a translation model, however, is its insistence on the message of the gospel as an unchanging message. As we will see below, tradition is not a model for daring and creative ways to state that message; it is conceived much more as a way of being faithful to an essential content. The values and thought forms of culture and the structures of social change are understood not so much as good in themselves, but as convenient vehicles for this essential, unchanging deposit of truth.

A SKETCH OF THE MODEL

THE TERMINOLOGY

When we speak of translation in this chapter, we do not have in mind a literal, word-for-word translation. This is what Charles Kraft speaks of as translation by formal correspondence,[6] and examples might be a translation of the English *table* into the Latin *mensa*, the Italian *tavola*, the Spanish *mesa*, the German *Tisch*, or the Ilokano *lamisaan*. People have such a literal translation model in mind when they ask what might be the Filipino equivalent for the Greek *homoousios* so that Filipinos might be able to express exactly what the Council of Chalcedon meant in its famous Christological definition, or how one might render *Being* in a language such as Japanese.

A formal-correspondence approach to translation can never get at the deep structures of a language, which are more than simple vocabulary and grammar correspondences. Words carry much more than denotative meanings; they are the vehicles of all sorts of emotional and cultural connotations as well. Languages such as Hebrew, from which one translates the Bible, and Ilokano, into which one translates, do not have the same ideas of subject, verb, object, voice as do western languages such as Latin or German or English. As Kraft observes:

> Word-for-word translation and the consistency principle are, however, the result of misunderstandings of the nature of language and of the translation process itself. The results of such emphases tend to be wooden and foreign-sounding. The literalists' focus sees but dimly the livingness of the original encoding of the message. Furthermore, it often ignores completely the contemporary cultural and linguistic involvement of any but the most theologically indoctrinated of the readers. Its aim is to be "faithful to the original documents." But this "faithfulness" centers almost exclusively on the surface-level forms of the linguistic encoding in the source language and their literal transference into corresponding linguistic forms in the receptor language.[7]

Any translation has to be a translation of meanings, not just of words and grammar. A good translation, as any student of foreign languages knows, is one that captures the spirit of a text, and a clear sign of having mastered a language is when one is able to understand jokes in that language, since humor often emerges in double entendres and idiomatic meanings. I will never forget the time during my student days when I was riding in the backseat of a car with a nun who had worked in the United States for several years but who had never quite mastered English. As we drove along, we were teasing the sister about something or other, and at a certain point the driver of the car told the sister not to worry; we were only "pulling her leg"—to which she emphatically remarked that that was not true; the two of us in the back seat were keeping our hands to ourselves! Her literal translation had clearly missed the point.

Translation, then, has to be idiomatic, or as Kraft says, it must be done by functional or dynamic equivalence.[8] In accepting this understanding of translation, Kraft is accepting the translation principle of the Phillips Bible, the New English Bible, and, in particular, the United Bible Societies (e.g., their English translation published as the Good News Bible [Today's English Version—TEV]; the UBS has been particularly active in translating the Bible into a large number of languages and making these versions available at a reasonable price). The aim of this dynamic-equivalence method of translation is to elicit the same reaction in contemporary hearers or readers as in the original hearers or readers. As Eugene Nida and Charles Taber put it, "a translation of the Bible must not only provide information which people can understand but must present the message in such a way that people can feel its relevance (the expressive element in communication) and can then respond to it in action (the imperative function)."[9] An example from the recently issued Ilokano Popular Version of the Bible might be helpful in understanding the freedom involved in such translation (Ilokano is the language spoken in many parts of northern Luzon in the Philippines). In translating Gen 1:1-2, the original Hebrew speaks about the *ruach elohim* (literally, the wind, or breath or spirit of God) moving over the surface of the watery chaos. The Old Ilokano Version translates *ruach* in the traditional, formal correspondence way (as does the Revised Standard Version) as "*ti Espiritu ti Dios*" ("the Spirit of God"). The new dynamic equivalent version, however, is less literal but much more faithful to the original Priestly author's intention when it translates *ruach* as "*ti pannakabalin ti Dios*" or "the *power* of God."[10]

After a thorough treatment of the nature and advantages of dynamic equivalent Bible translation, Kraft applies this kind of translation to theologizing. Basing his move on Bengt Sundkler's statement that "theology is, in the last resort, translation," Kraft says that

> *theological truth must be re-created like a dynamic-equivalence translation or transculturation within the language accompanying conceptual framework of the hearers if its true relevance is to be properly perceived by them.* Theologizing, like all Christian communication, must be directed to someone if it is to serve its purpose. It cannot be flung out into thin air.[11]

By the translation model, we do not mean a mere word-for-word correspondence of, say, doctrinal language of one culture into doctrinal language of another. Rather, we are concerned with translating the meaning of doctrines into another cultural context—and this translation might make those doctrines look and sound quite different from their original formulation. Nevertheless, the translation model insists that there is "something" that must be "put into" other terms. There is always something from the outside that must be made to fit inside; there is always something "given" that must be "received."

PRESUPPOSITIONS OF THE TRANSLATION MODEL

If there is a key presupposition of the translation model, it is that the essential message of Christianity is supracultural or supracontextual. Practitioners of this model speak of a "gospel core."[12] Another basic metaphor that reveals this presupposition is that of the kernel and the husk: there is the kernel of the gospel, which is surrounded in a disposable, nonessential cultural husk.

Just what this essence consists in, however, is a matter of some debate among advocates of the translation model. Krikor Haleblian notes that some theologians (he gives the examples of Saphir Athyal and Byang Kato) speak simply of the gospel core as "Christ incarnate." Donald McGavran, however, would hold that the essence of the gospel would have a bit more content. For him, the gospel is reducible to "the belief and allegiance to (a) the Triune God, (b) the Bible, and (c) the ordinances and doctrines set in the Bible."[13] Max Stackhouse outlines four basic doctrines that he considers basic to Christian orthodoxy and that "point to something true not only for those who already believe it, and not only for those formed in a particular socio-cultural-historical-linguistic system, but for everyone, everywhere."[14] These four doctrines are (1) that humanity is fallen and is in need of healing and salvation; (2) that, as is witnessed by the Bible, God's revelation takes place within human history; (3) that the doctrine of the Trinity articulates best what God is truly like and what faith in God means for life in the world; and (4) that Jesus is the Christ—that in Jesus men and women can find the true meaning of life.[15]

In any case, what is very clear in the minds of people who employ the translation model is that an essential, supracontextual message *can* be separated from a contextually bound mode of expression. The first step, therefore, in contextualizing a particular Christian doctrine or practice is to strip it of its wrappings—the contextual husk—in order to find the gospel kernel. Once the "naked gospel" has been revealed, one then searches the "receptor situation" for the appropriate terms or action or story to rewrap the message. When both are found and put together with the help of not only theology and anthropology but real religious and cultural sympathy, this particular aspect of the gospel, at least for this time and this place, has been translated relatively successfully. Since the important thing in the translation model is to translate the message, most translators will admit that while it is advantageous for the one translating to be a participant in the context into which the message is being translated, it is not absolutely necessary. What is important is that one be a person who has understood the Christian message and who is in creative touch with the experience, culture, or perspective in question.

Methodologically, it is important to note that the starting point in this process is always the supracultural, supracontextual essential doctrine. To turn around a phrase of Robert McAfee Brown, for the translation model, gospel content affects cultural and social context.[16] As Bruce Fleming puts its succinctly, contextualization is "putting the gospel into."[17] And Morris A. Inch reflects the same idea in the titles of two of his books: *Doing Theology across Cultures* and *Making the Good News Relevant*.[18] Several years ago a discussion arose in the Philippines as to whether theology in the Catholic colleges and universities was supposed to train Filipino Christians or Christian Filipinos. In terms of the translation model, the former answer would be the correct one.

This last remark points to another presupposition of the translation model, that of the ancillary or subordinate role of context in the contextualization process. Experience, culture, social location, and social change, of course, are acknowledged as important, but they are never as important as the supracultural, "never changing"[19] gospel message. If, for example, gospel values and cultural values come into conflict in the evangelization or contextualization process, there is no doubt that the content of the gospel message must be preserved, rather than the values and practices of the culture. Ultimately the gospel is the judge of all contexts, even though it seeks to work with and within all contexts.[20] The contextual situation, ultimately, is the vehicle of the message. The original gospel message was wrapped in a certain culture and embodied in certain persons and experiences, but these contextual particulars can, in many cases, be dispensed with in an encounter with other cultures and situations in other times. But context and message are always separate things, and context is clearly a secondary element. As Pope John XXIII expressed it in his opening speech at the Second Vatican Council, "the substance of the ancient doctrine of the deposit of faith is one thing, and the way in which it is presented is another."[21]

Everything we have said so far implies an understanding of divine revelation that is both propositional and quantitative. This is not true of every practitioner of the translation model, but it is certainly the notion of revelation of the great majority, particularly those of a more evangelical background.[22] In the first place, the emphasis on the priority of a message or gospel core points to the fact that revelation is understood as primarily, if not wholly, propositional. Revelation is conceived as a communication of certain truths or doctrines from God, and because they are from God, they are wholly culturally free or clothed in a culture that is divinely sanctioned. The gospel may be able to be stripped down to as little as one basic idea, such as the lordship of Christ, but this idea is a proposition that cannot be compromised. Second, revelation is understood as not only qualitatively different from human experience and culture but quantitatively different as well. The Christian message in an encounter with a new context and/or a new religion brings something that is *absolutely new* into that particular context. God's presence may not be wholly lacking in a non-Christian situation, but it only really becomes operative when the specifically Christian message is preached. This is why, in order to preach this message effectively, it must be clothed in language and patterns that the men and women of the new context can understand.

A final presupposition to be considered in regard to the translation model is its conviction, implied rather than stated explicitly, that all cultures have the same basic structure. Although there are ways of expression and modes of behavior that are unique to every culture, it is still possible to find some kind of rough correspondence between every aspect of one culture and every aspect of another. This presupposition is necessary if the basic point of the translation model is to be worked out in practice: that every concept of one culture can be translated in terms of another culture—if not exactly, then certainly equivalently. The procedure would be something like a person who would bring seed from one particular location to another. She or he would plant them in the new ground, confident that the soil is basically the same as in the original place of planting. The seeds would sprout and grow and really take root in the new ground, even though the *origin* of the seeds came from elsewhere. So the gospel is sown in the context of the experience of youth, or Asian culture, or among Hispanic/Latina women in New Jersey, or among Filipino farmers. It will take root in those contexts, but it will always be the *eternal* Word spoken in the context of the *changing* world.[23]

If we were to portray the procedure of the translation model in a diagram that captures its basic presuppositions, it would look like the diagram in Figure 3.

Figure 3
The Translation Model

Experience of the Past   Experience of the Present
   (Context)

                   → → → →

Scripture   Human experience (personal
                                 communal)
                      Culture (secular, religious)
Tradition   Social location
                      Social change

CRITIQUE OF THE TRANSLATION MODEL

Except perhaps for the countercultural model, which we will outline in Chapter 9, no other model that we will focus on in this book takes seriously the message of Christianity as recorded in the scriptures and handed down in tradition. The emphasis here is on Christian identity as more important than, though not exclusive of, contextual reality or cultural identity. Like the countercultural model, the translation model witnesses to the fact that Christianity does have something to say to the world and that its message is truly one that can bring light and peace to a dark and troubled world. It is important, therefore, that when preachers and teachers preach and teach and when women and men hear and read about Christianity, the message of life to which Christianity witnesses be heard and understood clearly, and not be presented in ways that automatically strike a person as irrelevant or as too accommodating.

Another important feature of the translation model is that it recognizes the ambivalence of contextual reality, whether that be a person's or a society's experience, a culture's or a religion's system of values, a person's social location or the movements of change in the world. For a practitioner of the translation model, it is not necessary to hold a fundamentalist faith in the goodness of every concept in the Bible or in the inspiring nature of every verse. Likewise, she or he does not have to defend every doctrine of the church or every action the church has taken in its long and often not-so-glorious history. So much of the Bible and of the formulations of tradition, the translator realizes, is simply the product of a culture and needs to be stripped down at every turn to the basic gospel message. By the same token, the person using the translation model will realize that not everything that is "genuinely African," for instance, is automatically good and that something that is very Asian might become a vehicle for something that transcends all cultures. The practitioner of the translation model is one who can accept the good in all cultures or contexts while still being committed to the transforming and challenging power of the gospel.

Third, the translation model is one that is able to be used by any person committed to a particular culture or situation, nonparticipant or participant. With a relatively brief introduction to a particular culture or society, one can begin "making the good news relevant" in homilies, religion classes, counseling sessions, and so forth. Especially when doing primary evangelization, this model of translating the message is absolutely essential. If no effort of translation is made, there is hardly any way people of another culture can come to know the life that Christianity holds out.

Nevertheless, there are some serious questions about an exclusive and even a preferred use of the translation model. One critique focuses on the idea of culture that underlies the model's theological method. The presupposition is that every culture is roughly similar to every other culture and that what is important in one will be important in another. As Robert Schreiter observes, "questions are rarely asked as to whether there really are such parallels, whether the parallels have the same significance in the new culture, or whether other more significant patterns might be drawn upon."[24] Polygamous marriages, for example, might seem against the teaching of Jesus (Mt 19:3-10) and have certainly not been the practice of the church, but in recent years both anthropologists and theologians alike have pointed out the importance of such marriage patterns for the order and cohesion of certain African societies.[25] What might seem on the surface, at least in terms of North American or European culture, a very un-Christian practice may actually be, if the deeper structures of a culture be known, something that can be interpreted in a profoundly Christian way.

Criticism can also focus on what is perhaps the key idea of the translation model: the supracultural or supracontextual nature of the Christian message. It is very improbable that there can exist such a thing as a "naked gospel." It is certainly important not to throw out the baby (doctrine) with the bathwater (context), and this is something that the translation model strongly affirms. The problem, however, is to know the exact difference between the two, because "we cannot have access to the gospel apart from some kind of human formulation."[26] A more naive, positivistic notion of culture, for instance, might allow for a supracultural content, but much more common today is a notion of culture that is all-embracing, the matrix of every human attitude and linguistic expression. Rather than the image of culture as a husk that covers a kernel, Krikor Haleblian suggests that culture is like an onion, with various layers. The message of Christianity is always inculturated, and rather than finding an essential core, one must find a way of discerning cultural patterns that incarnate or can incarnate Christian existence and meaning.[27]

Third, we might criticize as well the translation model's implicit notion of revelation as propositional. Revelation is not just a message from God, a list of truths that Christians must believe. Revelation is the manifestation of God's presence in human life and in human society, and if it is anything, the Bible represents the written record of that manifestation in particular times and within a particular society—that of Israel and the early Christian community. Contemporary scripture studies have made us well aware, as we have pointed out in Chapter 1, that the texts of the Bible are the results not of heavenly dictation, but of the struggles of women and men of faith to make sense out of that faith in the midst of lives where God's presence was often less than self-evident. Rather than a list of doctrines to be believed, the Bible—and to some extent the Christian tradition—presents various valid ways of wrestling with faith and doing theology, and acceptance of scripture and tradition as God's word is the acceptance of a challenge to imitate the writers of scripture and the giants of tradition in discerning God's ways in the present.[28] What this suggests is that, rather than looking for a kernel to wrap in a new husk, the theologian should be looking for God's presence at every layer of the onion and point that out in terms of the older and wider tradition.

The translation model can be neither rejected nor accepted uncritically. It seems to me that there are moments, such as the point of primary evangelization or an attempt to evangelize the culture of secularity and postmodernity, when a translation of one's own understanding of Christianity is necessary. And throughout the whole evangelization process, the integrity of the gospel and of the church's tradition must be safeguarded. The translation model, however, never moves beyond an accommodation or adaptation of a particular content. Ultimately it needs to take more seriously the world and the flesh within which, and not just by means of which, God became incarnate.

The Translation Model

Alternative Titles: *accommodation; adaptation*
Basis in Scripture and Tradition: *Acts 14:15-17; Acts 17:2-31; Cyril and Methodius; Ricci; de Nobili; John XXIII at opening of Vatican II*
Revelation: *tends to be interpreted as propositional, content-oriented*
Scripture/Tradition: *supracontextual; complete*
Context: *basically good and trustworthy*
Method: *kernel/husk; know the context so as to effectively* insert *the gospel*
Analogy: *bring seeds, plant in native ground*
Legend: *"putting the gospel into" (Bruce Fleming)*
Critique: *Positive: takes Christian message seriously; recognizes
            contextual ambiguity; can be used by participants and
            nonparticipants in a culture*
          *Negative: naive notions of culture and gospel; propositional
            notion of revelation*

EXAMPLES OF THE TRANSLATION MODEL

Out of a number of examples of theologians who practice a translation model of contextualizing theology—Byang Kato, Bruce J. Nicholls, Morris A. Inch, participants in the 1982 conference "Sharing Jesus in the Two Thirds World," Bong Rin Ro and members of the Asia Theological Association, and the "early" Louis J. Luzbetak[29]—I would like to focus on two. The first, David J. Hesselgrave, is a major spokesperson for the evangelical tradition of theology; the second, Pope John Paul II, has articulated his ideas about inculturation during his many journeys or pilgrimages in his capacity as head of the college of bishops of the Roman Catholic Church.

DAVID J. HESSELGRAVE

David J. Hesselgrave was educated at Trinity Evangelical Divinity School in Deerfield, Illinois, and the University of Minnesota (where he received his Ph.D.) and worked as a missionary to Japan for twelve years. He has contributed to various missiological journals, such as *Evangelical Missions Quarterly*, *International Bulletin of Missionary Research*, and *Missiology: An International Review*,[30] has edited collections of essays on missiological topics,[31] and has published important books on missionary communication, church planting, and cross-cultural counseling.[32] In 1989, with his colleague Edward Rommen (at the time, both were teaching at Trinity Evangelical Divinity School), Hesselgrave published *Contextualization: Meanings, Methods, and Models*, a wide-ranging summary and pointed critique of various approaches to the contextualization enterprise that concludes with several examples of contextual theology that are considered "authentic and relevant."[33] There is no doubt that Hesselgrave represents a rather conservative approach to the contextualization of theology and tends to be limited to Christianity's first encounter with a non-Christian culture, but his is a comprehensive and forceful articulation of one approach to what it means to be faithful to the Christian message while attempting to make it relevant to women and men of other cultural worldviews. It is an approach, I believe, that repays close study.

Hesselgrave's basic stance toward contextualization is very clear: contextualization is not optional; it is a missiological and theological necessity.[34] It is a process that is evident in the scriptures as well as in the history of the church and of theology.[35] One of the problems of missionary activity in the past has been that missionaries have been so preoccupied with the communication of their saving message that they forgot that, besides knowing the "message for the world," they needed to know "the world in which the message must be communicated."[36] Not the mere delivery of the message but the effective *communication* of the message is the best way to summarize what Christian mission is all about.[37]

Because communication is so essential to mission, Hesselgrave first anchors his ideas in a theory of communication. Expanding Aristotle's classic threefold components of speaker, speech, and audience, he speaks of the source, the act of encoding, the message, the act of decoding the message, and the receiver or "re-spondent." In the act of communication, the source (e.g., the missionary) has en-coded the message into terms or symbols meaningful to him or her, and as com-munication of the message takes place, the respondent decodes the message by encoding it into terms or symbols that are meaningful in his or her situation.[38] If an adequate communication of a message is to take place, the source needs to attempt to encode the message in such a way that when it is decoded by the respondent, he or she understands what has been communicated. The clearest example of this is language—the source person translates the phrase "here I am" into the Italian *eccomi* or the Ilokano *addaakon*. Communication can go wrong when the mes-sage is wrongly decoded (as in the case of the sister in the backseat of our car whose "leg" we were "pulling") or when the message is unable to be meaning-fully decoded (as in the case of Christian words such as "sin," "cross," or "salva-tion").[39]

Although in our human experience there is never a message that is not in some way encoded or contextualized in terms of culture, history, and context, Hesselgrave maintains that in communicating Godself to us, the human symbols of which God makes use take on supracultural and universal meaning.[40] "There was, and is, a 'gospel' or 'salvific' core (1 Cor. 15:1-4). This gospel core was determined by the Spirit and not by the evangelists; it was built upon and pointed to the whole coun-sel of God (Acts 20:27)."[41] Many things in Scripture, particularly in the Old Tes-tament, such as dietary laws and prescriptions about sacrifice, are culture-spe-cific, but there are principles by which this supracultural core can be discerned. Contextualization, therefore, becomes—here Hesselgrave borrows the definition of Bruce J. Nicholls—"the translation of the unchanging content of the Gospel of the Kingdom into verbal forms *meaningful* to the peoples in their separate cul-tures and with their particular existential situations."[42]

In order to effect this contextual communication of the gospel, Hesselgrave develops Eugene Nida's three-language model of communication into a three-culture model. The missionary is a subject of a particular culture; he or she needs to communicate the gospel message, which is wrapped in its cultural particularity, to subjects of another culture. In order to do this, one must take two steps: one must *decontextualize* the gospel in terms of one's own understanding by a thorough study of the scriptural text; then one must study the respondent culture in order to *contextualize* the message in its particular terms. As Hesselgrave summarizes:

> *Decontextualization* is needed in order to arrive at the supracultural message which is conveyed in culturally meaningful forms. The cultural wrappings must be folded back in order to get the gift of truth—the Western wrappings of the missionary's culture (where the missionary is a Westerner) and also the wrappings of biblical culture itself. When one comes to the Scriptures, he must be especially cautious, for in the Bible God Himself chose the language and forms by which the truth came to be unfolded. The words are God's; as well as the truths. . . .

As for *contextualization* it is needed to make the message meaningful, relevant, persuasive, and effective within the respondent culture.[43]

How does one actually communicate the gospel within the various, radically differing worldviews that exist in our world? In general, one must pay attention to oneself as source, to the gospel message as substance, and to style as the means of communication. Keeping in mind that contextualization is never a once-and-for-all accomplishment and that it is best done by participants of a culture,[44] one addresses these three components in terms of particular worldviews. Within the naturalist worldview, for example, the missionary must study philosophy and be careful of his or her arguments; the terms of the message must be translated in natural, scientific terms (Hesselgrave is a bit vague here); the missionary's style must not be a negative, "pulpit-pounding" one, but friendly, open, thoughtful. Within the tribal worldview, the missionary must cultivate an aura of power by demonstrating the powerful logic and historicity of Christian faith; the substance cannot compromise on monotheism, and the style must be respectful of people's ways, and especially respectful of their understanding of the sources of power. To give one more example, within the Hindu/Buddhist worldview, the missionary needs to be seen as a deeply religious person, a teacher, and above all a person of renunciation. The gospel must be presented in terms of forgiveness and personal peace, and the style has to be very spiritual.[45]

Throughout his works Hesselgrave gives various concrete examples of what he considers "authentic and relevant" contextualization, but in the fourth part of *Contextualization* he presents (with Edward Rommen) several proposals that are a bit more sustained.[46] Of these proposals, two are particularly clear examples of what Hesselgrave means when he speaks of contextualization.

The first of these is entitled "A Contextualization of the New Birth Message: An Evangelistic Tract for Chinese People."[47] The chapter begins by describing two tracts entitled "How Can a Man Be Born Again?"—both found on a rack of a Christian hospital in Hong Kong. One version was in English, the other was in Chinese, but both were "as identical in format and content as any two tracts in two languages as different as English and Chinese could possibly be."[48] Hesselgrave and Rommen point out that the Chinese version of the tract is a prime example of a translation that is really uncontextual; it is an example, as Nida and Kraft would say, of "formal correspondence."

Upon investigation it was discovered that a missionary obstetrician was giving these tracts to new parents whose children had been born at the hospital where she worked. But she was also suspicious that the way the message was presented (a message she totally agreed with) was inappropriate for Hong Kong people and Chinese culture. When the tract was referred to local people for their evaluation, they pointed out a number of defects in it from the point of view of their culture: to name a few, the cover pictured a Caucasian person; the "born again" theme could easily be confused with Buddhist ideas of reincarnation; it did not ask questions Chinese are asking; and it did not make use of Asian indirectness in its approach.[49]

In response to a request from the obstetrician, Hesselgrave and Rommen provided a more contextualized tract, which they entitled "New Life." They stipulated, however, that before publication it should be evaluated by several competent Chinese Christian leaders. In the chapter of *Contextualization* that we are summarizing here, an English version of the proposed tract is provided, and the reader can see how it tries to adapt the Christian message to the mentality and worldview of the Chinese. The tract begins by speaking about how the new baby will bear its parents' name and link the past with the future, and a little further on the text speaks about how children insure that parents will be cared for in old age, perpetuate the family name themselves, and contribute to the larger society. But then it raises the question about "spiritual life" and the need not simply to honor ancestors but the "true God of heaven." The responsibility of parenthood does not end when the umbilical cord is cut; the child must be clothed and nourished and cared for daily. But that is not all; the child is entitled to new spiritual life, and parents can provide that for the child through their faith in Christ.

The Chinese Christian leaders to whom the draft was submitted for evaluation liked the basic approach to the new tract and suggested a few changes—instead of saying that the child bears the parents' name, for example, they suggested that the text should speak of the child as becoming a family member. When the text was printed, a Chinese woman with a baby in her arms was pictured on the cover, and indications are that the contextualized version is "far more relevant and compelling to new Chinese parents"[50] than the one that was used before.

A second example of Hesselgrave's (and Rommen's) approach to contextualizing theology is entitled "The Doctrine of Justification by Faith Contextualized: Commentaries on Galatians 2 for Sixteenth-Century Europe and Twentieth-Century India." The authors' aim here is to follow up on a suggestion by Bruce J. Nicholls that "contemporary India needs the truth of justification by grace through faith as much as did sixteenth-century Europe, but that a contemporary commentary for India would be contextualized differently than Martin Luther's commentary on Galatians 2."[51] After a brief analysis of the context of first-century Galatia (the danger of Christianity remaining a Jewish sect) and sixteenth-century Germany (Luther's insight into the gratuity of God's love over against the selling of indulgences), the Indian context is described as one in which karma colors the whole Indian worldview. As described by D. T. Niles and the *Sanyatta Nikaya*, the essence of karma is that men and women have "responsibility within a situation that is ethical, given, personal, and shared. Karma is inexorable. In this existence no one can be free of it. Bad karma cannot be forgiven."[52] Paradoxically, all this is not really real, since the world and all happenings within it are only illusions. Salvation is being freed from karma through insight into its unreality.

Hesselgrave and Rommen then proceed to juxtapose three texts: that of Galatians 2, Luther's *Commentary on St. Paul's Epistle to the Galatians*, and their own text adapted to the Indian context within the Hindu worldview. The Indian commentary makes it clear that Paul's going up to Jerusalem (Gal 2:1-2) was not a response to insight gotten in meditation, but by the intervention of God; instead of Luther's aim at "papists" as "false brothers" (vv. 4-5), the Indian commentary aims at the error of holy people who think they are saving themselves through their own asceticism. Commenting on v. 6, "God does not judge by external appearance," Luther reflects on the wrong claims by the pope to be the center of Christian faith; in Indian context it is important to say that though people such as Moses, Vardhamana, Gautama, and Shankara are "teachers of the truth and good examples, . . . even the best of them were only men"[53] and so they should not be worshipped. Luther gets to the heart of things when he reflects on v. 20 and emphasizes that no work—no obedience, poverty, "shaven pate," or anything else—can save humanity; humanity is saved because it has been crucified with Christ and lives Christ's life: salvation is pure gift. In the Indian translation, emphasis is placed on the fact that it is "the only incarnate Son of God" who died, not a mythological avatar. It was Christ's free decision to die, and he did it for us. The result is *pattidana*, " 'man enjoying the merits of God's living and holy action in Christ.' This is true salvation. True salvation is not the denial of the reality of the *kamma* principle or the reality of this world. It is salvation in which Christ pays the penalty we incurred for breaking God's law."[54]

Hesselgrave and Rommen give two other examples in their book, but I think the ones that I have summarized here are sufficient to see how the points Hesselgrave has worked out in theory are put into concrete practice. In my opinion, Hesselgrave's principles are clearly enunciated, and he does succeed, to a certain degree, in taking culture (and to some degree, cultural change) seriously while preserving at all cost the purity and integrity of the gospel, at least as he understands it. I believe he would find somewhat of an ally in the next example of the translation model on whom we will focus: Pope John Paul II.

POPE JOHN PAUL II

There can be no doubt that the Roman Catholic Church in our time has witnessed a growing sense of the centrality and importance of human culture for genuine Christian existence and theological expression. When one considers the rather anticultural and ahistorical approach of Pius IX in the "Syllabus of Errors" in the last half of the nineteenth century (1864; see DS 2901-2980)[55] and Pius X's condemnation of "modernism" at the beginning of the twentieth (1907, see DS 3475-3500), the treatment of culture at the Second Vatican Council shows that a real "cultural conscientization" had been developing during the pontificates of popes such as Leo XIII, Pius XI, and Pius XII.[56] In the years after the Council, Pope Paul VI was strong in his conviction that not only individual persons but also their cultures need to be evangelized.[57]

Throughout his long pontificate, John Paul II has shown "a real and abiding interest in culture."[58] Before becoming pope, his philosophical writings on the human person give evidence that his interest in culture is not something that has only been forced on him by his papal responsibilities;[59] since he became pope, the question of culture—especially the dialogue between faith and culture—has been a constant subject of his voluminous writings.[60] In 1982 he created the Pontifical Council on Culture and charged it with the task of "giving the whole Church a common impulse in the continuously renewed encounter between the salvific message of the Gospel and the multiplicity of cultures, in the diversity of cultures to which she must carry her fruits of grace."[61] And as the pope "never tires of repeating, the Church's dialogue with present-day cultures is of crucial importance for the world's future."[62] Only through human cultures can human beings live out their humanity fully, and so the pope sees the immense importance of cultures being profoundly and vitally influenced by the humanizing message of the gospel. In fact, as he said in an address to cultural leaders, educators, and members of the business community during his 1988 visit to Peru, the very origin of culture is precisely in the relationship between religious faith and human development.[63]

Aylward Shorter has pointed out that, despite the fact that John Paul II has dealt with the question of faith and culture in the course of his many "pilgrimages" to the Third World, much of his concern is really with the secular cultures of the West, and particularly with the atheistic culture promoted by Communism. Such a concern, Shorter suggests, would explain a certain hesitation on the pope's part regarding the value of particular cultures, a hesitation that, "while seldom directly expressed," is "more often conveyed by a choice of phrase or the tone of a passage."[64] Whether or not Shorter is correct in determining the reason for the pope's somewhat negative attitude toward culture, one does indeed sense that, for him, while culture is important and central to human existence, it is nevertheless something thoroughly ambiguous and therefore something in need of purification and redemption.[65]

It is this hesitant attitude toward culture that colors John Paul's ideas about contextualization, or, as he calls it, *inculturation*. The pope introduced the term "inculturation" into official church language in an address to the Pontifical Biblical Commission in 1979, and a quotation from that address appears in the 1979 apostolic exhortation *Catechesi Tradendae*. Here, as elsewhere, inculturation is compared to incarnation—revealing, as Dennis Doyle puts it, that the process is described as starting from the top down. In other words, inculturation proceeds in such a way that "the underlying question is how a largely pre-set tradition and institution can have the greatest possible impact on any particular cultural situation while preserving what is good in that culture."[66] Such a "top-down" definition is given in *Redemptoris Missio*, in a quotation from the final document of the 1985 Extraordinary Synod: inculturation "means the intimate transformation of authentic cultural values through their integration in Christianity and the insertion of Christianity in the various human cultures."[67]

As Paul VI had insisted in *Evangelii Nuntiandi* (20), the evangelization of culture that the pope has in mind is not a superficial thing, a mere adaptation of the message of the gospel to a culture in a formal-correspondence mode. What is involved is, rather, a creative dynamic equivalent translation of the unchanging, supracultural, and supracontextual gospel by means of the symbols and thought forms of the other culture. Even more, the universal church itself is enriched in the inculturation process "with forms of expression and values in the various sectors of Christian life," thereby coming "to know and to express better the mystery of

Christ."[68] As one reads John Paul II, however, what becomes clearer and clearer is that, no matter how creative the translation of the gospel may be, it must always be a *translation* of the gospel (and of subsequent doctrinal formulations of the church). Time after time the pope warns against giving *culture*, and not the gospel, priority and distinguishes such "culturalism" from a genuine use of culture "*in order to re-translate* in new words and in new perspectives the biblical revelation that has been handed down to us."[69] Indeed, he admits that there are some cultural expressions (philosophical viewpoints, languages, scientific systems) that have nothing at all to offer the gospel message and need only to be opposed and corrected.[70]

Foremost in the pope's mind, it seems, is the preservation of the unity of the faith, and for him this can be accomplished only by emphasizing a primary universality of ecclesial communion and doctrinal expression. This idea is expressed with particular clarity in an address given at a general audience on September 27, 1989. Referring to the Pentecost experience where people from many nations and cultures heard the disciples speaking of "the mighty acts of God" in their own tongues (Acts 2:11), the pope concludes "*that the Church came into being as a universal Church, and not merely as a particular Church, that of Jerusalem.*"[71] He goes on to say that in this way "*Christian Universalism*" (his emphasis) is inaugurated, expressed from the beginning in the diversity of cultures. The methodological effect on the process of inculturation is subtle but profound: one always begins with a universal (necessarily supracultural) message, which can be expressed in or translated into particular cultural forms. And because the important thing is the faithful transmission of this universal message, it stands to reason that even though inculturation "must involve the whole people of God and not just a few experts, since the people reflect the authentic *sensus fidei*,"[72] the bishops "must be watchful, . . . and see to it that the work of adaptation is done by teams controlled by the episcopate so that Catholic doctrine will be expressed correctly and in its entirety."[73] As the pope emphasized in an address to the first national congress of the Ecclesial Movement of Cultural Commitment, "only the full truth about man, given to us by faith" and "thought out under the guidance of the Magisterium of the Church," can enable Christians to harmonize "the ever greater diversity of the elements that constitute modern culture: the unification and harmonization in which wisdom consists."[74]

Throughout the years of his pontificate, the pope has held up several examples of the correct interaction between faith and culture. In his 1980 address to the Zairean bishops, the pope gave as an example of authentic inculturation his own country of Poland, where, after centuries, "a profound harmony has developed between Catholicism and the national characteristic pattern of thought and action."[75] The culture and way of life of Poland have been thoroughly penetrated by Christian values, so much so that for the last half century Poles found resources in their culture to resist the competing culture of Communism. This high level of inculturation has taken centuries to develop and has involved a great amount of "theological clarity, spiritual discernment, wisdom and prudence,"[76] but the result is a Christianity that is fiercely loyal to the church's tradition and authentically Polish to the core.

In 1982, addressing participants of an international congress on the life and thought of the Jesuit missionary Matteo Ricci, John Paul praised the work of Ricci as equal to the work of Justin Martyr, Clement of Alexandria, and Origen "in their effort to translate the message of faith in terms understandable to the culture of their times."[77] Ricci's task in China, as one of his companions explained in a letter to a friend, was to become Chinese, "*ut Christo Sinas lucrifaciamus*"—to win China for Christ.[78] At first, as the pope rehearses the story, Ricci and his companions went among the Chinese in dress similar to Buddhist monks, only to realize that if they were to have genuine impact on Chinese society and culture, they needed rather to present themselves as scholars, as men who in the Chinese context had more power and status. It was only after acceptance by the highest levels of society that Ricci could really succeed in his work of effectively preaching the gospel. Eventually, with the help of a number of Chinese collaborators, Ricci succeeded in the seemingly impossible task of "devising Chinese terminology for Catholic theology and liturgy, thus making Christ known and embodying His Gospel message and the Church in the context of the Chinese culture."[79] The pope is careful to point out that even though Ricci's methods were considered radical and even scandalous to some, what "assured fruitfulness to his work, gave him the strength to overcome difficulties and discouragement and prevented him from making wrong choices" was the conviction that he was not carrying on a purely personal work but was a representative of the Holy See and the Society of Jesus.[80] The pope does not say it explicitly, but he seems to point to Ricci's fidelity to the universality of the Christian message as the crucial factor in his success as an agent of inculturation. What is important is to discover the resources within a culture that can be used to make the gospel relevant:

> In speaking of the Gospel, he knew how to find the cultural means appropriate for whoever was listening to him. He began with the discussion of subjects dear to the Chinese people, namely, morality and the rules for social living, according to the Confucian tradition whose great human and ethical values he recognized with sensitivity.
>
> Then he introduced, in a discreet and indirect way, the Christian point of view of the various problems and so, without imposing himself, he ended up by bringing many listeners to the explicit knowledge and authentic worship of God, the Highest Good.
>
> This message, so concrete and full of hope but at the same time respectful of all the positive values of classical Chinese thought, was understood by his disciples and sensed by numerous friends and visitors.[81]

On the occasion of the eleventh centenary of Saints Cyril and Methodius, the Apostles of the Slavs, the pope issued a special encyclical that commemorated the lives and work of these two missionary pioneers. Here the pope talked specifically about these saints' work of evangelization as a model of contextualization. In order to best bring the gospel to the Slavic peoples, Cyril and Methodius, blood brothers, immersed themselves in Slavic culture and made great efforts "to gain a good grasp of the interior world of those to whom they intended to proclaim the word of God in images and concepts that would sound familiar to them."[82] Then, through catechesis, they were able to "transpose correctly biblical notions and Greek theological concepts into a very different context of thought and historical experience."[83] In this way, the Slavs to whom the brothers were sent were able to hear God's word "proclaimed in a way that completely fitted their own mentality and respected the actual conditions of their own life."[84]

At the same time that Cyril and Methodius were making efforts of inculturation, they (especially Methodius) were making efforts to preserve the unity of the faith as well. The pope commends the saints for preserving "a resolute and vigilant fidelity to right doctrine and the tradition of the perfectly united church, and in particular to the 'divine teachings' and 'ecclesiastical teachings' on which, in accordance with the canons of the ancient councils, its structure and organization was founded."[85] Like Matteo Ricci, it was this creative fidelity to the gospel and the church that enabled them to be so successful in their work.

Aylward Shorter calls *Slavorum Apostoli* "a celebration of John Paul II's conception of culture."[86] As he explains it, the pope's idea is that the best form of culture is like that of Poland: a culture permeated with gospel values. While all people are people of culture, there is a great gulf between cultures that are evangelized and those that are not. As Shorter concludes, "St. Justin's concept of the 'seeds of the Word' is not found in the Pope's writings, nor does he often dwell on the Christian potentialities of non-Christian culture."[87] Pope John Paul II has certainly made some significant contributions to the question of the contextualization of Christianity, however. His approach may not be as open to the possibilities of culture as the other models I will discuss in the following chapters, but as one who is pledged to be the guardian and protector of the rich Christian tradition, his openness is in many ways very remarkable.

5

The Anthropological Model

The anthropological model of contextual theology is almost at the opposite end of the spectrum from the translation model. If the primary concern of the translation model is the preservation of Christian identity while attempting to take culture, social change, and history seriously, the primary concern of the anthropological model is the establishment or preservation of cultural identity by a person of Christian faith. In the context of the anthropological model, therefore, the answer to the question as to whether one is aiming to become a Christian Filipino or a Filipino Christian is very definitely the former option. What is important in this model is the understanding that Christianity is about the human person and her or his fulfillment. This does not mean that the gospel cannot challenge a particular context, but such a challenge is always viewed with the suspicion that the challenge is not coming from God as such, but from a tendency of one (western, Mediterranean) contextual perspective to impose its values on another.

If the translation model has recourse to a passage such as Acts 17 on which to base its authenticity, the anthropological model could cite Mt 15:21-28 (par. Mk 7:24-30), in which pericope Jesus is shaken out of his prejudice by the Syrophoenician woman, learns from her, and is edified by her faith.[1] From tradition, proponents of this model might cite Justin Martyr's idea that other religions (and cultures) contain "seeds of the word."[2] Or they might cite certain passages from recent church documents: a passage from Vatican II's decree on missionary activity, for example, says that today's missionaries, as contemporary disciples of Jesus, "can learn by sincere and patient dialogue what treasures a bountiful God has distributed among the nations of the earth. But at the same time, let them try to illumine these treasures with the light of the gospel, to set them free, and to bring them under the dominion of God their savior."[3] Similarly, an Orthodox advisory group to the World Council of Churches Commission on World Mission and Evangelism, meeting in 1990, insists, "We are called to study the strange and sometimes offensive voices in various cultural milieus not only for the purpose of combatting or converting them, but also to learn from them and to deepen our insights and understanding of the gospel."[4]

A SKETCH OF THE MODEL

TERMINOLOGY

The anthropological model is "anthropological" in two senses. In the first place, this model centers on the value and goodness of *anthropos*, the human person. Human experience, as it is limited and yet realized in culture, social change, and geographical and historical circumstances, is considered the basic criterion of judgment as to whether a particular contextual expression is genuine or not. It is within every person, and every society and social location and every culture, that God manifests the divine presence, and so theology is not just a matter of relating an external message—however supracultural or supracontextual—to a particular situation; rather, theology chiefly involves attending and listening to that situation so that God's hidden presence can be manifested in the ordinary structures of the situation, often in surprising ways. Rather than correspondence with a particular message, the more general human categories of life, wholeness, healing, and relationship become the standards by which genuine religious expression is judged to be sound.

Second, this model is anthropological in the sense that it makes use of the insights of the social science of anthropology. By means of this particular discipline, the practitioner of the anthropological model tries to understand more clearly the web of human relationships and meanings that make up human culture and in which God is present, offering life, healing, and wholeness. This second sense of the anthropological model points to the fact that the main emphasis of this approach to contextual theology is on culture. For this model, it is particularly in a study of, and sympathetic identity with, a people's culture that one finds the symbols and concepts with which to construct an adequate articulation of that people's faith. It is not that the practitioner of this model denies the importance of scripture or of the Christian tradition, nor does he or she ignore the reality of particular personal and communal experiences, social location or social and cultural change. But what gives shape to this particular model is the special concern with authentic cultural identity.

The term *indigenization*, once used by many as a general term for the entire contextual process, might be used as an alternate way to describe what we mean by this model. Although the term is a bit awkward in English, it expresses well the idea that this model is concerned with what is indigenous or proper to a people and their culture. Robert Schreiter, citing a term used by the Ecumenical Association of Third World Theologians, speaks of various "ethnographic models" that focus on cultural identity and continuity.[5] This term is also illustrative of what the anthropological model is about, since ethnography is another name, perhaps more preferred in Europe, however, for the same discipline as anthropology. The term *inculturation* is often proposed as well to express the importance of culture in the construction of a true contextual theology.[6] Nevertheless, I prefer the term *anthropological* because of the richness of the double sense described above. This model, more than any other, focuses on the validity of the human as the place of divine revelation and as a source (*locus*) for theology that is equal to the other two sources of scripture and tradition.

PRESUPPOSITIONS OF THE ANTHROPOLOGICAL MODEL

In what has become quite a famous passage, M. A. C. Warren pleaded eloquently for

> a deep humility, by which we remember that God has not left himself without a witness in any nation at any time. When we approach the man of another faith than our own it will be in a spirit of expectancy to find how God has been speaking to him and what new understandings of the grace and love of God we may ourselves discover in this encounter.
>
> Our first task in approaching another people, another culture, another religion, is to take off our shoes, for the place we are approaching is holy. Else we may find ourselves treading on men's dreams. More serious still, we may forget that God was here before our arrival.[7]

These words express perhaps more clearly than any I know the central and guiding insight of the anthropological model: human nature, and therefore the human context, is good, holy, and valuable. The anthropological model would emphasize that it is within human culture that we find God's revelation—not as a separate supracultural message, but in the very complexity of culture itself, in the warp and woof of human relationships, which are constitutive of cultural existence. Rather than approaching the Bible as a particular message or set of doctrines that are wrapped or clothed in foreign but ultimately similar cultural trappings, the practitioner of the anthropological model understands that the Bible is the product of socially and culturally conditioned religious experiences arising out of the very life of Israel and the early Christian community. Rather than understanding the doctrinal formulations of tradition as directly inspired words from heaven, the anthropological model sees doctrines as conditioned at all times by the various cultures and sociopolitical concerns of western Europe.

While the person who uses the translation model basically sees himself or herself as bringing a saving message into the context and making sure that it is presented in a relevant and attractive way, the practitioner of the anthropological model looks for God's revelation and self-manifestation as it is hidden within the values, relational patterns, and concerns of a context. Robert T. Rush characterized the change that had taken place in mission theology since Vatican II by speaking of a change of imagery of the missionary. Whereas formerly the missionary might be pictured as a "pearl merchant," Vatican II and the theology of mission since have begun to discover that a better image might be that of a "treasure hunter."[8] While the scriptures and the Christian tradition can serve as a map, which, in order to be helpful in the search, needs to be translated, the real work involves digging deep into the history and tradition of the culture itself, "for it is primarily there that the treasure is to be found."[9] The treasure, of course, is God's grace in Christ, and this healing, redeeming presence is hidden in every culture and in every religious way within particular cultures.[10] Practitioners of the anthropological model would insist that while the acceptance of Christianity might challenge a particular culture, it would not radically change it. The anthropological model sees a mutual benefit for both the particular culture and wider Christianity.

In Chapter 2 we made the distinction between a creation-centered theology and one that was redemption-centered. Depending on which basic theological orientation one chooses, we said, one gives more or less room for a particular historical or cultural context to function as a valid theological source. A redemption-centered theology, even though it might acknowledge the importance of contextual actors, would not provide much room for them methodologically in the actual theologizing process. A creation-centered orientation, however, would tend to regard the stuff of human experience in general and of culture in particular as revealing God's presence in a particular situation. For one to be a practitioner of the anthropological model, I believe, such a creation-centered theology must be taken as one's basic theological stance. The anthropological model rests on a conviction of the goodness of creation, shot through and through with, as Gerard Manley Hopkins expressed it, "the grandeur of God." Those who employ the anthropological model might often take it to the extreme, but at the heart of this model lies the strong sacramentalism characteristic of true Catholic thinking.[11]

The starting point, therefore, of the anthropological model is, broadly speaking, present human experience, with a particular focus on human culture, secular or religious. In a paper delivered at a missionary congress in 1983, Simon Smith spoke of what for him was the true meaning of inculturation. Speaking out of his experience as a missionary in Africa, Smith first stressed what inculturation is not. It is not "liturgy with drums or dance or tinkling bells or flowers or incense; the existence of an indigenous clergy or even hierarchy," and the like.[12] These types of practices fail truly to be inculturations because they all "presuppose that there exists a certain body of data, a message, a body of doctrine, a certain minimum which we have to adapt, adjust, clothe or I don't know what."[13] The problem was with the starting point; it took something basically non-African as the primary factor in Christianity and sought ways to *adapt* it. What needs to be done, however, is to begin from the opposite pole of culture:

> In order to understand what I am trying to say, listen to this conversation I had a few years ago in Africa with a group of African theologians (I say *African* theologians, not theologians in Africa). When one speaks of inculturation in Africa, one has to recognize the primacy of culture. *We* are accustomed to stress revelation or dogma or some other given thing when we speak of inculturation. But for Africans it is *culture* which is primary.[14]

Whether every African would agree with Smith or not, his statement is one that points to a key presupposition of the anthropological model: it is culture that shapes the way Christianity is articulated. Or to refer once more to the title of McAfee

Brown's essay, the anthropological model holds that "context affects content."[15]

Especially in its more radical or purer forms, the anthropological model sees a particular context as unique, and the emphasis is on this uniqueness rather than what participants in this context have in common with other groups. As a consequence, the anthropological model relies very little on insights from other traditions and other cultures for the articulation of faith. If they are used at all, other ways of thought need to be thoroughly adapted. If they are not, says Leonardo Mercado, they will produce false results. The production of a Filipino theology, says Mercado, needs to work with Filipino categories of thought and Filipino images and values. Ideas from other Asian cultures might also be helpful, but particular care should be taken when using western thought. "Although Western theology has its merits, the Filipino who is steeped in Western categories will find himself a prisoner. A knowledge therefore of Filipino and other Oriental categories will help him in theologizing with the people."[16]

Mercado's remark also makes mention of a final presupposition: for the anthropological model, the experience of the ordinary cultural subject, the ordinary person, is where one must look for manifestations of culture. The people are the best contextualizers, and the less touched they are by dominant western models, the better.[17] The role of the trained theologian, therefore, is not that of an expert who tells people the best way to express their faith. Rather her or his role is that of reflector and thematizer, the one who is able to provide the biblical and traditional background that will enable the people to develop their own theology. Her or his role is very much like a midwife—assisting at a birth with lots of experience and expertise, but not really directly involved in the birthing itself.[18] Nevertheless, even the theologian should be a participant in the culture in which the contextual theologizing is done. She or he is at an advantage if she or he has experience with other cultures or contexts, but the theologian must always be a participant—or a highly gifted person with genuine sympathy for the situation or culture.[19]

By applying the techniques of anthropology and sociology, therefore, the practitioner of the anthropological model attempts to listen to a particular context in order to hear within its structure (especially within the complex structure of culture) the very Word of God, hidden there like a dormant seed since the beginning of time and ready for sprouting and full growth. An analysis of the Filipino *sakop* orientation, for example, whereby the Filipino understands herself or himself first as a member of a group rather than as an individual, might be the way that Filipinos can live out the mystery of God's church.[20] An analysis of popular religious movements such as the African Independent Churches or groups such as the Philippine Benevolent Missionary Association, Inc., might provide clues to the authentic religious genius of a particular people.[21] Reflecting closely on the experience of being a woman will yield new ways to understand the scriptures, traditional sources, and the entire doctrinal tradition.[22]

In the same way, since within a language is found the entire way that a people or culture views the world, a "metalinguistic" analysis of language is very helpful in getting at the heart of a culture where God manifests God's self.[23] Dionisio Miranda, for example, begins his construction of Filipino ethics with an in-depth analysis of the Tagalog word *loob*.[24] Along the same line, my colleague John Kaserow has pointed out a whole theology of priesthood (which I have thought could be as validly applied to the church) in an analysis of the Chinese character *shen fu*, and I have always been amazed at the depth of meaning of the ordinary Ilokano word for "going to Mass," which is *makimisa*—literally, "doing the Mass together."

Finally, the anthropological model uses the wisdom gleaned from interreligious dialogue as material from which a truly culturally sensitive theology can be articulated. In 1974 the East Asian bishops, speaking of the need to develop an Asian spirituality, endorsed this particular method. "It behooves us," they said, "to find out what are the elements in oriental culture, which can be used to develop an East Asian spirituality. The traditional forms of asceticism, classical Chinese ethical teaching and practice, oriental methods of meditation and prayer, are some of the fields in which such an incarnation could be promoted."[25]

Figure 4 portrays the basic procedure of the anthropological model, along with its presuppositions.

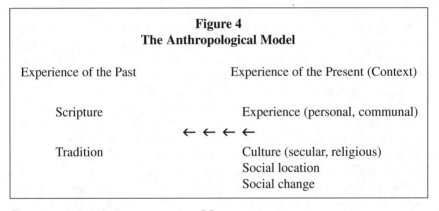

Figure 4
The Anthropological Model

Experience of the Past	Experience of the Present (Context)
Scripture	Experience (personal, communal)
	← ← ← ←
Tradition	Culture (secular, religious)
	Social location
	Social change

CRITIQUE OF THE ANTHROPOLOGICAL MODEL

The strength of the anthropological model comes from the fact that it regards human reality with utmost seriousness. It attests to the goodness of all creation and to the lovabilty of the world into which God sent God's only son (Jn 3:16). Its idea of revelation surpasses that of the translation model in that it recognizes that revelation is not essentially a message, but the result of an encounter with God's loving and healing power in the midst of the ordinariness of life. Its understanding of scripture and tradition as a "series of local theologies"[26] is much more faithful to contemporary scholarship than the view that these theological sources are only accidentally culturally conditioned. As I said in the beginning of this chapter, this model has some basis in both classical and contemporary Christian thought.

This model also has the advantage of allowing men and women to see Christianity in a fresh light. Christianity is not automatically the importation of foreign ideas. Rather it is a perspective on how to live one's life even more faithfully in terms of who one is as a cultural and historical subject. To be a Christian, insists the anthropological model, is to be fully human; it is to find perhaps more challenging but always more abundant life. This is a whole new way of doing theology.

A third positive aspect of the anthropological model is that it starts where people are, with people's real questions and interests, rather than by imposing questions asked out of other contexts. Anthropologist Jon Kirby has pointed out that evangelization in Africa has been less than successful since Christianity has not been presented as a system that solves problems that Africans really have. "African Christians continue to deal with their problems outside the boundaries of Church authority (and hopefully without anybody noticing). How may we speak of the growing 'African Church,' or 'indigenization,' or of 'contextualizing the gospel' without first opening our eyes and ears to people's problems as they are experienced and understood by them?"[27] The anthropological model would try to answer this question by initiating "a dialogue with Christian tradition whereby that tradition can address questions genuinely posed by the local circumstances, rather than only those questions that the Christian tradition has treated in the past."[28]

A major danger, however, with this model is that it easily falls prey to a cultural romanticism. On the one hand, this romanticism is evidenced by what is often a lack of critical thinking about the particular culture in question. Despite the fact that he explicitly denies such uncritical acceptance of Filipino culture,[29] one gets the impression when one reads Mercado that if something is genuinely Filipino, it is good, holy, and revelatory.[30] On the other hand, such cultural romanticism is blind to the fact that the idyllic picture of a culture that practitioners of the anthropological model paint does not really exist. The fact is, as Aylward Shorter points out, that acculturation, or the encounter of one culture with another, is happening all the time, even despite efforts of some societies to seal a culture off.[31] Cultures are changing all the time, and they change because of all sorts of factors, not least of which is an encounter with Christianity and its expression in often radically different cultural forms. If a theology or a particular church resists cultural change in the name of the contextualization of Christianity, such resistance, rather than opening a culture to its greatest potential, functions as a conservative force and actually works against the good of a culture. Muslims in Iran are certainly in touch with Iranian culture, as were the Taliban in Afghanistan with Afghan culture, and they practice an Islam that is thoroughly indigenous and, as much as possible, sealed off from western influence. But whether this isolation is ultimately in the best interest of their respective peoples is far from certain. It would be a shame, in my opinion, to create a U. S. American Christianity that did not at the same time take account of the role of the United States in the world today. The whole situation of humanity at the dawn of the twenty-first century is characterized by the need to be interdependent and globally conscious, not sealed off into neatly definable cultural groups.[32]

Use of the anthropological model is often more easily said than done. It was pointed out in the beginning of the previous chapter that in some way or another every effort of contextual theology is an effort of translation: not only the present—experience, culture, social location, and social change—needs to be attended to; the experience of the past—scripture and tradition—needs to be attended to as well. Simply to discover the gospel emerging from a particular situation is the ideal of the anthropological model, but that is, to my knowledge, never the real situation. Even radical practitioners of the model such as Mercado and Panikkar speak in categories of sin, grace, justice, trinity, and so forth. And as much as the anthropological model tries to fend off influence from other cultures, the fact that its method hinges on the western science of anthropology and other social sciences is indicative of the fact that it cannot be a method that is totally isolated.

The insight of the anthropological model is that the theologian must start where the faith actually lives, and that is in the midst of people's lives. It is in the world as it is, a world bounded by history and culture and a particular language, that God speaks. To ignore this would be to ignore the living source of theology. But to listen only to the present and not to the past as recorded in scripture and tradition would be like listening to a symphony in monaural when, by the flick of a switch, it could come alive in full stereo.

The Anthropological Model

Alternative Titles: *indigenization; ethnographic model*
Basis in Scripture and Tradition: *Mt 15:21-28; Mk 7:24-30; Jn 3:16; movement of Acts; Justin Martyr—"seeds of the word"; GS 44; AG 11; CT 53*
Revelation: *tends to be understood as "personal presence"*
Scripture/Tradition: *culturally conditioned; like all human expressions, incomplete*
Context: *basically good and trustworthy; equal to scripture and tradition*
Method: *know the culture to "pull the gospel out of it"*
Analogy: *seeds are already in the ground; just need to be watered to sprout*
Legend: *"take off your shoes" (Max Warren)*
Critique: *Positive: takes context seriously; provides fresh perspectives of Christianity; starts with where people are*
    Negative: prey to cultural romanticism

EXAMPLES OF THE ANTHROPOLOGICAL MODEL

ROBERT E. HOOD

African American or black theology is often associated with the theology of liberation, and so it is considered an example of the praxis model of contextual theology—the model we will consider in the following chapter. In the United States, the name usually connected with such a theology is James H. Cone, whose pioneering works *Black Theology and Black Power*, *A Black Theology of Liberation*, and a number of other works over the last three decades have made him not only the foremost black theologian in the United States but also one of the most important voices of liberation theology throughout the world.[33]

There is another approach, however, to doing theology in the African American context that, while not ignoring the importance of working for and theologizing out of the struggle for liberation, insists that—methodologically speaking— any genuine African American theology will take as its starting point the riches of black culture, which are inescapably intertwined with black religion. In *The Identity Crisis in Black Theology*, for example, James Cone's brother Cecil Cone argues that black religion, formed in the crucible of black Americans' African religious heritage as well as their experience of slavery and oppression, is the only proper point of departure for the construction of African American theology.[34] This is especially true because, he maintains, the Christianity of African Americans is not and never was conventional Christianity. Rather, instead of becoming Christians by submitting themselves to the worldview and doctrinal system of the Christian church, African Americans appropriated them into their traditional religious systems.[35]

It is this more anthropological approach to theology that has been developed by African American theologian Robert E. Hood, and it is on his work that I propose to focus here. Hood is a priest of the Episcopal Church in the United States and is currently Professor of Church and Society at General Theological Seminary in New York City. He completed his doctoral studies, with a dissertation on Karl Barth, at Oxford University and has published a number of articles, mostly on issues relating to the black church.[36] In 1985 he published *Contemporary Political Orders and Christ: Karl Barth's Christology and Political Praxis*, in 1990 he published *Must God Remain Greek? Afro Cultures and God-Talk*, and in 1994 he published *Begrimed and Black: Christian Traditions on Blacks and Blackness*.[37]

Hood's short program for Afro-Anglican theological education, given at a conference in 1985, provides an overview of his concerns in doing theology. Among other recommendations, including an insistence that theology should always connect with issues of justice and liberation, Hood urges that biblical studies should include "stress on the role of Egypt and such people and nations as Ethiopia and Nubia" and on "concepts which have parallels in Afro traditions, religions, communities, cultures."[38] He further recommends that church history include the development of Anglicanism in other areas besides England and North America, that liturgical studies be taught in a way that includes "the preaching, singing, religious customs of indigenous cultures of Afro-Anglicanism even if it means neglecting or dropping the *Book of Common Prayer*,"[39] and that the Spirit be recognized as active in everyday life and "in the religious traditions of Africa and the African Diaspora."[40]

All of this is part of a project on Hood's part to demythologize what he considers an all-too-Graeco-Roman, Eurocentric tradition, in order that the values and cultural expressions of other nonwestern, non-Greek-influenced cultures can find expression in Christian theology and worship.[41] For various reasons, he says, among which is the assumed superiority of western culture coupled with an assumed inferiority of the African and Asian races, Greek-influenced western thinking had "control of the past" and so never allowed for anything significant to emerge from other cultures or other worldviews. It is time now, however, especially in the light of the fact that Christianity is growing most rapidly in the very cultures that have for so long been ignored or repressed, to ask some fundamental questions: Could unity in faith mean that a plurality of different worldviews needs to be cultivated when it comes to constructing theological formulations? Could there possibly be several orthodox formulations about, say, the nature of Christ and the Spirit? Is it possible to allow other cultures as well as Greek culture to set the agenda for theology and doctrine?[42] Hood's answer to these questions would be a resounding "yes," and in answering in this way, he reveals that for him the essential way to be faithful to the gospel and to Christian tradition is to attend first to context. His model for doing theology is anthropological.

Although Hood has employed his method to reflect on the doctrines of God, Christology, and the saints, perhaps the best example of how his method might change theological and doctrinal content is his reflection on the doctrine of the Spirit. What Hood attempts in this reflection is to show a link between the traditional notion of God the Holy Spirit and the various good spirits whose existence and role are so "crucial for understanding the African and Caribbean worldview as well as the traditional religion that has shaped it."[43]

The biblical worldview regarding the Spirit of God, Hood argues, is very similar to the African worldview regarding the spirits. It is the Spirit that "will not speak on his own authority, but whatever he hears he will speak" (Jn 16:13), and this is similar to the African belief that the spirits are given authority by God to act in certain ways in the world.[44] Like the Spirit that inspired the prophets, and John in the book of Revelation, the spirits in African religions are power-giving; and like the seven spirits standing before God's throne, the spirits in African religion act as messengers throughout the earth and to men and women.[45] Spirits in the Bible are called in Hebrew *mal'akim*, messengers of God, and "are used by God (Yahweh) for inflicting vengeance on enemies (2 Kings 19:35; Ps. 35:5f.) and creating disorder in the natural realm (2 Sam. 24:16)."[46] In the New Testament, says Hood, under the influence of popular Judaism and Persian religion, these same spirits are called demons (*daimonia*), but such a development into a negative idea about the spirits is due to cultural change in Judaism and is not central to Christian faith.[47]

The dogmatic tradition as well leaves room for a possibly different understanding of the nature of the Spirit. The doctrinal formulation that the church has espoused in its official creeds is really the creation of theologians such as Athanasius and especially Augustine, and their ideas about the consubstantiality of the Spirit were solidified through the development of western theology. Other theologians, however, such as Tertullian and Origen as well as Basil, Gregory of Nyssa, and Gregory Nanzianzen, were less insistent on the technical definition of the divinity of the Spirit, although the latter three "did write and preach endlessly about its inclusion within the godhead."[48]

In African traditional religion, explains Hood, God is—though not always—sovereign and above all spirits; but God normally relates to humankind and the natural world *through* the various spirits—"sons of God," as Ghanaian theologian Kwesi Dickson calls them, or God's "executioners" or "spokesmen."[49] Africans also acknowledge evil spirits, but they might more accurately be called " 'mysterious powers' rather than spirits because, whereas spirits are essentially good, these forces in Africa are seen as the personification of evil."[50] Such spirits do not in any way come from God but are often harnessed by evil human beings.[51]

What Hood proposes is an alternate theology of the Holy Spirit, based on the African worldview and his reading of scripture and tradition in its light. Such a theology, he admits, would not be possible within the framework of the Greek, Eurocentric worldview, which controls the theological possibilities of the Christian tradition today, but he insists that it is completely plausible within the context of Africa and cultures of the African diaspora such as black culture in the United States. The Holy Spirit, he suggests, can be interpreted as the "Ministering Spirit" of God. As Ministering Spirit, God's Spirit is sovereign over a host of lesser spirits who, while not equal to divinity, are nevertheless not merely created. These spirits are the way God relates to and acts in the world: they provide strength, consolation, healing, inspiration, ecstasy, warning; sometimes they even carry out divinely ordered consequences for human misbehavior. While evil spirits or "mysterious powers" also exist, Hood maintains that God's Spirit, made manifest in Jesus as Christ, is stronger than evil and ultimately victorious over it. For African religion, the worship of spirits as God's messengers—even worship in the form of sacrifices—is the same as the worship of God as such.

Hood's ultimate point in all of this is that African American religion could be made more relevant to black people if some of these ideas were admitted into its mainstream. It is clear many African beliefs have always been present in black religion throughout its history, he says, and it is time now for these beliefs to be fully recognized by the African American church as theologically, pastorally, and spiritually valid and enriching.

Hood's reinterpretation of the doctrine of the Holy Spirit points to the radical revision of Christian doctrinal thought and theological formulation that use of the anthropological model might make possible. Starting with the African roots of the African American experience and taking seriously the thought and beliefs of unsophisticated (i.e., untainted by western thought) Africans and African Americans, the contextual theologian is led to the articulation of a theology that, while radically different from traditional formulations, earnestly claims authentic fidelity to its deepest spirit.

VINCENT J. DONOVAN

Vincent J. Donovan, our second example of the anthropological model, served for a number of years in East Africa and, during the 1980s and 1990s, in African

American parishes in Dayton (Ohio), Chicago, and North Carolina, and worked as a campus minister at Duquesne University in Pittsburgh. Now deceased (1999), he was a priest in the Roman Catholic Congregation of the Holy Spirit, and did graduate studies at Fordham University in New York and at the Gregorian University in Rome. Donovan is most well known for his *Christianity Rediscovered*,[52] a charming and provocative book about his work among the Masai people in Tanzania, but he also published several articles, and a second book entitled *The Church in the Midst of Creation*.[53]

A basic idea for understanding Donovan's thought, and especially basic for understanding his approach to the contextualization of theology, is a distinction he makes between evangelization and a people's response to evangelization (what he calls the "refounding" of the church).[54] As he repeats several times in *Christianity Rediscovered*, the task of the missionary is to present the gospel, and the task of the people who respond to it is to express that gospel and its meaning in their own language and within their own thought forms: "the field of culture is theirs. Ours is the gospel."[55] The gospel alone is "revelation" ("what God wants us to know and do"); everything else is "religion" ("what *we make* of that revelation").[56]

For Donovan, the missionary or evangelizer needs to approach a non-Christian religion and/or culture with the "naked gospel," the "stripped-down skeletal core" of the gospel, the "final and fundamental substance of the Christian message."[57] Rather than burden a non-Christian people with a message that is really western, Eurocentric culture masquerading as religion, all the evangelizer needs to bring is the supracultural message of the gospel, unencumbered by anything, as clear and straightforward as possible.

From one point of view, the gospel can be put in an abbreviated, basic form.

> It is a message of God who is a Spirit totally beyond us, yet is the creator of this world, a God who loves this world and is saving it; who loves good and evil people, forgives all who turn to God, is prodigal (generous in gifts and calling), continues to create to wipe out suffering and injustice, promises to save all men and women, all nations—the whole world. We are called to be perfect as God is perfect, forgiving all, reaching out to the suffering, in the sacred task of building the earth.[58]

From another point of view, however, the "naked gospel" is not articulated so easily. Donovan admits that he really does not know what the "final and fundamental substance of the Christian message" is. In fact, he says, no one does, because it is something that will only emerge in the future. The essence of the gospel message will only become clear when all cultures hear it from messengers who have understood it from their own cultural point of view and who are convinced that it is of value to the world. Then, when all cultures have been evangelized by the gospel and when the church community has been evangelized by the cultures of the world, the meaning of the gospel will at last be known.[59] In the meantime, evangelization needs to be done with humility. The evangelizer should approach another culture with the conviction that God is already present within it, even though that culture, like all cultures, is also deeply flawed. His or her role is to bring God to full recognition within that culture and thus to contribute to the full expression of the gospel.[60] Ultimately, the gospel is not a message at all, but a Person, "a God-human named Jesus Christ"[61]; evangelization is fueled with the faith that this Person is present through his Spirit in all of history.[62]

The method of this kind of evangelization, therefore, is not one in which the messenger enters a culture or situation simply to communicate a message, no matter how stripped down it is. Rather, with the conviction of the basic goodness of a context, the evangelizer presents the message with as few accretions from his or her own context as possible and invites his or her hearers to "play back" what they have heard. Evangelization, conceived in this way, is more of a dialogue; and as in every dialogue, the outcome cannot be predicted. Both evangelizer and evangelized are changed, and as a result, the gospel message takes on a shape and content that it never had before. Donovan, when asked how he convinced the Masai in Tanzania that the gospel was indeed for them, describes the process in this way:

> With great reverence to the Masai culture, we went back to the naked gospel, as close as we could get to it, and presented it to them as honestly as we could. We let them play it back to us—that was the system, to let them play it back. As it was played back we began to see different lights on the very message we were trying to bring to them. I would present it as clearly as I could, and they would play back what they heard me saying. That would startle me. There was this constant playing it back and forth, until something emerged that I thought they or we had never heard before. At the end, we began to see that what was emerging was the God of the gospel—one that we did not recognize before we started this thing.[63]

Christianity Rediscovered tells the story of how this kind of evangelization took place. The Masai could not accept a God who was understood in wholly male images; this opened Donovan up to the deeply biblical images of God as female. The story of the Good Samaritan was hard for the people to accept, but they honestly grappled with it and brought to it a new and rich meaning. In telling the story of Abraham, and as the people questioned him, Donovan had to admit that even *his* people (Christians) had not yet found the High God. The dialogues between Donovan and the Masai opened them up to the possibility of a "future tense" in their lives and gave them hope in a life beyond this one. The image of a lion stalking and killing its prey opened up a fresh understanding of faith and provided a startling image of God.[64] Donovan was the messenger, yes; but in a way, his method made him more of a catalyst. In a real way, to allude to the words of Paul VI and John Paul II (EN 75 and RM 21), the Holy Spirit was the principal agent in the evangelizing of the Masai.

When a people or a culture accepts the truth of evangelization and commits itself to the Christian God through baptism, Donovan says that the way that they express their faith is completely their concern. The missionary, he says, presents the gospel; the rest is up to the people hearing the message. They can reject it, and that is that; but if they accept it, *how* they accept it is up to them. The missionary, no matter how hard he or she tries, can never get away from the image of the church, the content and hierarchy of Christian doctrines, that he or she has learned. So he or she should be as uninvolved as possible in the people's response, which is the church. The missionary's task is the gospel; the people's task is everything else:

> The way people might celebrate the central truths of Christianity; the way they would distribute the goods of the earth and live out their daily lives; their spiritual, ascetical expression of Christianity should they accept it; their way of working out the Christian responsibility of the social implications of the gospel—all these things, that is: liturgy, morality, dogmatic theology, spirituality, and social action would be a cultural response to a central, unchanging, supracultural, uninterpreted gospel.[65]

Donovan gives a number of examples of this response in *Christianity Rediscovered*, but perhaps the most striking is the way that the people chose to celebrate Eucharist.[66] As he describes it, the Eucharist was something that people celebrated throughout the whole day. There was no dichotomy between sacred and profane, between daily life and prayer life; the whole day was a prayerful celebration of the community's renewal as Christ's body in this world, as the *orporor sinyati*, or holy brotherhood/sisterhood/*koinonia*.

The celebration would begin long before Donovan would arrive, but when he did arrive, he would scoop up a handful of grass and hand it to the elders who came to greet him. Grass was a sign of peace among the Masai, and so, when they received it, they would pass it on throughout the village as a sign of reconciliation. If the grass would ever stop—that is, not be accepted by one person or one family—the Eucharist could not be celebrated. In the meantime, however, as the grass was being passed from family to family in the village, the singing and dancing would begin. Donovan never told the people what to sing or how to dance: "They sang what they wanted to sing and when they wanted to."[67]

The celebration continued in different parts of the village and in many different ways at the same time. Donovan would walk around the village during all of this, visiting with a woman who was repairing the roof on her hut, instructing other people for baptism, visiting the village's sick, giving deeper instruction to the village leaders. Later on, if and when the elders decided it was fitting, Donovan would say the words over bread and wine. This did not always happen, but when it did, it was more than just "the saying of a few words in the right order." Rather it was a celebration of the fact that "This—not just the bread and wine, but the whole life of the village, its work, play, joy, sorrow, the homes, the grazing fields, the flocks, the people—all this is my Body."[68]

In the last chapter of *The Church in the Midst of Creation*, Donovan presents the story[69] of a group of African American Christians who discover the power of the "naked gospel" in a Bible study group and who respond by creating their own culturally rooted community. It all began with a "forlorn group of black parishioners"—seven women and four men—"and a white priest meeting in the church office."[70] After they had read the first chapter of Luke's gospel, the priest began talking about some technical aspects of the gospel, but he was soon interrupted by one of the women who talked about how surprised she was that women like Elizabeth and especially Mary spoke so freely against the traditional ways of doing things. Mary was seen as an unwed, pregnant teenager, and her language in the "Magnificat" was seen as pretty radical.

The next week twenty people showed up for the Bible study, and the woman who had started the previous week's discussion sat at the head of the table while the priest moved to the side. As the discussion proceeded, the group began to move from studying the Bible to reflecting on problems and situations in their own lives in the Bible's light. And so by the next meeting the group had grown to thirty, and soon the group saw that it had to divide into two groups. As the group began to discuss the Holy Family, there was an unexpected turn:

> That family did not seem so flawless and tranquil and perfect after all. There was that threat of divorce hanging over the family from the beginning. There was grinding poverty—the offering of two pigeons in the Temple was the best the family of Nazareth could come up with, to redeem their first-born. There was the incident of the runaway child of twelve, with Jesus being scolded by his mother for his efforts, and the beginning of a generational conflict between mother and son, which continues through the Gospel. And it seems the family turned into a one-parent family, with Joseph disappearing from the scene. The Holy Family was becoming very familiar to the black group discussing it.[71]

Eventually the group broke up into three groups. Prayer became less awkward, Jesus became more human, his parables were discovered to reflect quite accurately much of the life of the inner city. The priest couldn't attend every group meeting, or even any group meetings in some weeks, but grassroots leadership emerged and the communities still flourished. The groups' discussions became much more than study groups; they began to reflect on how they might begin to change things in their neighborhoods and in their city. They also became more prayerful and began to make up ceremonies—"*agapes*, with bread and grape juice. (They were wary of alcohol and what it was doing to black society.)"[72] They began having naming ceremonies when babies were born, ceremonies that reflected their African roots and that were strangely soul-stirring. Their image of Jesus changed; he was now seen as a man who was really on their side, someone who identified with them, black like them. They began attracting non-Catholics to their gatherings as well.

What was happening, one realizes, was that this community was responding in its own way to the gospel that it had so strongly experienced. And in the process a new kind of church, a new kind of doctrine, a new kind of ministry was being developed. It was not something closed and exclusive, but it was theirs. It was not an adaptation or translation of a traditional structure; it was something that grew out of their experience and their cultural identity. Context was affecting content.

Donovan was not a professional theologian, and sometimes his ideas are not always consistent, but reading his works, especially his book on his experiences with the Masai, is an incredibly moving experience. His sensitivity to the importance of culture, his critical commitment to its goodness, his contagious humanity, and his inspiring faith are all reasons for taking his work as a serious attempt to show that constructing a contextual theology starts not with a predetermined message or content, but with God's living, challenging, life-giving presence in the midst of human life.

6

The Praxis Model

If the translation model focuses on Christian identity within a particular context and seeks to preserve continuity with the older and wider tradition, and if the anthropological model focuses on the identity of Christians within a particular context and seeks to develop their unique way of articulating faith, the praxis model of contextual theology focuses on the identity of Christians within a context particularly as that context is understood in terms of social change. Virginia Fabella, in the introduction to the proceedings of the Asian Theological Conference held in Sri Lanka in 1979, uses other terminology but points to the emergence of a way of doing theology that is significantly different in its scope and starting point from efforts that start with the need either to adapt the gospel message of revelation or to listen to the context.

> Though theologians continue to employ adaptation, which seeks to reinterpret Western thought from an Asian perspective [what I have described as the translation model], or indigenization, which takes the native culture and religion as its basis [my anthropological model], there is the newer thrust to contextualize theology. . . . As a dynamic process, it combines words and action, it is open to change, and looks to the future.[1]

This last "newer" way of doing theology is what we mean by the praxis model, a model usually identified with what has come to be called the theology of liberation but that has also come to be used in the emerging discipline of "practical theology."[2] As Fabella has described it, all these aspects are important for understanding this model of doing theology. It is a never-ending process that gets its considerable power from the recognition that God manifests God's presence not only, or perhaps not even primarily, in the fabric of culture, but also and perhaps principally in the fabric of history. The praxis model is a way of doing theology that is formed by knowledge at its most intense level—the level of reflective action. It is also about discerning the meaning and contributing to the course of social change, and so it takes its inspiration from neither classic texts nor classic behavior but from present realities and future possibilities.

As the translation model might appeal to Paul's efforts to translate the message of Jesus in terms of Greek categories as a biblical basis for its model, and the anthropological model might appeal to contemporary understandings of the formation of the Bible, as well as to texts from the patristic witness, the praxis model also has a rough precedent in Christian tradition. The prophetic tradition that insists on not only words but also action (Isaiah, Amos), the New Testament dictum of the need not only to *hear* the word but to *do* it (Jas 1:22), and the close connection of ethical behavior with theological thought are ample evidence that if the praxis model has some aspects that are new on the theological scene, they are not totally without precedent. A phrase attributed to Karl Barth insists that "only the doer of the word is the true hearer," and Justo González argues that because his theology emerges out of his pastoral practice as a bishop and pastor, a concern for praxis has patristic roots in the work of Irenaeus of Lyons.[3]

A SKETCH OF THE MODEL
TERMINOLOGY

All too often the term *praxis* is used as a trendy alternative to the words *practice* or *action*. For example, one might hear a "practical type" say to a more "professorial type," "That is all very well, but how will it work out in *praxis*?" This use of the word, however, is wrong. *Praxis* is a technical term that has its roots in Marxism, in the Frankfurt school (e.g., J. Habermas, A. Horkheimer, T. Adorno), and in the educational philosophy of Paulo Freire.[4] It is a term that denotes a method or model of thinking in general, and a method or model of theology in particular.

Several years ago, at a meeting of Latin American theologians in Mexico City, Jon Sobrino, a theologian working in El Salvador, made the point that one difference, if not the most significant difference, between what he called "European" theology and Latin American theology is rooted in a different response to two "moments" of modernity.[5] It is an understanding of the nature of these moments, and how they differ quite radically from each other, that we can come to understand the correct notion of praxis.

The first moment of modernity, characterized by the thought of Descartes and especially Kant, introduced the idea of rationality and subjective responsibility. This modern turn to the subject was deeply revolutionary, for from then on it became clear that "nothing is either true faith or right morality which is not our own; and that, in consequence, external authority is, in principle, an unsound basis, and individual judgement, not merely a right but a duty."[6] After this revolution in thinking, which almost immediately began to permeate the way men and women viewed the world, theology could no longer seriously argue solely from authority if it was to be credible in the world. What became necessary for theological method, therefore, was not to continue to quote "proof texts," whether from the Bible, from church teaching (what came to be called magisterium), or from eminent theologians (the fathers and doctors). What became necessary was, first, by rigorous use of the historical-critical method, to find out what the church truly did believe, why it believed it, and whether such belief was necessary still (positive theology).

Then, in a second movement of rational reflection, theology sought to probe the meaning of what was to be believed (speculative theology). It was in this way of meeting the challenge of rationality posed by the Enlightenment that European (and North American) theology developed its understanding of what theology was all about. All the great modern theologians—from Schleiermacher and Möhler in the nineteenth century to Barth, Tillich, and Rahner in this century—were all struggling to make sure that what Christians believed was both accurately stated and meaningfully appropriated.

In his talk in Mexico City, however, Sobrino pointed out that modernity has a second, perhaps more significant, moment, and this is the moment characterized by Karl Marx. Marx's breakthrough was his discovery that rationality or intellectual knowledge was not enough to constitute genuine knowledge. Even personally appropriated knowledge, while infinitely better than believing on someone else's authority, was not enough. We know best, Marx insisted, when our reason is coupled with and challenged by our action—when we are not just the objects of historical process but its subjects. This is perhaps best summed up in the famous sentence in Marx's critique of Feuerbach: "the philosophers have only *interpreted* the world in various ways; the point is to *change* it."[7] Within this way of understanding, theology becomes much more than simply thinking clearly and meaningfully. It becomes a way of articulating one's faith that comes out of one's Christian commitments to a particular way of acting and sets the agenda for an even more thoughtful and committed plan of action in the future. Latin Americans, says Sobrino, orient themselves to this understanding of theology. For them, theology finds its fulfillment not in mere "right thinking" (*ortho-doxy*), but in "right acting" (*ortho-praxy*).

When we speak of the praxis model of contextual theology, we are speaking about a model the central insight of which is that theology is done not simply by providing relevant expressions of Christian faith but also by commitment to Christian action. But even more than this, theology is understood as the product of the continual dialogue of these two aspects of Christian life. The praxis model employs a method that "in its most profound sense is understood as the unity of knowledge as activity and knowledge as content."[8] It works on the conviction that "truth is at the level of history, not in the realm of ideas."[9] As Philip Berryman characterizes it by referring to its use by Paulo Freire, praxis is "action with reflection."[10] It is reflected-upon action and acted-upon reflection—both rolled into one. Practitioners of the praxis model believe that in this concept of praxis they have found a new and profound way to do theology, a way that, more than all others, is able to deal adequately with the experience of the past (scripture, tradition) and the experience of the present (human experience, culture, social location, and social change).

What we are naming the praxis model is often also referred to as the "liberation model."[11] The reason for this is chiefly that it has been the political theologians (e.g., J. Moltmann and J. B. Metz) in Europe and especially the liberation theologians, particularly those in Latin America, who have developed this particular model in its fullest sense. Another reason, however, is more aligned with the basic commitment to praxis as a theological method. Practitioners of the praxis model stress that Christian action, as one of the key components of theology, will inevitably come up against the fact that such action takes place within a sinful world and a world of sinful structures that condone the sins of those who support them and oppress those who do not. True Christianity, it becomes clear, must work against such oppressive structures not just by seeking to change certain features, but by seeking to supplant them completely. Liberation and transformation, not just gradual development or friendly persuasion, is the only way that men and women can fulfill their call to be genuine children of God. As practitioners of the praxis model began to reread the Bible and Christian tradition, they began to discover many forgotten things about Christianity and its roots in Hebrew religion: that the Bible itself is a product of struggles for human freedom; that Jesus' message is a message not primarily of doctrines but of structure-shaking attitudes and behavior; that sin must be opposed not by compromise but by radical reordering of one's life. Social change—and the social location of the poor and the oppressed—began to be seen as a privileged source of theology. Commitment to social change in terms of Christian principles and from the perspective of the poor and marginalized led not only to social transformation but to a deeper and more challenging knowledge of God as such.

As closely associated as the theology of liberation is with the praxis model, however, I choose to continue speaking of it as a praxis model for two reasons. First of all, this way of approaching the contextualization of theology does not necessarily have to take on liberation themes. It may well be possible, for instance, to do theology with a particular context where structural injustice is not very rampant. In this instance, one could still theologize by acting reflectively and reflecting on one's actions—this is the insight of practical theology.[12] Second, I would like to keep the term *praxis model* because the term reveals more clearly than *liberation model* that the specificity of the model is not one of a particular theme but one of a particular *method*. As valid as liberation theology is, its revolutionary impact has come more from its method as "critical reflection on praxis."[13]

PRESUPPOSITIONS OF THE PRAXIS MODEL

As should be evident from the preceding paragraphs, the key presupposition of the praxis model is the insight that the highest level of knowing is intelligent and responsible doing. While, for more traditional ways of doing theology, theology might be described as a process of "faith seeking understanding," the praxis model would say that theology is a process of "faith seeking intelligent action." In 1976 a group of Third World theologians met at Dar es Salaam, Tanzania, to speak about the new kind of theology that was emerging from their countries. In their concluding statement they wrote the following hard-hitting words: "We reject as irrelevant an academic type of theology that is divorced from action. We are prepared for a radical break in epistemology which makes commitment the first act of theology and engages in critical reflection on praxis of the reality of the Third World."[14] Leonardo Boff says much the same thing when he says that, for the theologian who takes praxis seriously, the first word is spoken by what is done, that is, by a conscious act aimed at changing social relationships. It is therefore an inductive theology. It does not start with words (those of the Bible or the magisterium) and end in words (new theological formulations), but stems from actions and struggles and works out of a theoretical structure to throw light on and examine these actions.[15]

By first acting and then reflecting on that action in faith, practitioners of the praxis model believe that one can develop a theology that is truly relevant to a particular context. What becomes clear is that theology done in this way cannot be conceived in terms of books, essays, or articles. Rather than something concrete, permanent, and printed, theology is conceived more in terms of an activity, a process, a way of living. It is certainly true that there are practitioners of the praxis model—the liberation theologians of Latin America, for example, or feminist theologians throughout the world—who are true scholars, but much more theology is generated in the writing of throwaway leaflets, in unrecorded homilies, group discussions, and in people's hearts.[16] As Cuban American Ada-María Isasi-Díaz writes powerfully:

> Hispanic women protesting the lack of city services in the South Bronx, emptying a bag of trash on the desk of the city official who could order the garbage to be picked up more frequently in the area where the women live— that is doing Hispanic women's liberation theology. A woman struggling in a meeting controlled by Hispanic men to pass a resolution that would insure a certain percentage of women in each of the delegations to an important national meeting—that is doing Hispanic women's liberation theology. Four women testifying in front of a group of Roman Catholic bishops about the oppression of Hispanic women in Church as well as in society, finishing their presentation by giving each of the bishops a stone and telling them "We have asked for bread and you have given us a stone. Put these stones on your altars when you celebrate Eucharist and remember us Hispanic women, struggling for our liberation and the liberation of our people"—that is doing Hispanic women's liberation theology.
>
> But the reflection that led to such actions, reflection about self-identity, about our participation in making decisions that affect us and our families, about our willingness to risk—doing such reflection is doing Hispanic women's liberation theology. Meeting after an action . . . is doing Hispanic women's liberation theology.[17]

The practitioner of the praxis model presupposes the importance of the culture aspect of context in developing an understanding of faith.[18] More than the translation and anthropological models, however, he or she would go beyond seeing culture as human or religious values and ways of behavior. Constitutive of culture itself is cultural and social change, and this needs to be taken into account as much as do traditional customs, values, and expressions of language. It follows that political and economic systems make up part of culture as well, and any kind of articulation of faith cannot be politically or economically neutral.[19] Praxis theologians would be very sensitive to newer understandings of culture as hybrid identity and products of social conflict.[20]

Since context is a human (or more exactly a *humanizing*) product, the praxis theologian would see cultural existence as essentially good. But any context can be perverted and in need of liberation and healing. The seeds may very well be in the soil of a particular context, but healthy growth demands constant weeding and cultivating. United States Americans, for instance, might be highly appreciative of the high ideals of freedom and participation of U.S. culture, but as they reflect on their experiences in ministry or just being with friends, they might become more and more convinced of the perversion of U.S. American individualism and the need for a greater sense and exercise of community.[21] The rereading of the gospel and Christian tradition within this context, coupled with continual (communal) reflection on ways to develop more of a community sense, might develop a most challenging brand of theologizing within the U.S. context. In a more forthright liberation vein, we might quote the Third World theologians from their powerful Dar es Salaam statement once more. In paragraph 32 they affirm very clearly "the basic goodness of creation and the continued presence of God's spirit in our world and history." Nevertheless, they caution,

> it is important to bear in mind the complex mystery of evil, which manifests itself in human sinfulness and the socio-economic structures. The inequalities are diverse, and account for many forms of human degradation; they necessitate our making the gospel the "good news to the poor" that it is.[22]

A key presupposition of the praxis model is its notion of God's revelation. If the translation model works largely out of the presupposition that revelation consists in a supracontextual and unchanging message, and if the anthropological model understands revelation in terms of a personal and communal encounter with divine presence, the praxis model understands revelation as the presence of God in history—in the events of everyday life, in social and economic structures, in situations of oppression, in the experience of the poor and the marginalized. The God revealed in history, however, is not just *there*. God's presence is one of beckoning and invitation, calling men and women of faith to locate God and cooperate with God in God's work of healing, reconciling, liberating. We best know God by acting in partnership with God. As Sobrino puts it, "to know the truth is to do the truth, to know Jesus is to follow Jesus, to know sin is to take away sin, to know suffering is to free the world from suffering, to know God is to go to God in justice."[23]

God's presence and invitation to work beside God are available to all women and men equally. This is why an important presupposition of the praxis model, like that of the anthropological model, is that all women and men are called to theologize. In fact, by their lives of reflective action, they already do. In basic ecclesial communities or in bible-sharing groups there is emerging a theology that belongs not to one individual but to the community as a whole. The role of the minister or theologian in such a community is to midwife the birth of such theologizing, to order it, to provide it with the perspective of tradition, to organize the people's experience, and to assist them to articulate it more clearly.

As Figure 5 makes plain, the basic movement of the praxis model is circular. Praxis theologians make it clear that committed action is a first requirement,[24] but it makes sense to say that one might come into the circle at any point. Ideally, however, committed action is a first step. One needs faith in order to do theology, and faith, according to the praxis model, is more than believing propositions or opening up to an encounter; it is "doing the truth." Then in a second step, a "theory" is developed, based equally on (1) an analysis of one's actions and of the particular situation (experience, culture, social location, movement of social change) in which one acts and (2) a rereading of the Bible and Christian tradition. This theory, however, is anything but theoretical. As Philip Berryman explains it, referring to Latin American thinkers, theory is constructed "as a tool for cutting through the appearance and getting at the heart of things."[25] Armed with a new theory rooted in concrete action and critical reflection, the third step of the praxis model is to action once more, but this time action more refined, more rooted in the Bible, and more rooted in contextual reality. This third step is really the first step of another circle, a circle that really becomes a spiral. "Theology follows as fruit of critical reflection on socially transformative praxis. Change occurring or brought about ceaselessly in persons and societal realities dictates continuing change in our interpretation of the Bible and of Church teaching. To quote J. L. Segundo: '. . . each new reality obliges us to interpret the Word of God afresh, to change accordingly, and then to go back and re-interpret the Word of God again, and so on.' "[26]

Where is the theology here? Some theologians have located theology in the second, or reflective, stage of the process. "Contemplation and practice together make up a *first act*; theologizing is a *second act*," as Gustavo Gutiérrez says.[27] However, one might do better to think of theologizing as taking place in the entire process. As one acts, one knows in a way that is only augmented by reflection and (to refer to Gutiérrez) contemplation; and as one acts more consciously, one knows even more clearly. The articulation of faith is in the intelligent action (praxis) itself.[28] Care of one's garden is a never-ending task, but as one continues to weed and water and cultivate, the garden becomes more lush and beautiful.

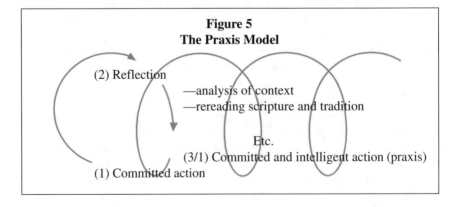

Figure 5
The Praxis Model

(2) Reflection

—analysis of context
—rereading scripture and tradition

Etc.
(3/1) Committed and intelligent action (praxis)

(1) Committed action

CRITIQUE OF THE PRAXIS MODEL

The great strengths of the praxis model are its method and its undergirding epistemology. Sobrino is correct in seeing that Marxist analysis has broken radically from a preoccupation with rationality and meaning, and the Marxist perspective on the primacy of praxis is a much more comprehensive way of knowing than that of mere intellectual affirmation. That this praxis perspective is not narrowly Marxist is evidenced by a similar perspective being proposed by thinkers quite different from Marx in many ways—people such as Max Scheler, Karl Mannheim, Maurice Blondel, and Bernard Lonergan.[29] As a theological method, the praxis model is by its very nature wedded to a particular context. It will never be a theology that does not have its "feet on the ground."[30] Although most writing about this model has been by those who have taken liberation as a main concern, the model has wider applications. In an essay from which I have quoted several times in this chapter, Leonardo Boff speaks about the method employed by liberation theology as a method involving "*seeing* analytically, *judging* theologically, and *acting* pastorally or politically, three phases in one commitment in faith."[31] The reference to "see, judge, act" calls to mind the cardinal principles of older movements such as Young Christian Workers, Young Christian Students, and the Christian Family Movement. A theology that is not in some way rooted in praxis cannot be considered an adequate theology today. From another perspective, practical theologians propose a method of theological procedure and reflection that, while attending to and being nourished by tradition, is thoroughly rooted in *praxis* from beginning to end.

Doing theology as a critical reflection on praxis makes theology capable of being a powerful expression of Christianity. Roger Haight has written that liberation theology has provided an "alternative vision" for theology, one that infuses traditional doctrinal positions with new energy.[32] To call to mind once more the link between our praxis model and the YCW, YCS, and CFM movements from the 1930s to the 1960s, it is important to remember that it was in the context of these movements that a fresh notion of the role of the laity was discovered and that it was here that much of the renewal of Vatican II, in terms of ecclesiology, ecumenism, and liturgy, had its roots.[33] By constantly reflecting on one's daily activity in terms of scripture and tradition (and vice versa), Christianity is understood to bring much to bear on the realities of daily life, and daily life can help sharpen expressions of Christian faith.

It was pointed out in Chapter 2 that one of the criteria for judging the authenticity of a theological expression is its power to challenge and nourish other particular expressions. Certainly in terms of liberation theology, which is a major but not the only practitioner of the praxis model, we can see proof of this model's validity. It is generally acknowledged as the most important development in theology in the latter half of the twentieth century,[34] and it has inspired and challenged other theologians, helping them to articulate their own concerns more clearly. Black theology in the United States and South Africa, feminist theology in the United States particularly but with growing power in all parts of the world,[35] and "Minjung" theology in Korea are just a few variations of the many theologies that have liberation concerns and take praxis seriously.[36]

I believe that the praxis model as such is basically sound. It is based on an excellent epistemology, its understanding of revelation is very fresh and exciting, and it has deep roots in theological tradition. The model has come under some criticism, however, in its concrete form of liberation theology. Some feel uncomfortable with liberation theology's use of Marxism;[37] others point out its selectivity and even naïveté in terms of its reading of the Bible;[38] still others criticize liberation theologians' concentration on what is negative in society and their "inability to see intermediate manifestations of grace" in society or expressions of popular religiosity.[39] While some of these critiques are valid and some a misunderstanding of liberation theology's deepest concerns, this is not the place for an extended critique. Many excellent and constructive critiques are available, as well as some eloquent defenses.[40]

The praxis model gives ample room for expressions of personal and communal experience, cultural expressions of faith, and expressions of faith from the perspective of social location. At the same time it provides exciting new understandings of the scriptural and older theological witness. In some ways this model takes the concrete situation more seriously than any other model, with the possible exception of the countercultural model, on which we will reflect in Chapter 9. This is because it regards theology not as a generally applicable, finished product that is valid for all times and in all places, but as an understanding of and wrestling with God's presence in very particular situations—a movement for fairer housing laws,

---

The Praxis Model

Alternative Titles: *situational theology; theology of the signs of the times; liberation model*

Basis in Scripture and Tradition: *prophetic tradition; Jas 1:22; Irenaeus; Karl Barth*

Revelation: *envisioned as God at work in the world, calling men and women as partners*

Scripture/Tradition: *culturally conditioned, like all human expressions; incomplete*

Context: *basically good and trustworthy but can be distorted; should be approached with some suspicion; can be equal to scripture and tradition*

Method: *practice/reflection/practice—in unending spiral*

Analogy: *garden needs to be constantly weeded; the work never ends; practice makes one a better gardener*

Legend: *"to know Christ is to follow him" (Alfred Hennelly)*

Critique: *Positive: strong epistemological basis; provides an "alternate vision"; influence on theology*
     Negative: critiqued for close connection with Marxism

a campaign for voter registration, an earthquake in a particular part of the world, a moment of transition in a particular parish, an immense tragedy such as that of September 11, 2001. There is a certain permanence and even generality needed in the theological enterprise, of course, but the praxis model offers a corrective to a theology that is *too* general and pretends to be universally relevant.

EXAMPLES OF THE PRAXIS MODEL

Because of the immediate and necessarily transitory nature of theology done out of the praxis model, it is rather difficult to identify genuine examples of its use from published sources. Very often, for instance, the language of liberation does not necessarily mean that the full method of liberation theology—critical reflection on praxis—is operative in various theologies in which liberation is a major theme. A case in point is one of the most important liberation theologians, Leonardo Boff. Boff is certainly aware of the importance of praxis in the theological enterprise, but several of his books do not immediately reflect the method of praxis at the heart of their construction. Boff's books on Christology, grace, and the Trinity[41] all reflect liberation themes, and they do speak about the "primacy of orthopraxis over orthodoxy" and about theology as "reflecting critically on the praxis of Christian faith."[42] Perhaps more operative methodologically, however, is the classical approach of positive and speculative theology. In *Ecclesiogenesis*, however, and in some essays in the collection entitled *Church: Charism and Power*, Boff reflects on the concrete experience of the basic ecclesial communities, and so the actual method of praxis is in much more evident use.[43] The actual *being* church of the small community sheds new light on what it means to be church. The basic communities are actually reinventing ecclesiology, bringing to the fore questions never asked before or at least never taken seriously (the ecclesiality of the local church, the church as the "Sacrament of the Spirit," the possibility of a layperson presiding at Eucharist and women being admitted as officeholders in the church). Boff is certainly among those who employ the praxis model, but even he does not use it all the time. What I have called the anthropological model and the synthetic model also play a major role in his construction of a theology in the Latin American Brazilian context.

The theologians on whom I would like to focus more closely in this section, Douglas John Hall and a number of Asian feminist theologians, also employ other approaches to doing theology. Nevertheless, like Boff and other liberation theologians, their use of the praxis model is what characterizes the basic direction of their thought, and their works point to fresh ways of thinking about Christian faith.

Douglas John Hall

Douglas John Hall is a minister of the United Church of Canada and is Professor Emeritus of Christian Theology at McGill University in Montreal. He was born in Ontario in 1928, received a B. A. from the University of Western Ontario in 1953, and then spent the next several years (until 1960) studying under the likes of Paul Tillich, Reinhold Niebuhr, and Robert McAfee Brown at Union Theological Seminary in New York. Ordained in 1960, he pastored a parish for two years and completed his doctorate at Union in 1963. Before taking up his position in Montreal, he served as principal of St. Paul's College in Waterloo, Ontario (1962-1965), and taught theology at St. Andrew's College in Saskatoon, Saskatchewan (1965-1975). Among his publications are *Lighten Our Darkness* (1976), *Has the Church a Future?* (1980), *The Steward* (1982), *The Stewardship of Life in the Kingdom of Death* (1985), *Imaging God* (1986), *God and Human Suffering* (1986), and, between 1989 and 1996, a three-volume systematic theology with the titles *Thinking the Faith*, *Professing the Faith*, and *Confessing the Faith*—all with the subtitle *Christian Theology in a North American Context*.[44]

Although they have been developed and refined over the years, Hall's basic concerns were present in the first book mentioned above. The subtitle is *Toward an Indigenous Theology of the Cross*, and in the book he tries to present a theology that is "indigenous to our North American experience as [Hall quotes George Grant] 'the most realized technological society which has yet been.' "[45] The way toward that theology is the construction of a "practical theology" that "could become meaningful only if it were elaborated and incorporated into the living structures and programs of the Church."[46] In other words, Hall wants to construct a theology that deals with the experience of contemporary North Americans as they deal with the reality of their technological society. But even more, that theology will only be real if it is put into action in a Christian life by a church that has the courage to go against the mainstream of both modern culture and the ecclesiastical tradition of triumphalism. In subsequent works, "indigenous" has been changed to "contextual," and "practical theology" has become more fine-tuned as "praxis." But the themes of "theology of the cross," the post-Constantinian *krisis* of the church, and concern for the destruction of humanity and nature through the abuse of technology all remain key to his theological thought.

An image that somehow sums up all these concerns is that of the steward—a biblical symbol, says Hall in another book's subtitle, that has come of age. It is by reflecting on the deeper implications of this symbol that Hall does theology according to the praxis model.

North American theology, in either its Canadian or U.S. variety, has not been noted for great theoretical depth or originality. It has basically been a follower of European trends and has at best adapted European concerns to a very different national and cultural context. More than ever before, however, North Americans need to develop their own theology, but where are they to begin? One point of entry, Hall suggests, is to reflect on some of the actual practices operative in Canadian and U.S. American Christianity. There are, he says, "perhaps hidden depths of potential theological importance in *some* of the practices that inform everyday life in North American churches."[47] When one reflects "upon these practices with sufficient imagination to wrest from them their deeper meaning," permitting this "new depth of understanding" to shape and inform one's subsequent action, one engages in what theologians have come to call praxis.[48]

Doing theology in this way differs quite significantly from theology's "conventional pattern."[49] This way of doing theology attempts first to work out a theory—of church, Christ, grace, and so forth—and then apply it to a particular situation. As Hall says, the hidden assumption here is that the more removed from actual situations, the more real an idea is; situations become more real the more they are shaped by the abstract idea or theory. The order is first knowing, and then doing. "Praxis thinking," however, insists that real theory emerges out of action and evokes more responsible, more real activity. Rather than truth being worked out apart from life, praxis thinking holds that truth can only be grasped in a dialogue with life as it is actually lived, suffered through, and celebrated.

It is the tradition of stewardship in the North American church that Hall singles out as particularly worthy of reflection by North American theologians. The reflection must be in terms of praxis, however. It is not a matter of developing a theology of stewardship and then applying it to the North American context. Rather, Canadian and U.S. theologians need to reflect on stewardship *as it is practiced* in the light of a rereading of the Bible and church tradition, and then a proper contextual theology will emerge. "Somehow, our *thinking* about stewardship has to incorporate and draw upon that experience, that practice. *Praxis* means that our reflection upon the theological meaning of stewardship involves, not a withdrawal from the practice of it, but 'critical reflection on historical practice.' "[50]

Having established that he will reflect on the actual practice of stewardship (what I have called above the "committed action" from which reflection flows), Hall first investigates the origin of the idea within the Bible and finds that the image is so rich that it needs to be regarded as more than a metaphor. It is rather a symbol that contains *in nuce* the entire message of Judaic and Christian faith.[51] Then, in a second chapter, the reasons are explored as to why this powerful symbol was not taken up with full seriousness. The church developed into a power in league with or in rivalry with the state, and the humility involved in stewarding (being only a representative of the Master) was simply not relevant. But particularly in North America, where the church functioned in relative independence of the civil government and could not depend on the state for support, the practice of stewardship began to emerge. Even then, however, being confined to the practical (largely financial) needs of the church, it was not utilized to the full. Today, in the light of the bankruptcy of modern rationalism and technology (e.g. the ecological and nuclear crises), the practice of stewardship can come into its own and play its full symbolic role. "Thus to 'think stewardship' today is . . . to be plummeted into the center of the spiritual struggle of late 20th century humanity, the struggle to find a future that is neither the pretentious lordship of the universe . . . nor on the other hand the cowardly slinking away from all thought, planning, and action that aims at change. Stewardship . . . belongs to the essence of things."[52] As Hall continues to develop his reflection on the symbol, acting as stewards means acting on behalf of justice (in terms of First World/Third World), getting involved in movements for ecological responsibility, and committing oneself to the cause of world peace. In a sequel to *The Steward*, Hall insists on stewardship as constitutive of the very mission of the church. "To engage in Christ's mission in the world today is to be stewards of life in the kingdom of death."[53] In subsequent books, steward-ship is developed as the way human beings discover not only their humanity but also the God in whose image they are created; this is done by participating in the suffering of the world's victims, identifying with wounded nature, testifying to the world, and accepting the resulting opprobrium.[54]

The first volume of Hall's three-volume systematic theology, *Thinking the Faith*, is a virtual *summa* of his previous books and contains sustained reflection on his theological method. The crisis facing the church today, he says, is a crisis of think-ing. In a world experiencing the failure of the optimistic vision of modernity, and in light of the tendency of women and men either to despair of all meaning or to repress their terror by the mindless pursuit of pleasure, a *thinking* faith is neces-sary, and "only a thinking faith can survive." Indeed, "only a thinking faith can help *the world* survive."[55]

Thinking the faith, however, is no exclusively theoretical enterprise. Rather, the thinking that Hall has in mind "involves entering at depth into the historical experiences of one's own people."[56] Thinking the faith means the doing of theol-ogy, and such doing inevitably involves the theologian in the art of praxis. Never-theless, the point must immediately be made that the method of praxis does not absolve the theologian from hard thinking. As Hall puts it:

> The point of praxis is not to substitute act for thought, deed for word, but to ensure that thinking is rooted in existence—and committed to its transforma-tion. To say that the summons to contextualization is a call to faithful Christian praxis is *not* to say, "Let us leave off all this wearisome business of theology and get on with *doing* the truth!" It means, rather, to pledge oneself to the overcoming of the (after all, artificial) gap between thought and act, and so to become more serious *about both*.[57]

This whole notion of theology as critical reflection on praxis is summed up in a famous line of Luther: "a person becomes a theologian by living, by dying and by being damned, not by understanding, reading and speculating."[58] The point is, Hall comments, not that thinking and reading are not necessary components of the theological enterprise, but that genuine understanding of faith comes only when believers are *more*, not less, involved in their world. "Concentration upon the 'object' of theology implies at once—not even as a second step—an intensified awareness of ourselves as subjects engaged upon this search."[59]

An authentic North American theology, therefore, has to start with the commit-ment of persons to be involved in the transformation of their world. Rather than succumb to the alternatives of despair and (more commonly) cynicism or repres-sion and (often subsequently) *sup*pression,[60] the Christian is called upon to face the world today with a "prophetic realism," ready to face the consequences of the fact that "a society based on happiness cannot survive; only a society based on truth can survive."[61] Theology that is faithful to the North American context needs to be in touch with the victims of affluent and powerful North American society; it needs to heed the voices of its prophets, artists, novelists, dramatists, poets, and musicians. It needs to reread, wrestle, and dialogue with Christianity's sources, especially in the scriptures. It needs both to be deprofessionalized and done in the context of communal dialogue—"the experience of one has to be tested against the experience of another."[62]

A North American theology, Hall says, must be a theology of the cross. It needs to acknowledge from the outset that "the single most far-reaching ecclesiastical factor conditioning theological reflection in our time is the effective disestablishment of the Christian religion in the western world by secular, political, and alternative religious forces."[63] For North American theology to be genuine, it needs to be humble in its articulation of Christian truth in a world of many religious ways and to direct special efforts toward dialogue and reconciliation with Judaism. It needs to be aware, with the help of the critics of economic globalization, of the structural evil created and maintained by Canadian and U.S. prosperity. North American theology can only be authentic if it is done out of commitment to reversing the harm our culture does to the natural world and to warding off the specter of nuclear destruction. Finally, as a *thinking* faith, theology can never accede to the "simplism" and apocalypticism that can result from the stress of today's postmodern world.[64]

Hall's now completed three-volume systematic theology is a major effort to do theology in terms of praxis. There are parts of all three books that could be enhanced by an even greater stress on committed action and involvement, but on the whole his thinking is remarkably consistent and provocative. While much of his later work especially might also be classified as an exercise of what we will call the countercultural model, it remains a fine example of the power and potential of doing theology out of committed action, and rigorous reflection on that action as well.

ASIAN FEMINIST THEOLOGIANS

In the last several years a number of collections of works have appeared containing some of the first tentative theologizing of Third World women theologians, and in each one the praxis model is claimed as the most adequate way for Third World women to do theology. In 1988 Filipina Virginia Fabella and Ghanaian Mercy Amba Oduyoye edited *With Passion and Compassion*, a collection of essays that had been written in preparation for the International Women's Conference at Oaxtepec, Mexico, in late 1986.[65] Held immediately prior to the seventh international conference of the Ecumenical Association of Third World Theologians (EATWOT), this conference of African, Asian, and Latin American women was the realization of a demand by the women of EATWOT for a clearer voice in an organization that claimed to be about liberation but often found itself stuck in the mire of sexism and gender discrimination.[66] In 1988 as well, Letty M. Russell, an Anglo-American feminist theologian, together with Kwok Pui-lan (Hong Kong),

Ada María Isasi-Díaz (Cuban American), and Katie Geneva Cannon (African American), edited a volume entitled *Inheriting Our Mothers' Gardens: Feminist Theology in a Third World Perspective.*[67] While the volume edited by Fabella and Oduyoye deliberately excluded minority women from First World contexts (a policy hotly contested by North American black and Hispanic/Latina women at the EATWOT conference), Russell and company's volume includes contributions of U.S. American black and Hispanic/Latina women, as well as women from Ghana, Korea, and El Salvador. The year 1989 saw the publication of an English translation of a volume of eight essays, together with a final statement of a women's theology conference held at Buenos Aires in 1985. The collection was entitled *Through Her Eyes: Women's Theology from Latin America*[68] and was edited by Latin American theologian Elsa Tamez. The volume includes reflections by Protestant and Catholic women, as well as by North American women who have devoted their lives to the poor of Latin America. In 1990 Virginia Fabella and Korean theologian Sun Ai Lee Park edited a collection that attempts to provide a sampling of the theologizing efforts of Asian women: *We Dare to Dream: Doing Theology as Asian Women.*[69] This volume is composed of a number of presentations from various women's conferences throughout Asia and also includes three essays previously published in Fabella and Oduyoye's 1988 collection.

Each one of these books might provide a number of examples of the praxis model. What I propose to do here, however, is to focus on several of the essays in the third book I have mentioned—on the emerging theology of Asian feminist theologians. Not only do the essays in this book represent clear examples of the praxis model; they also show this model at work in contexts (Asia and the experience of women in Asia) not readily associated with the liberating action to which the praxis model often leads.

The first example on which I would like to focus is Virginia Fabella's essay, "Christology from an Asian Woman's Perspective." Fabella, one of the editors of the collection, is a Maryknoll sister from the Philippines who holds an M. A. from the Maryknoll School of Theology in New York and a Doctor of Ministry degree from San Francisco Theological Seminary. She has been active in EATWOT since its beginning in 1976, and for many years served as EATWOT's Asian coordinator. Her essay is really only an outline of a Christology that needs to be worked out in more detail in the future. Nevertheless, it presents an overview that shows how a "liberational, hope-filled, love-inspired, and praxis-oriented christology"[70] might well look. Fabella recognizes at the start that a truly Asian Christology needs to be rooted in the reality of Asian culture and especially needs to deal with the various soteriological claims of the venerable Asian religions. Nevertheless, she insists, unless Christology deals specifically with women's experience and calls on Christians to cooperate in the task of liberating women from situations of oppression, abuse, and domination within highly patriarchal Asian cultures, Christology will neither have relevance for Asia as it really is nor be faithful to Jesus as he was remembered in the Christian scriptures. Christology, therefore, is not simply intellectual or speculative activity; it is reflection on the meaning of Jesus, who makes a difference in people's lives and calls them to strive for the humanity that he came to bring. Here we see clearly the committed starting point: solidarity with Asia's poor, and particularly with Asia's poor women.

Fabella proceeds to a rereading of the scriptures and the tradition (social analysis goes on throughout her essay). Jesus' message is not so much a message about himself as it is a call to action. Jesus' preaching of the reign of God is an invitation for people "to reform their lives, believe in the good news, and be saved. To enter the kingdom meant to change one's ways of behaving and relating."[71] Furthermore, the message of Jesus is preached not only in word but also—even primarily—in deed. Jesus manifested the reality of the reign of God by his solidarity with the marginalized of his society: sinners, outcasts, women. Jesus was not only considerate of such people; he "even acted contrary to the prevailing customs and practices. Women were among the non-persons of society, mere chattel. But Jesus never ignored them when they approached him for healing; they were human beings worth making whole again. . . . He not only valued them as friends but affirmed their trustworthiness and capability to be disciples, witnesses, missionaries, and apostles."[72]

This radical inclusive action, instanced by Jesus' association with sinners, his healing on the Sabbath, his prophetic critique of his culture, led inevitably to his death. But the disciples' transformation soon afterwards was the basis for their faith that Jesus had triumphed over death and that his continuing life was empowering them to live and act as he did. Resurrection faith, Fabella implies, is not a matter of believing this or that theory of how Jesus "came back to life," but of being gripped by the truth of Jesus' life-giving and transforming Spirit. It was reflection on Jesus' life and on his continuing presence in the church that called forth doctrines of Jesus' divinity. In the context of the Hellenistic culture of the Roman Empire, such doctrines were expressed in metaphysical categories. For Asians today these doctrines might not be very meaningful and may even get in the way of dialogue with other religious traditions. If Jesus' identity is to make sense in Asia today, it will not be in terms of claims of metaphysical uniqueness, but by the way faith in Jesus empowers people—especially Asia's women—to work and struggle for justice and equality.[73]

Fabella's Christology is fundamentally shaped by her basic commitment to the liberation of Asian women. What is important in Jesus' life is not a message about his own identity or the nature of the world; rather it is the way Jesus acted and the action to which he calls men and women. Faith in Jesus today is not about believing Nicean or Chalcedonian formulas (though it does not exclude them), but about being transformed and empowered by Jesus' vision of equality and liberation. The more one believes in Jesus, the more one will commit oneself to living like Jesus; the more one does that, the more one will come to understand who Jesus is. Christology is developed in the context of critical praxis.

Asian feminist theology, says Yong Ting Jin, a Malaysian theologian who has worked in Hong Kong as the regional secretary of the World Student Christian Federation, also has far-reaching ecclesiological implications.[74] Working out of the conviction that "oppression of women is SINFUL" and that the root of this sin is the all-embracing system of patriarchy,"[75] Yong points out how the church is thoroughly patriarchal, and then shows how a rereading of the scriptures unmasks this development as unfaithful at every turn to the vision and practice of Jesus and the reality of the early church.[76]

As women realize how both Asian and ecclesiastical society oppresses and abuses them, they will begin to assert their God-given rights to celebrate their God-given dignity. When this happens—and it is beginning to happen already—all sorts of new ways of understanding and being church will emerge: "Every person, female and male, is summoned to participate in the building processes of the new. When the new era comes, it cannot leave the old structures and lifestyles intact."[77] Central to the new structures and lifestyles will be a new role of women, working as partners with men and not dominated by them. Women will contribute to a new understanding of power and authority in the church; they will contribute to a new way (the praxis model) of doing theological reflection; they will lead the church in its struggles for peace and justice. The church will be transformed into the true church of Jesus Christ and a community relevant to Asian reality as it acts according to the vision of Jesus Christ.

While I could provide several more examples of the praxis model from the essays in the book, let me conclude with a brief overview of the contribution of Philippine scholar Mary John Mananzan, a Benedictine nun, writer, educator, and social activist with a Ph.D. in philosophy from Rome's Gregorian University. Mananzan's presentation focuses on what it means to be a religious woman (i.e., a nun) in the context of the contemporary Philippines and begins with an articulation of the praxis orientation:

> To be a Christian today in a land where injustice and oppression abide is a challenge. To be a woman religious in such a situation is doubly so. It calls for a radical re-thinking of the meaning of being a Christian and of the imperative of religious commitment. It precipitates a spiritual crisis. It demands a consequent revision of one's way of life—a true conversion, a *metanoia*.[78]

Most of the article is a chronicle of Mananzan's involvement with and transformation by social justice concerns over the last two decades. Solidarity with strikers and slum dwellers, participation in intense retreats of shared experiences and fears, aligning herself with the "No Nukes" movement in the Philippines, and acting as national chairperson for the Philippine women's organization GABRIELA (to name but a few of her activities!)—all have shaped a very definite understanding of the vowed life that is quite different from "convent life" as it is often conceived ("When I hear a young woman answer the question 'why do you want to enter the convent' with 'because I want to have peace and quiet,' I just smile").[79] In the red-hot forge of action on behalf of justice, poverty becomes more than just "economizing or asking of permission," celibacy is revealed as the freedom to risk and to be available, and obedience begins to mean more than community loyalty as one begins to listen carefully to the voice of the people and let them set the agenda.[80]

By using the praxis model, Mary John Mananzan goes a long way in the reconstruction of religious life that is being called for from other quarters.[81] The more universal appeal is a strong indication of the model's validity, not just for purely political and social concerns but for many other concerns as well. The praxis model is perhaps the newest way of doing contextual theology, but it promises to be one of the most powerful.

7

The Synthetic Model

In a 1964 commencement address, the late Filipino historian Horacio de la Costa pointed to the significance of statesman José P. Laurel's diary, written during the Second World War when Laurel was being held at Sugamo Prison in Manila. Since there was no paper available, Laurel made entries in his diary in the blank spaces of a western book. De la Costa calls this fact "oddly symbolic" because it reveals something very meaningful about the Filipino condition and presents a kind of model for the construction of Filipino thought. As de la Costa continues to comment:

> we, as a nation, have received a rich intellectual legacy from the West: our religious faith from Spain, our democratic institutions from America. But this legacy, rich as it is, has blank spaces which, in the providence of God, we are meant to fill.[1]

This conception of the way Filipino thought is to be developed is a perfect example of the fourth model operative in the construction of contextual theology, the synthetic model. This is the model that tries to balance the insights of each of the three models presented so far, as well as the insights of the countercultural model to be presented in Chapter 9, and reaches out also to insights from other people's contexts—their experience, their cultures, and their ways of thinking. Like Laurel in writing his diary, it makes creative use of whatever is at hand.

The synthetic model is a middle-of-the-road model. It appears in Figure 2 (see p. 32) at the center of the continuum, midway between emphasis on the experience of the present (i.e., context: experience, culture, social location, social change) and the experience of the past (scripture, tradition). It might rely for scriptural justification on the whole process of the formation of the various biblical books. The Bible came about gradually, through a collection of individual books, each of which was formed within the context of present concerns interacting with contemporary culture, neighboring cultures, and ancient traditions.[2] The synthetic model might rely as well on theories of doctrinal development that understand doctrine as emerging from the complex interaction of Christian faith and changes in culture, society, and thought forms. It would also invoke some passages of the Roman magisterium that try to walk a theological path between mere adaptation on the one hand and a broad culturalism[3] on the other. Paul VI articulates some important aspects of what I call the synthetic model in the following passage from *Evangelii Nuntiandi*:

> The more an individual Church is attached to the universal Church by solid bonds of communion, in charity and loyalty, in receptiveness to the Magisterium of Peter, in the unity of the *lex orandi* which is also the *lex credendi*, in the desire for unity with all the other Churches which make up the whole—the more such a Church will be capable of translating the treasure of faith into the legitimate variety of expressions of the profession of faith, of prayer and worship, of Christian life and conduct and of the spiritual influence on the people among which it dwells. The more will it also be truly evangelizing, that is to say capable of drawing upon the universal patrimony in order to enable its own people to profit from it, and capable too of communicating to the universal Church the experience and the life of this people, for the benefit of all.[4]

It is true that this passage speaks in terms of *translating* the faith into other cultural contexts, but it seems to go beyond the translation model in that it acknowledges mutual enrichment of cultures toward the end of the passage.

The synthetic model is "both/and." It takes pains to keep the integrity of the traditional message while acknowledging the importance of taking all the aspects of context seriously.

A SKETCH OF THE MODEL

TERMINOLOGY

When we speak here in terms of a model that is synthetic, we do not mean that the model is artificial. The synthetic model does not have a meaning analogous to synthetic rubber or synthetic diamonds. Every model, as was pointed out in Chapter 3, is synthetic in this sense, since every model is an artificially constructed case. But this is not the point here.

The word *synthetic* functions in several other ways as a description of a particular model of theological method. In the first place, this way of doing contextual theology looks to a *synthesis* of all the other models described in this book. It tries to preserve the importance of the gospel message and the heritage of traditional doctrinal formulations while at the same time acknowledging the vital role that context has played and can play in theology, even to the setting of the theological agenda. In addition, the synthesis will include the importance of reflective and intelligent action for the development of a theology that does not ignore the complexities of social and cultural change. Second, the synthetic model reaches out to the resources of other contexts and other theological expressions for both the method and the content of its own articulation of faith. In this way there develops a synthesis between one's own cultural point of view and the points of view of others as well. Third, and perhaps most profoundly, this model is synthetic in the Hegelian sense of not just attempting to put things together in a kind of compromise but of developing, in a creative dialectic, something that is acceptable to all standpoints. Another name, therefore, for this model might be the "dialectical model." Or since this model involves constant dialogue and employment of what David Tracy has named the analogical imagination,[5] the model might also be spoken of as the "dialogical model," the "conversation model," or even the "analogical model. " This is the model, I believe, that theologians such as Aylward Shorter mean when they speak of the "inculturation" or "interculturation" of theology as "the on-going dialogue between faith and culture or cultures . . . the creative and dynamic relationship between the Christian message and a culture or cultures."[6]

PRESUPPOSITIONS OF THE SYNTHETIC MODEL

A fundamental presupposition of the synthetic model is the composite nature of the human context as the situation in which men and women live. Practitioners of the synthetic model would hold that every context has both elements that are unique to it and elements that are held in common with others. This is something that practitioners of the anthropological model might admit in theory,[7] but their emphasis is much more on the uniqueness of a particular culture or situation. What is important for the synthetic model is to emphasize *both* uniqueness and complementarity, since one's identity emerges in a dialogue that includes both. Thus, for instance, to speak of oneself as an Indonesian is to speak about oneself against the background of being Asian, of sharing in much of Malaysian culture and linguistic patterns, as being influenced by the Muslim worldview and as colonized by a western culture (Holland). What it means to be an Indonesian, therefore, includes much of what it means to be Asian, Malaysian, Muslim, and Dutch, and yet there is something to being Indonesian that none of these cultures have, nor do they have the other four characteristics in exactly the same mixture.

This composite makeup of every culture means that every culture can borrow and learn from every other culture and still remain unique. In the area of politics, this means that Indonesians can learn much by studying western-style democracy—or Marxism—and not feel that by setting up certain structures in Indonesia they are submitting to cultural domination. The use of computer technology, to give another example, does not have to destroy the values involved in more traditional forms of communication. For theology, and this is a key idea for the synthetic model, this means that the Indonesian can profit as much from a critical reading of Karl Rahner or Karl Barth as she or he can from another theologian who shares the culture. As Vietnamese thinker To Thi Anh puts it, eastern and western values need not be in conflict. Each can learn from the other, and each can profit from the other.[8]

Context, within the parameters of the synthetic model, is looked upon as ambivalent. Some features of a culture, for example, such as clothing and styles of music, are totally neutral; some features of a culture, however, are clearly good or clearly bad. Few critics of culture would disagree with the underlying spirit of freedom that founds so much of U.S. American life; and yet few would fail to point out the wrongheadedness of U.S. American "manifest destiny" or jingoist thinking. Similarly, one can clearly admire the beauty of Kalinga weaving while absolutely condemning the former custom of head-hunting. Most features of a culture, however, are more ambivalent than anything else; they can be good or bad, depending on how they are used and developed. It is an important value for Filipinos, perhaps the central Filipino value, to be in harmony with both nature and society.[9] But while this thirst for harmony can lead to a sense of connectedness with all things and produce a deep responsibility to the earth, to human society, and to transcendent reality, it can also be perverted into "getting along" in society or into having one's life directed by others and never by oneself. U.S. American individualism, on the other hand, can either make United States Americans isolated, lonely, and empty or undergird a culture of personal responsibility to the greater whole.

The practitioners of the synthetic model would say that it is only when women and men are in dialogue that we have true human growth. Each participant in a context has something to give to the other, and each context has something from which it needs to be exorcised. As men and women read literature, philosophy, and history produced by people with different experience, from different ages, from other cultures, and from other social locations, and when they can come together in some form of conversation, each person will recognize her or his uniqueness. In terms of theology, it will be recognized that it is not enough to extol one's own experience as the only place where God can speak. One can also hear God speaking in other contexts and—perhaps in a particular way—in the contexts in which the Hebrew and Christian Scriptures were written. Attention to one's own context can perhaps discover values in other contexts that had never been noticed before, and attention to others (including the Hebrew and Christian Scriptures) can transform and enrich one's own worldview. As David Tracy points out, "the self finds itself by risking an interpretation of all the signs, symbols, and texts of its own and other cultures."[10]

God's revelation, therefore, is understood to be something that is historically circumscribed within the particular contexts in which the scriptures came to be written, and so has a particularly contextually conditioned message. But it is also understood at the same time to be operative in one's own context, calling men and women to perfect that context through cultural transformation and social change. Revelation is both something finished, once and for all, of a particular place—*and* something ongoing and present, operative in all cultures, and uncircumscribable in every way.

In regard to the persons who actually construct a contextual theology, the synthetic model would hold that while it might be ideal that the theology comes from the ordinary subjects of a particular culture, that is not always possible nor is it necessarily the best procedure. In his book *Toward a Theology of Inculturation*, Aylward Shorter refers to a book by Cameroun theologian Jean-Marc Éla. Éla strongly insists that the work of inculturation can only be done by cultural subjects—in his case, by people from Cameroun: "Missionaries cannot carry out inculturation. They are merely at the start of the process. They listen, stimulate and canalize. Africans themselves cannot carry out inculturation, as long as they are in cultural and socio-economic bondage to non-Africans."[11] While this is true, says Shorter, Éla tends to overreact. The church of Africa is certainly burdened by European structures and European mind-sets, but he judges that it is not necessary to go as far as Éla does "in order to uphold the right of Christians in Africa to take their rightful place in the Church. The argument for African inculturation is not strengthened by denigrating the parent Church of Europe."[12] The outsider, it seems, has some part to play in constructing a local theology, even though it may be quite limited and auxiliary.[13]

A few pages later, in the next chapter, Shorter emphasizes that while "Inculturation is essentially a community process," it also needs the presence of experts—"even sometimes missionaries from overseas, to give the community encouragement and to help it make the necessary discernment and the necessary critique of its own culture, and to promote the discovery of the seeds of the Word."[14] Shorter, as a practitioner of the synthetic model, is extremely sensitive to culture and insists that the contextualization or inculturation process should start with the local culture and not "Christianity's previous inculturations."[15] And yet there is an openness to and respect of the wider Christian tradition in his method that is much more evident than in the anthropological or praxis models as I have characterized them. Theologians such as Mercado or Boff would want to assign much more value, almost an exclusivity, to the role of the ordinary cultural subject in the fashioning of a theology in context.

The procedure of the synthetic model, one realizes, is very complex. However, the procedure is much more like producing a work of art than following a rigid set of directions. One needs to juggle several things at one time, but it is not a matter of just keeping everything moving smoothly. One needs, rather, to place emphasis on message at one point, while at another point one needs to emphasize cultural identity. At one point traditional practices (such as the rosary or stations of the cross) might need to be cultivated. Perhaps in another set of circumstances they need to be resisted. To use our horticultural example, the synthetic model sees the need and value of cross-pollination so that new and sturdier plants might be developed to be better suited to a particular environment. Figure 6 illustrates the elements that one needs to keep in creative tension if one adopts this particular method of contextualizing theology.

Robert Schreiter, whose synthetic model for constructing local theologies has also been described as a semiotic model,[16] presents a "map" of his method that might indicate one way to deal with the complexities illustrated in Figure 6. While one must always take into account what Schreiter calls previous local theologies (ranging from scholastic understandings of God to practices of popular religiosity), one begins with listening to culture for basic patterns and structures, analyzing culture in order to discover its basic system of symbols. Out of such a "thick description" will emerge basic themes for the local theology. At the same time,

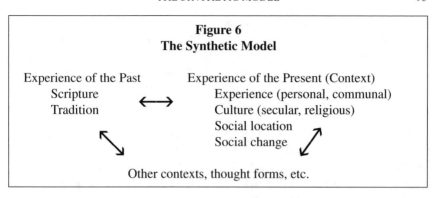

Figure 6
The Synthetic Model

Experience of the Past   Experience of the Present (Context)
      Scripture   Experience (personal, communal)
      Tradition   ⟷   Culture (secular, religious)
                                        Social location
                                        Social change

Other contexts, thought forms, etc.

however, these themes need to be in dialogue with the basic themes in gospel and tradition, which are normative inasmuch as they are acknowledged by the community as relatively successful local theologies in times past and in varying cultures. This dialogue between culture and tradition is the heart of Schreiter's process and has a mutually transforming effect on both conversation partners. If, as we have seen, the translation and anthropological models can be illustrated as direct lines going from gospel/tradition to context, or vice versa, and if the praxis model and general synthetic model can be imaged respectively as a spiral and the interacting sides of a triangle, Schreiter's expression of the synthetic model can be pictured as two parallel columns in constant interaction and dialogue with one another.[17]

CRITIQUE OF THE SYNTHETIC MODEL

Perhaps the strongest aspect of the synthetic model is its basic methodological attitude of openness and dialogue. In our contemporary, postmodern world so filled with what David Tracy speaks of as plurality and ambiguity, truth will not be reached by one point of view trying to convince all the others that it alone is correct. That is neither possible nor, as the situation has revealed, even desirable. It was possible in a world that saw truth as a simple correspondence between concept and reality; but that same world was one that also prescribed one culture and one way of thinking for all. It was, as Shorter calls it, a worldview of monoculturalism.[18] Contemporary postmodern thinking, however, is moving away from this correspondence understanding of truth and understanding truth more in terms of relation, conversation, and dialogue. It is encouraged in this regard by the radical pluralism and multicultural consciousness that is emerging, at least implicitly, everywhere. Truth in this scheme of things is understood not so much as something "out there" but as a reality that emerges in true conversation between authentic women and men when they "allow questioning to take over."[19]

Such a dialogical way of understanding truth does not mean that anything goes or that personal convictions and traditional, classic formulations of faith are watered down or sold out. As Tracy insists,

Conversation is a game with some hard rules: say only what you mean; say it as accurately as you can; listen to and respect what the other says, however different or other; be willing to correct or defend your opinions if challenged by the conversation partner; be willing to argue if necessary, to confront if demanded, to endure necessary conflict, to change your mind if the evidence suggests it.[20]

The synthetic model really makes an effort to make theologizing an exercise in true conversation and dialogue with the other so that one's own and one's culture's identity can emerge in the process. Such a dialogical process puts sometimes needed emphasis on the fact that contextual theology is not a once-and-for-all project, but is something that must be ongoing. Aylward Shorter warns that the inculturation of theology cannot be limited to the "first insertion" of a faith into a culture.[21] The contextualization of theology must become an attitude. Christians have to give up the notion that there is such a thing as "plain theology" or "just theology." Theology *as such* does not exist. Because contexts constantly change, theology has constantly to change as well.

Perhaps more than any other model, the synthetic model witnesses to the true universality of Christian faith. The fact that every person in every context can learn from every other person and the fact that the present can continue to learn from the past point to the reality of "something," however elementary or however preconceptual, that is a constant in Christian identity. The synthetic model is much more sophisticated in its understanding of this constant than is the translation model, for its understanding of revelation is much less locked into the idea of a set of propositions.

A final positive aspect of the synthetic model can be expressed in the words of Robert Schreiter:

> Especially when wielded in the hands of local leaders, it can quickly help achieve the twin goals of some authenticity in the local culture and respectability in Western church circles. The theology which emerges from such a model is replete with the categories, names, and concerns of a local culture, yet looks like Western theology and is relatively easily understood by Westerners. Moreover, it makes dialogue between North Atlantic and other churches much easier, since fundamentally similar frameworks are in use. It can give younger Churches a sense of equal status with older, more established churches.[22]

But there is another aspect to this last positive trait of the synthetic model, and it is that the model is always in danger of "selling out" to the other culture, tradition, or social location and so always needs to be appropriated with some suspicion. Openness is a good thing, and it cannot be discarded, but the theologian must always be aware of the power and subtle manipulations of a dominant culture (such as U.S. American, French, or Roman) as well. This is not totally to discredit this model, but only to warn its practitioner of some built-in dangers.

In the same vein, a theology that operates within the parameters of the synthetic model might fall prey to the criticism that it is too weak, too wishy-washy. Theology done according to this model in Papua New Guinea, for example, can appear to be faithful neither to traditional concerns of Christianity nor to traditional concerns and contemporary problems of, say, Sepik River society. If the theologian is not careful, what can emerge is a theology that is not a true synthesis in the Hegelian sense that we mentioned at the outset of this chapter, but a mere juxtaposition of ideas that really do not enhance one another.

When done well, however, the synthetic model can be a powerful, creative model for contextual theologizing. In the hands of theologians such as Vitaliano Gorospe and José de Mesa from the Philippines, the Japanese missionary to Thailand and United States-based Kosuke Koyama, African missionary Aylward Shorter, and African Charles Nyamiti, Christian faith finds new, vital, and deeply rooted expression.

The Synthetic Model

Alternative Titles: *dialogical model; analogical model*
Basis in Scripture and Tradition: *formation of the Bible; development of doctrine; EN 64*
Revelation: *elements of all three previous models*
Scripture/Tradition: *culturally conditioned; incomplete*
Context: *ambiguous and incomplete; needs the "other" for completion*
Method: *conversation with all partners*
Analogy: *cross-pollination*
Legend: *"between the lines" (Horacio de la Costa)*
Critique: *Positive: attitude of dialogue; emphasis on ongoing process; witness to universality; easy to dialogue with other churches*
               Negative: danger of "selling out;" might seem "wishy-washy"

EXAMPLES OF THE SYNTHETIC MODEL

Kosuke Koyama

Our first example of the synthetic model, Kosuke Koyama, has been called "one of the most imaginative and widely-read Asian theologians"[23] and is generally acknowledged as one of Asia's leading theological thinkers.[24] Koyama was born in Japan in 1929 and was baptized a Christian in 1942. From 1960 until 1968 he taught at Thailand Theological Seminary, and from 1968 until 1974 he lived in Singapore, where he was executive director of the Association of Theological Schools in Southeast Asia, dean of the Association's graduate school, and editor of of its journal, the *South East Asia Journal of Theology*. In 1974 Dr. Koyama moved to the University of Otago in Dunedin, New Zealand, and in 1980 he became Professor of Ecumenics and World Christianity at Union Theological Seminary in New York City. Koyama retired from Union in 1996 and now lives in Minneapolis, Minnesota. Koyama has published five books, the first four of which are collections of essays, Bible studies, and meditations.[25] Only *Mt. Fuji and Mt. Sinai* represents a longer, sustained theological reflection.[26] Selections from these books have been included in several volumes of the Mission Trends series, in Gerald H. Anderson's *Asian Voices in Christian Theology* and in Douglas J. Elwood's *Asian Christian Theology*, and other essays and reflections have appeared in journals as diverse as *Theological Education, Missionalia, Missiology,* and *Christian Century*.[27] As Koyama has developed over the past several years, his theological focus has changed from trying to make sense of Christianity in Thailand and Singapore to trying to make sense of his Christian faith as a Japanese person. While his earlier books refer to himself as Japanese and speak somewhat of Japanese reality, *Mt. Fuji and Mt. Sinai* is taken up entirely with the question of doing theology within a specifically Japanese cultural, religious, and historical context.

One of the first things readers will notice about Koyama's writings is that they are indeed "imaginative and creative." Koyama's humor and simplicity have a way of engaging his readers or hearers in his theological process, and his profundity has a way of sneaking up on them. Speaking to an audience in an Indonesian seminary, for example, he asked the students what they saw when they saw chickens—the seminary runs a poultry farm. One student saw economic opportunity, another a gift of God, another a model for family life, and Koyama commented that this reflection was the best way to begin talking about the meaning of theology. Just as everyone sees something more in chickens than just the chickens themselves, so theology is a way of seeing more in the world and human experience, and talking about it. "Indeed, we must be able to see the power of the Creator himself in a chicken, even though a few hours later it will become 'fried chicken.' "[28] Along the same lines, Koyama's writings are filled with colorful, almost flippant images. Readers are warned against having a "middle kingdom complex," by which one's culture or religion is understood to be the most viable or the best;[29] contextual theologians are urged to do theology with a "crucified mind";[30] and the God of love is often described as a "three mile an hour God," who walks the same speed as finite creatures but who is "hot" with passion for them.[31]

In the preface to *Waterbuffalo Theology*, Koyama describes his method as a "theology from below." His approach to theology, he says, is determined not so much by what theologians such as Aquinas and Barth have said, but by the everyday realities that Thai farmers experience: water buffaloes, pepper, bananas, cock fighting, sticky rice. "I begin speaking," he writes, "from where they are (i. e., cock-fighting). From talking about the human situation I go on to call God into this real human situation."[32] The God who is called into the situation is the God of the Bible, but because Koyama has taken pains to take account of the religious and cultural context, the biblical message "comes through,"[33] if not always in Thai or Buddhist terms, at least in a way that is fresh and comprehensible to the Thai mind. As David Hesselgrave and Edward Rommen describe Koyama's method: "He wrestles with the text. At the same time he searches for religious and cultural materials at hand that will make the text come alive, allowing it to speak to persons in their existential situation. The results are either happy or unhappy, depending upon where one sits."[34]

Koyama speaks occasionally about what he does as "translation." More prominent is the idea of "re-rooting," which he describes as discerning the inner meaning of the gospel and then "guarding, watering, and nurturing it as it roots itself in the native soil."[35] In any case, he tends to see the possibility of a supracultural message, a "universal word,"[36] that can become meaningful (and so translated) when it is spoken with reverence to a particular cultural and religious context.

One outstanding example of this method at work appears as a short reflection on Mt 15:21-28—the story of the Canaanite woman with the sick daughter who wouldn't take no for an answer from Jesus. Koyama relates how, when he first preached on the story to the farmers in Thailand, he relied heavily on Luther's interpretation of the story, an interpretation that illustrates the need for strong faith in God, faith that holds on despite seeming rejection. "Those who have no understanding of doubt, turmoil, pangs, tremor, panic, despair, desolation and desperation are bound to fall short of the crucial message of this story. The basic fact about faith is that faith is faith when it believes in spite of *assault*!"[37] When he preached Luther's interpretation of the passage, however, in his broken Thai, the result was disastrous—"my audience went home with the impression that some kind of neurosis constitutes a vital part of the Christian faith."[38]

Koyama then tells how he began to rethink (reroot) the passage from the Thai point of view and became excited by what he found. What he realized was that the text could be interpreted in quite another way. Instead of focusing on the faith of the woman in spite of her rejection by Jesus, Koyama focused on the strong love of the woman for her sick daughter that was at the root of her insistence. This natural love, which was transformed into faith in Jesus, was something that the Thai people (and other Asians) could understand. Koyama's interpretation did not negate the sixteenth-century German interpretation; it simply provided an interpretation that was more sensitive to another culture and another time: it effectively rerooted or translated the gospel message into another soil so that it could be communicated in a more relevant way.

There are other examples of ways in which Koyama employs a kind of translation model in his theologizing,[39] but as one reads his works, one senses that more is going on than the mere translation of scriptural/doctrinal categories and language into those of the Asian cultural world. I find a strong dialectic in much of what he writes between a high sensitivity to cultural reality on the one hand and a strong sense of the truth of the gospel message on the other. In one of the major essays in *Waterbuffalo Theology*, for example, Koyama introduces a distinction that he will use many times to describe the reality of Christianity: the distinction between "cool *arahant*" (an enlightened Buddhist monk) and "hot God." For the Buddhist, salvation consists in noninvolvement, self-emptying, escape from the world of *dukkha* (suffering), but for the Christian, salvation is the acceptance of a God who is impassioned and involved, bidding humanity not to escape suffering, but to transform it through loving action in history. Christianity recognizes the values expressed in the Buddhist way but calls for a "warming" of these values through covenant with the "hot" God of Jesus Christ.[40] More is involved here than just the translation of Buddhist categories in terms of Christian ones. A real dialogue is taking place in which Buddhist values are treated with respect but ultimately critiqued in the name of the gospel.

The same dynamic goes on in an earlier chapter of the same book, a chapter entitled "Will the Monsoon Rain Make God Wet?"[41] The Thai people, Koyama says, live in a world of "many-time-ness," of recurring seasons, of life being renewed at regular intervals, and this opens the way to a view that sees God as part of nature, and religion as the acquiescing to nature's harmony. Christianity, on the other hand, has a linear view of history, with God as sovereign over nature and history. For Christianity to have an impact on Thai life, however, some of the Asian sense of harmony and recurrence has to play a part in its worldview. Koyama suggests that both the Asian cyclic sense of history and the Christian (with western influence) linear sense need to be replaced by a spiral view that includes both in a creative tension. "Is not this image helpful and even necessary in the land of the monsoon orientation? Is not this at least one way to see the signs of the times in Thailand? Will this not bring the presence of God closer to the people of Thailand?"[42]

It is in his later works, however, that Koyama is most clearly revealed as a practitioner of the synthetic model of contextual theologizing. In a review of *Mt. Fuji and Mt. Sinai*, Catalino G. Arévalo remarks that the book is " 'unsystematic' in the accepted or expected sense."[43] In a certain sense this might be true, but I believe that there is a system in the book nonetheless. It is a system, however, that tries to take account of a number of concerns all at once and tries to synthesize Christian particularity (scripture and tradition) with sensitivity to Asian (particularly Japanese) culture in a changing world. *Dialogue* is a word that does not appear in the book's index, but is a key word for understanding what Koyama is trying to do. Both Japanese culture (particularly its world-negating Buddhist strain) and the Judaeo-Christian tradition have positive points that need the benefit of "creative two-way traffic between them."[44] Japanese culture needs to be enriched by Judaeo-Christian insistence on God's transcendence as "maker of heaven and earth," and it can be enriched as well as it rediscovers its Buddhist roots in self-denial and detachment. Theological reflection within the Japanese context cannot compromise the Christian message, and it can be enriched from the wealth that the Judaeo-Christian tradition (philosophy, theology, general culture) can provide. It can also learn from some of the deepest insights of the Buddhist tradition. Koyama concludes that this can perhaps best be expressed in terms of a theology of the cross that reveals a God who is deeply and passionately engaged in human history through a denial of self and by siding with the marginalized in incarnation. Ultimately, neither Mt. Fuji nor Mt. Sinai have the power to save. God's power comes from the broken one on Mt. Calvary.

In an address to the American Society of Missiology in 1984—just as *Mt. Fuji and Mt. Sinai* was being completed—Koyama spoke of "The Asian Approach to Christ."[45] To speak of Christ in Asia today, he said, God has to be understood in four ways. First of all, God must be imaged as impassioned, over against the basic Asian idea of salvation as noninvolvement. Second, God must be imaged as discontinuous, again over against the Asian idea of salvation as blending in harmoniously with the cycles of nature. Third, God needs to be seen as embracing reality in divine involvement rather than simply as transcendent of it. And fourth, God must be understood as on the periphery of life, in solidarity with the oppressed and abandoned of this world. But because it is *God* at the periphery, the periphery is revealed as the true center. These four images, Koyama says, are triggered by a study of the spiritual life of the East. At one and the same time they critique this spiritual life in the light of the Christian gospel, draw from the riches of this great religious tradition, and get their language from the tradition's vocabulary. It seems to me that Koyama's reflections here represent a strong exercise of what I have called the synthetic model. It is extremely complex, but every element of what makes up contextual theology is given its due.

José M. de Mesa

In contrast to Koyama, the second theologian on whom we will focus is not very well known outside his native country of the Philippines. In the Philippines, however, among both professional theologians and increasingly among members of the church at large, José M. de Mesa is regarded as one of the most articulate and creative theologians his country has yet produced. While Koyama might be characterized as representing a more conservative use of the synthetic model, in many ways gravitating toward the translation model in his concern for the preservation of the experience of the past recorded in tradition and preserved in tradition, de Mesa might be illustrative of a more liberal use of the synthetic model, gravitating both toward the anthropological model in his concern for a positive appreciation of culture and toward the praxis model in his concern for a theology that comes out of committed concern for the underside of society.[46]

De Mesa is a lay theologian, born and raised in the Philippines, and holds a Ph.D. in religious studies from the Catholic University of Louvain in Belgium. He is currently on the faculty of De La Salle University in Manila but has served also as Professor of Systematic Theology and Dean of the Graduate School at Maryhill School of Theology in Quezon City (Metro Manila) and a member of the faculty of the East Asian Pastoral Institute in Manila. He is a popular lecturer throughout the Philippines and around the world and a regular contributor to a number of Filipino theological journals, and has published a number of books—two of them with his colleague at Maryhill School of Theology, Belgian missionary Lode Wostyn.[47]

A study of his writings reveals that de Mesa does not lay down a particular theological method and then follow it with consistent regularity and rigor. This does not mean that he is not methodologically sophisticated, however; rather, it points to a flexibility that employs a number of approaches in a truly *synthetic* way. In the introduction to theology written in collaboration with Wostyn, a four-step method is sketched out that approaches theology along the lines of what I have called the praxis model.[48] In their book on Christology, de Mesa and Wostyn employ a model based on three "hermeneutical principles." This model, while still rather praxis-orientated, seems to be much more inclusive of other theological approaches: "We follow as it were a spiral which starts with our experience, moves through the successive experience-interpretations in history, and ends up with our own experience-interpretation."[49] In a very distinct methodological essay in *In Solidarity with the Culture*, however, de Mesa proposes a related yet rather different approach: one does theology in Asia today through a mutually respectful yet critical dialogue between Judaeo-Christian tradition on the one hand and culture (including what I have called social change) on the other.[50] Although one can start at either pole, of tradition or context (de Mesa's emphasis is particularly on culture), the way one begins this dialogue in Asia (Philippines) today is to make a methodological option to emphasize the positive resources and potential of the culture. In this way the gospel can better be communicated and understood within the Asian context, and the reflection on culture can contribute to a better understanding of the gospel itself.[51] But having said this, de Mesa can still theologize in ways that are best suited to the translation model. In an essay on the doctrine of Providence in lowland Filipino context, for example, de Mesa concludes that the two concepts *bahala na* and *malasakit* present the doctrine in "culturally intelligible terms."[52]

The breadth of de Mesa's learning, as well as the extent of his creativity, is wonderfully illustrated in an essay entitled "The Resurrection in the Filipino Context."[53] The essay begins with a survey of reasons to hold that the Filipino has little interest in the Resurrection or the risen Christ—" 'The Christ of the Filipinos,' writes Frank Lynch, 'is pre-eminently a suffering Christ. He is the beaten, scourged, humiliated, and defeated Christ.' "[54] However, a deeper analysis of Filipino religiosity and of the scriptural sources can reveal the possibility that the Resurrection does indeed play an integral part in the faith life of Filipinos. The *Pasyong Mahal*, a long poem, read in daily sections in Filipino homes during Lent and the Triduum, that details Jesus' life, includes no less than eight stanzas that speak of the Resurrection; the practice of the *Salubong* or the dramatization of the meeting of Jesus and Mary on Easter morning is an integral part of Easter celebrations throughout the country; and the famous passion play held yearly on the island of Marinduque includes the Resurrection as an integral part of the script. More subtly, yet very significantly, the popularity of the feast of *Cristo Rey* or *Kristong Hari* (Christ the King) points to the fact that Filipinos do not just focus on the suffering or dead Christ: "Triumph, exaltation, glory. The feast of Christ the King is undoubtedly these. This fact also indicates that Filipinos believe in the 'resurrection' without actually using the concept."[55] And upon further analysis, says de Mesa, the idea of resurrection needs to be understood as not the only way the triumph of Jesus over evil can be or even was portrayed in the scriptural sources. Relying on the thought of Edward Schillebeeckx and James Mackey, he insists that "there are other ways of speaking of [Jesus' transformation after death] in our Tradition: the ascension (Jesus going to the Father), exaltation/vindication (Jesus as Lord sitting at the right hand of the Father) and the *parousia* (The Lord is coming). This implies that it is possible to speak about the same reality using imageries other than the Resurrection."[56]

Perhaps there is a way of speaking of the Resurrection in Filipino context that takes into account Filipino attention to the suffering Christ on the one hand and the rather implicit faith in Christ's triumph on the other. What de Mesa suggests is that the Filipino idea of *pagbabangong-dangal* can capture both Filipino sensibility and traditional faith. *Pagbabangong-dangal* can be roughly translated "the raising up of one's honor," and the closest English equivalent would be something like "vindication" or "restoration of honor. "

To the "objective" observer, it would seem as if Jesus' ministry ended in failure and shame (*hiya*). Not only was Jesus' message rejected by the political and religious leaders of Israel; it was rejected by the majority of the people as well. And not only that—this general rejection led Jesus to a most shameful death. The conclusion could only be drawn that Jesus was wrong, "wholly and entirely: in his message, his behavior, his whole being. His claim about the Kingdom of God and His Father (*Abba*) is now refuted, his authority gone, his way shown to be false."[57] And yet, not many days after Jesus' shameful death, his scattered disciples found themselves drawn back toward one another, their courage restored, their own shame at deserting the master forgiven. Confident that only a living person could be experienced as so present and so powerful in their midst, the disciples fearlessly began to proclaim that Jesus was indeed alive. Jesus' life did not end in failure; it had blossomed into the power of God's empowering and forgiving Spirit. This is the meaning of the Resurrection: Jesus' vision was right! "The shame and dishonor were taken away; Jesus—his person, his message, behavior and commitment—was vindicated."[58]

De Mesa admits that this imagery of vindication/exaltation is not the only way of speaking of what happened to Jesus after his death. Other complementary, more traditional images and metaphors, such as "ascension into glory," "seated at God's right hand," and "risen from the dead" are necessary. But this particular way of speaking certainly is relevant in a culture in which shame is one of the main things to be avoided and in which vindication plays such an important part. In addition, he says, this way of speaking has two other advantages in the Philippine context. In the first place, speaking of the Resurrection as *pagbabangong-dangal* can avoid the common mistake that Jesus' triumph over the forces of evil and death is something merely physical, the "resuscitation of a corpse." Rather, it can emphasize that Resurrection is something that can go on in people's daily life—in their own daily living and struggling, whether individually or as a people. Living according to principles *does* issue in some kind of justification. Second, this particular interpretation of Jesus' Resurrection provides a foundation for courageous action on behalf of justice and liberation and provides a theological background for understanding the *pagbabangong-dangal* experienced in events such as the "EDSA Revolution" of 1986 when justice was vindicated in the fall of the dictator Marcos.

In the light of contemporary scholarship, de Mesa concludes, and in the light of a key concept in Filipino psychology, to speak of the Resurrection of Christ in terms of vindication may be the best way of articulating the doctrine to Filipinos today.

Even though de Mesa recognizes that theology in the Philippines can only be "an occasional enterprise, one dictated by circumstances and immediate needs rather than the needs for system building,"[59] he and his colleague Lode Wostyn have succeeded in developing a full-blown systematic Christology. The work is, by their own admission, neither finished nor polished, but it does go a long way to providing a disciplined and thoughtful presentation of the mystery of Christ that is faithful to the Christian tradition, in touch with contemporary scholarship, and responsive to the needs and concerns of Filipino Christians today. As in their previous book on doing theology (and in many of his other writings), the text is enlivened by de Mesa's original cartoon sketches, and these serve to summarize and emphasize the book's basic ideas.[60]

De Mesa and Wostyn proceed in constructing their Christology by following three hermeneutical principles, which they set out at the beginning: (1) revelation happens in and through human experiences; (2) experience is always interpreted experience; and (3) experience and its interpretation in the past has to be critically correlated with present-day experience in a particular local and cultural context.[61] The book is developed in three parts, and in each part all three hermeneutical principles are operative, while each part also emphasizes one principle in particular. In the first part, the "Christological question" is set up in terms of what might be the experience in which humanity in general and Filipinos in particular might expect to discover God's revelation. The answer is the experience of needing "salvation," which is best expressed in the Filipino context as *ginhawa*. In Part 2 the person of Jesus is remembered in terms of what he did, what he said, how and why he died, and how he was experienced as risen. This is done not only through a study of the scriptural witness (Jesus as eschatological prophet) but also through a correlation of that witness with the Filipino longing for *ginhawa* (and so Jesus is remembered as both "liberator" and "*ang taong maganda at kalooban*" [roughly: a person of graciousness and kindness]). Finally, in Part 3 the reader is led through the process of how the New Testament church correlated its experience with that of the risen Lord, how this process took place within the Hellenistic world (the context for what are called the "classical dogmatic formulations" of Christological and trinitarian theology), and how the process needs to take place in today's Philippines. De Mesa and Wostyn suggest in this final section that it is only by living as disciples—and therefore in a Christian praxis—that one can really "Christologize" the experience of Jesus today.

This brief overview of the book, however, does not begin to describe its intricacy. De Mesa and Wostyn are constantly listening to Philippine culture for clues of the Christological experience; they provide a number of possible translations of traditional theological terms and concepts; they dialogue extensively with contemporary western scholarship, particularly that of Edward Schillebeeckx; and they heed the call of liberation theologians to make theology not just something in books but something that arises out of and bears fruit in intelligent action. De Mesa's work by himself and his work with Lode Wostyn show some of the best possibilities of the synthetic model of contextual theology. It is rich in scholarship, rich in creativity, and the work of a person who seeks sincerely to understand his faith.

8

The Transcendental Model

In one of his "Peanuts" cartoons, the late Charles Schulz depicts Linus struggling with his math homework and being completely flustered. After a series of frames in which Linus's grimaces reveal his almost desperate difficulty in understanding, Linus exclaims in the last frame: "You can't learn the new math with an old math mind!" In the gospel of Mark, Jesus says that a new patch cannot be put on an old garment and new wine cannot be put into old wineskins (Mk 2:21-22).

All three of these parables illustrate very clearly the key insight for understanding the transcendental model of contextual theology: there are some things that we cannot understand without a complete change of mind. Some things demand a radical shift in perspective, a change in horizon—a *conversion*—before they begin to make sense. Until we make this shift, whatever we are trying to understand will defy understanding. Without this shift or conversion, we are struggling to find an answer to what amounts to an inadequate question.

The transcendental model proposes that the task of constructing a contextualized theology is not about producing a particular body of any kind of texts; it is about attending to the affective and cognitive operations in the self-transcending subject. What is important is not so much that a particular theology is produced but that the theologian who is producing it operates as an authentic, converted subject. In the same way that Bernard Lonergan speaks of metaphysics, a contextual theology will not appear primarily in books, but in men's and women's minds.[1]

A SKETCH OF THE MODEL

TERMINOLOGY

The term *transcendental* is meant to refer to the transcendental method that was pioneered by Immanuel Kant in the eighteenth century and developed in the twentieth century by thinkers such as Pierre Rousselot, Joseph Maréchal, Karl Rahner, and Bernard Lonergan, all of whom attempted to interpret what they discovered to be a genuine "intellectualism" in Thomas Aquinas in terms of modern subjectivity and historical consciousness.[2]

Transcendental method proposes a basic switch in the process of coming to know reality. Instead of beginning with the conviction that reality is "out there," existing somehow independently of human knowing, it suggests that the knowing subject is intimately involved in determining reality's basic shape—and so one needs to begin one's quest for knowing what "is" by attending to the dynamic of one's own consciousness and irrepressible desire to know. The switch is one from beginning with a world of objects to beginning with the world of the subject, the interior world of the human person. "Genuine objectivity is the fruit of authentic subjectivity," Lonergan writes. Objective knowledge, knowledge of the real, can only be achieved "by attaining authentic subjectivity."[3] It is in attending to one's transcendental subjectivity, therefore, as it reaches out naturally toward truth, that one finds oneself doing an authentic contextual theology.

PRESUPPOSITIONS OF THE TRANSCENDENTAL MODEL

A fundamental presupposition of the transcendental model is that one begins to theologize contextually not by focusing on the essence of the gospel message or the content of tradition as such, nor even by trying to thematize or analyze a particular context or expressions of language in that context. Rather, the starting point is transcendental, concerned with one's own religious experience and one's own experience of oneself. When one starts with oneself, however, it is important to understand that one does not and can not start in a vacuum. Very much to the contrary, one realizes that as an individual, as a subject, one is determined at every turn by one's context: I am precisely who I am because I exist at this particular point in time, because I am a recipient of a particular national and cultural heritage, because I have a particular set of parents and have received a particular amount and quality of education, and so forth. What might seem at first glance to be a very personal and even individualistic starting point is really one that is extremely contextual and communal.[4] Because of this inevitably contextual nature of the subject, one could easily speak of starting from one's own *community's* religious experience and from one's own *community's* experience of itself. From this transcendental starting point, therefore, theology is conceived as the process of "bringing to speech" who I am or who we are—as a person or persons of faith who are in every possible respect a product of a historical, geographical, social, and cultural environment.

The questions one asks, therefore, when one does theology according to the transcendental model are not questions about how a particular theology will *look*—i.e., what themes it might have so that it takes on a kind of North American or Asian or African shape, or the language one needs to use to sound convincingly Hispanic/Latino or Filipino. Much more basic will be questions that try to evaluate one's own authenticity as a religious and cultural subject. So, rather than questions such as "How can I express the Reign of God in a Hispanic/Latino way?" or "How can I show how Lakota customs both reflect and challenge Christian values?" the practitioner of the transcendental model asks, as she or he tries to live a Christian life: "How well do I know myself? How genuine is the religious experience I am trying to interpret, how well does my language express this experience? How free of bias am I? Do I feel comfortable with a particular expression of my religious experience? Why or why not? Do I really understand what I am trying to articulate?"[5]

This first presupposition leads naturally into a second: that which might seem so private and personal is really something that can articulate the experience of others who share one's basic context—members of one's generation, members of one's culture, members of one's nation. Given the fact that, as Lonergan insists, the only way to true objectivity is through radical and authentic subjectivity,[6] or given the fact that, as psychologist Carl Rogers says, the most personal is the most general,[7] the practitioner of the transcendental model would argue that what might seem like a rather narrow starting point in individual experience is actually the best starting point for doing theology that speaks to other individuals—historically and culturally determined subjects—who share one's own worldview.

A third presupposition of the transcendental model is in regard to the notion of divine revelation. God's revelation is not "out there." Revelation is not in the words of scripture, or the doctrines of tradition or even hidden within the labyrinthine networks of human culture, social location, and social change. The only place where God can reveal Godself truly and effectively is within human experience, as a human person is open to the words of scripture as read or proclaimed, open to events in daily life, and open to the values embodied in a cultural tradition. Revelation, in other words, is only revelation—revealing God's self and offering friendship to men and women—when men and women are actually attending to the fact that God is always pouring love into our hearts by the Holy Spirit (see Rom 5:5). Revelation is understood as an event, not as a content; it is something that happens when a person opens himself or herself to reality. Theology is possible only for the converted subject, only for the person who in full openness has allowed God to touch and transform his or her life.[8] Perhaps even more accurately, one could say that theology happens as a person struggles more adequately and authentically to articulate and appropriate this ongoing relationship with the divine.

A fourth foundation stone on which this model rests is the conviction that while every person is truly historically and culturally conditioned in terms of the content of thought, the human mind nevertheless operates in identical ways in all cultures and at all periods of history. What this means is that when an Asian or an African inquires or understands, the concepts and images by which he or she understands will be radically different from, say, a North American or a European, but the basic cognitive operations will be the same. As real as historical and cultural differences are, in other words, a historical or cultural subject's way of knowing transcends those particular differences.[9] No matter where one knows or when one knows, one begins the process in experience, organizes this experience by means of concepts, judges the truth or falsity of one's conceptual understanding in judgment, and integrates the knowledge arrived at in judgment by means of a decision. What the transcendental model claims is that if one gives full rein to this transcendental, transcultural process as one tries to express one's faith, one will necessarily come to an expression of faith that is truly one's identity as a historical and cultural subject.

Because the transcendental model puts so much emphasis on the authenticity of the subject who is trying to express his or her experience as a person of faith and a person of a particular context, it is clear that the best person to do theology within a particular context is the subject of that context as such. The development of a truly contextual theology is something that takes place as a person both wrestles with his or her own faith and shares that faith with others who share his or her cultural parameters. But because of the transcultural nature of the working of the human mind as it comes to know, conversations with persons of other cultures or other periods of time (e.g., with the classics of Christian tradition or members of other cultures working in one's own) are not excluded. One might say that the transcendental model works here through a method of both sympathy and antipathy—sympathy in that a person of integrity might learn much from another person of integrity from another context; antipathy in that if a person analyzes why he or she is repulsed by or not attracted to a particular way of doing theology, he or she has already taken a first step to doing contextual theology as such. A theologian from Papua New Guinea, for example, might read with great profit the works of a Schleiermacher or an Aquinas. He or she might be greatly stimulated by a guest professor from North America or Southeast Asia, even if he or she ultimately will have to disagree with him or her; and study in a great university such as Cambridge or Tübingen might be of immense value in helping him or her understand the authentic cultural and faith expressions of other peoples and other ages. The only thing that is important, however, as a person from one context encounters a person from another, is that one must never relinquish one's authenticity as a particular historical or cultural subject. These positive or negative encounters with others can be extremely fruitful for one's own theological thinking, but never provide ready-made answers. But as one tries personally to appropriate the ideas of another, as one runs these ideas through the filter of one's own context, one can be challenged to greater authenticity and to broader horizons. To use the horticultural metaphor once again, a person can be inspired to work in his garden because of the example—or lack thereof—from others working in their own gardens.

Not only professional or trained theologians are capable of doing theology, however. The transcendental model easily admits the fact that any Christian who authentically tries to appropriate his or her faith is participating in the theologizing process and is doing genuine contextual theology. Like both the anthropological and the praxis models, the transcendental model insists that the ordinary Christian believer is a theologian, perhaps even of primary importance.[10] What the transcendental model emphasizes, however, is that every authentic Christian theologizes not by virtue of how much he or she knows or by the accuracy with which he or she is able to express doctrine. Rather, to the extent that a person of faith obeys the transcendental precepts—"Be attentive, Be intelligent, Be reasonable, Be responsible"[11]—in trying to articulate and deepen his or her faith, he or she is doing genuine theology. And to the extent that a person does this as an authentic human subject—conditioned by history, geography, culture, and so forth—he or she is doing genuine contextual theology.

In several places in his writings, Bernard Lonergan uses the image of a scissors' action to explain the process of interpretation.[12] Although we might use the image here in a slightly different way, the image of scissors might be a good one to explain the process of theologizing in terms of the transcendental model. The upper blade of the scissors, we might say, stands for the person as subject, in his or her existence as a member of a particular history and a particular culture; the lower blade stands for that subject's experience of God, illumined and deepened in the context of the Christian symbol system. In terms of the transcendental model, the subject theologizes when these two imaginary blades are brought together. The theologian attempts to conceptualize or "bring to speech" his or her experience of God, as experienced in a particular spatiotemporal or cultural milieu. This activity is theology, and because it is necessarily the activity of a contextualized subject, the resulting content is a contextualized theology.

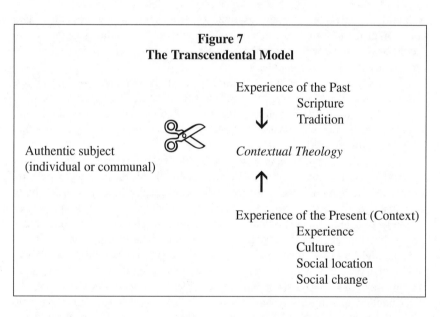

Figure 7
The Transcendental Model

Experience of the Past
Scripture
↓ Tradition

Authentic subject
(individual or communal)   *Contextual Theology*

↑

Experience of the Present (Context)
Experience
Culture
Social location
Social change

It is quite possible that modes of expression other than discursive, expository ones would lend themselves to this model of contextual theology. As consciousness grows that theology is a wider activity than writing books and articles and that it perhaps might best be done as a sermon or a hymn, contextual theologians might take these activities more seriously. The activity of the artist might be a better analogy for doing theology than that of the philosopher or mathematician. Perhaps the work of novelists as diverse as Soshaku Endo of Japan, Nick Joaquin of the Philippines, and Walker Percy of the United States, as well as artists and musicians from various cultures, might be worth investigating for the development of this model.

CRITIQUE OF THE TRANSCENDENTAL MODEL

The transcendental model points to a new way of doing theology. With its emphasis on theology as activity and process rather than theology as a particular content, it rightly insists that theology is not about finding out right answers that exist in some transcultural realm, but about a careful but passionate search for authenticity of expression of one's religious and cultural identity. The transcendental model highlights the active, never-ending aspect of Anselm of Canterbury's definition of theology as faith *seeking* understanding and highlights as well the tentative expression that is sought—*understanding* rather than certitude.[13]

A second advantage of this model is that it clearly recognizes the contextual determination of the person who theologizes. The "turn to the subjective" espoused by transcendental method clearly includes a turn to the historical and the cultural as genuine theological sources and *loci* of revelation. God's love floods a person's heart where he or she is, and theology is understood as the search for understanding one's recognition of such gracious action.

Third, the universal structure of human knowing and consciousness provides a common ground for mutual conversation and interaction. In this way, one's own theologizing can be both sharpened over against the "other," and challenged and purified by the other's questions.[14]

The reaction of many people to the transcendental model, however, is that it is too abstract, too hard to grasp. It is difficult to make the shift from thinking of theology as some kind of content to be studied, written about, or lectured on to thinking of it as the actual activity of seeking understanding as an authentic believer and cultural subject.[15]

A more serious objection, however, is that the very universality that is one of the model's advantages is not really universal at all, but is the product of western, male-dominated cultural thought forms. Do people really come to understand in the same way, or are there really different ways of knowing?[16] Is the transcendental model of contextual theology just another subtle way that western (and perhaps patriarchal) thought attempts to domesticate attempts to think in alternative ways?[17]

One might also ask, if subjective authenticity is the criterion for authentic theology, what or who provides the criterion of subjective authenticity? Is Lonergan's dictum about objectivity arising out of true subjectivity really true? The danger is that attention to subjectivity in the transcendental sense might degenerate into subjectivity in the sense of relativity, or, as Robert Bellah and his coauthors warn, into "expressive and utilitarian individualism."[18] John Stacer notes that the subjectivity that Lonergan and others (e.g., James, Royce, Marcel, Hocking) espouse does indeed prepare one to "understand persons from all around the world." But he also warns that this can degenerate into a "therapeutic mentality" that tends to cut us off from genuine dialogue with the other.[19]

Finally, since it is so hard to be an authentic believer and an authentic human being, it might seem that a theology that depends on these criteria would never get started. The transcendental model might simply be too ideal or at best only a "metamodel" that lays down the condition for the possibility of any contextual theological thinking.

The Transcendental Model

Alternative Title: *subjective model*
Basis in Scripture and Tradition: *Mk 2:21-22*
Revelation: *tends to be understood as personal presence, encountered in subjective (personal, communal) experience*
Scripture/Tradition: *culturally conditioned; incomplete*
Context: *good and trustworthy; individual experience is clue to wider experience; individual experience is conditioned by the radical communal nature of humanity*
Method: *sympathy and antipathy*
Analogy: *if I cultivate my garden, another will be inspired to cultivate his or hers*
Legend: *"the most personal is the most general" (Carl Rogers)*
Critique: *Positive: emphasizes theology as activity; recognizes contextual nature of all theology*
　　　　　Negative: too abstract; false claim to universality; too ideal to be practical

---

EXAMPLES OF THE TRANSCENDENTAL MODEL

Precisely because of its character as a metamodel, every authentic theologian might be cited as an example of the transcendental model at work. As I pointed out in Chapter 1, no genuine theology has ever been a theology that has been developed outside some specific context; and so, from the writers of the various Christian scriptures ("Luke," Paul, the author of Hebrews) through Origen, Augustine, Aquinas, Hildegard, and Catherine of Siena to Luther, Calvin and Bellarmine, the "classics" of the Christian tradition have been the products of men and women who were both true cultural subjects and people of living faith. And as I have intimated above, if we widen the notion of theology to include music, literary expressions, and the plastic arts, the number of practitioners of this model would be enormous, including the hymns of Ephrem, the music of Mozart, Duruflé, Dave Brubeck, and Bruce Springsteen, the novels of Endo, Percy, and Flannery O'Connor, the poetry of Rilke and Emily Dickinson, and the works of countless anonymous icon painters and African sculptors, not to mention inspiring and thought-provoking works by Michelangelo, Matisse, and Robert Lentz.

Nevertheless, it seems to me that some contemporary theologians illustrate this model in a particularly clear way: they are thinkers rooted deep in their cultural traditions, social location, and religious faith, but their theological thought develops methodologically neither from mere contextual identity (anthropological model) nor from a concern for the preservation of the Christian tradition within a particular context (translation model). Some of them may be aware of the importance of theologizing out of praxis (praxis model), and some may attempt to balance culture, tradition, and societal and/or personal transformation in their theological endeavors (synthetic model), but what emerges as their overarching concern and methodological lodestar is their commitment to their own integrity as Christian human beings. From among such theologians I have chosen to focus on Sallie McFague and Justo L. González.

SALLIE MCFAGUE

Sallie McFague, Professor of Theology at Vanderbilt University in Nashville, Tennessee, is a prime example of someone who could be said to do theology out of the transcendental model. McFague was educated at Smith College and Yale Divinity School, and since 1970 she has been a member of the faculty at Vanderbilt, serving as Dean of the Divinity School from 1975 to 1979. She also served as editor of *Soundings: An Interdisciplinary Journal* (1967-1975), and in addition to a number of articles in journals and books, she has published *Speaking in Parables: A Study in Metaphor and Theology*; *Metaphorical Theology: Models of God in Religious Language*; *Models of God: Theology for an Ecological, Nuclear Age*; *The Body of God: An Ecological Theology*; *Super, Natural Christians: How We Should Love Nature*; and *Life Abundant: Rethinking Economy and Theology for a Planet in Peril*.[20]

"The purpose of theology," McFague writes in the first line of her first book, "is to make it possible for the gospel to be heard in our time."[21] This sentence is programmatic, for if we examine what McFague means by "the gospel to be *heard* in our time" and then see what she means by "the gospel to be heard *in our time*," we can better understand how she goes about her theological craft.

First of all, when McFague talks about the importance of the gospel, or the Christian message, being able to be heard again today, she is not talking about a mere translation of the message or a rewording of the various traditional Christian symbols. Rather, for the gospel to be heard today, a radically different way of doing theology, a different theological method, needs to be developed—one that can place contemporary men and women in situations of genuine encounter with the word so that by a "certain shock to the imagination" (Amos Wilder) people can be helped to say, " 'Yes,' not simply with their heads, but with commitment to be lived out in their entire lives."[22]

Such a style of doing theology, however, is not exactly a radical departure from tradition. In fact, what McFague proposes is a return to the method of Jesus, who preached and taught in the genre of the parable, which she defines—and this is key—as an extended metaphor. Like the metaphor, the parable uses the familiar in an unfamiliar context; it involves the person hearing or reading it to such a degree that he or she becomes aware of the world or of life's possibilities in a new and fresh way. Like the metaphor, one comes to this new understanding and awareness *through* the parable—not by figuring out what it means, but by living within the tension it provides.[23] And like the metaphor, the parable has both an "is" and an "is not" quality to it:[24] God is a rock—but of course God is not; God is a father (or mother), but not literally. The reign of God is a woman searching for a lost coin, or a merchant finding a pearl of great price, or a wedding feast to which those invited refused to come and then to which anyone was invited—yes . . . and no. A good parable, like a good metaphor, often invites insight through shock; in fact, "a metaphor that has lost is shock (its 'is not' quality) loses as well its recognition possibilities (its 'is' quality), for the metaphor is no longer 'heard': it is taken to be a definition, not a likely account."[25]

What McFague proposes is a metaphorical theology, that is to say, an intermediary theology that, taking its clue from the metaphorical nature of Jesus' parables, "relies on various literary forms—parables, stories, poems, confessions—as a way from religious experience to systematic theology.[26] Theology, to be heard today, cannot be in the form of a purely conceptual systematic (constructive) thought; but neither can it simply tell stories or propose poetic images. What is needed is a middle way between primary, imagistic language and secondary, conceptual expressions of thought.[27]

McFague suggests that the model, as a "metaphor with staying power,"[28] might be employed to provide such a way. On the one hand, the model retains all the tentative, imaginative, and "is/is not" properties of the parable, poem, or story; on the other hand, as a "dominant metaphor,"[29] it has already moved toward reflection, interpretation, and conceptualization. Reflection on various models—tentative, engaging, even playful reflection on metaphors that shock, surprise, and provide new insight—is the method by which McFague believes theology can be "heard" in a new way in today's world. Although it is not new (indeed, McFague argues that it is quite traditional, at least in its roots), what we have is a method of contextualization that proposes not so much an alternative *content* but an alternative way of doing theology.

McFague's books are each progressive steps in the development of a theology that tries to work out of this alternative method. She is honest about the fact that there may be other ways of allowing the gospel to be heard in our contemporary world, but she proposes hers as *one* way—"a limited, biased, and finally personal way . . . influenced by my own tradition of Protestantism as well as by my own sensibility and personal faith."[30] As she makes clear at the beginning of *Models of God*, her starting point is her own social location as a white, middle-class woman, strongly influenced both by liberation theology in general and by feminist theology in particular. Nevertheless, her work does not call directly for "programs of revolutionary action," either in the wider political arena or with respect to the emancipation of women; rather, it works out of the conviction "that a new imaginative picture of the relationship between God and the world must precede action," as revolutionary as that action might be.[31]

To move to the second aspect of McFague's initial, programmatic sentence, her proposal is to do theology so it can be heard *in our time*. *Our* time, for McFague, is North America in the last quarter of the twentieth century and the beginning years of the twenty-first, seen from the point of view, as I pointed out above, of a white, middle-class woman with a global sense on the one hand and a sense of tradition on the other. Our *time* is that of "postmodernity,"[32] a time characterized by a growing suspicion of values and products of the western, Enlightenment-influenced modern world. Any characterization of the elements of postmodernity will vary, McFague says, but they will usually include

> a greater appreciation of nature, linked with a chastened admiration for technology; the recognition of the importance of language (and hence interpretation and construction) in human existence; the acceptance of the challenge that other religious options present to the Judeo-Christian tradition; a sense of the displacement of the white, Western male and the rise of those dispossessed because of gender, race, or class; an apocalyptic sensibility, fueled in part by the awareness that we exist between two holocausts, the Jewish and the nuclear; and perhaps most significant, a growing appreciation of the thoroughgoing, radical interdependence of life at all levels and in every imaginable way.[33]

At the end of *Metaphorical Theology*, and in a more systematic and sustained way in *Models of God* and *The Body of God*, McFague presents several "thought experiments"[34] that attempt to do theology in the alternative way that she has proposed and that come out of and speak to the context of contemporary, postmodern North America. Using an extended feminist analysis in *Metaphorical Theology*, she concludes that while the term *father* need not result in making of God an idol that reflects our sinful, patriarchal society, a recognition of the metaphorical nature of the word can open us up to other metaphors that are perhaps more appropriate—certainly less dangerous—for our time. While the metaphors of mother, brother, or sister might also do (Mechtild of Hackeborn speaks of God as Father in creation, Mother in salvation, Brother in dividing up the Kingdom, Sister in sweet companionship[35]), the metaphor—or more precisely, model—of "friend" is proposed as an image that is even more appropriate for our age: it is radically relational, gender/race inclusive, and able to stress "mutuality, maturity, cooperation, responsibility or reciprocity."[36] This one alternative model for speaking of God in our time is extended to three in *Models of God*, where God is named, in addition to "friend," as "mother" and "lover." Another provocative metaphor, "the world as God's body," is traced in a chapter in *Models of God* and developed in more detail in *The Body of God*. McFague freely acknowledges that other models can be used as well, but she argues that these models of God as mother, lover, and friend and the world as God's body are particularly adequate to express an understanding of God in an age threatened by nuclear holocaust or ecological suffocation. Each one of these images, in its own way, points to the way that God loves (gratuitously, passionately, challengingly), the way God acts (creating, saving, sustaining), and the way God relates (in justice, as healer, as companion) in a way that affirms God's transcendence on the one hand and human responsibility on the other.

To my mind, McFague has articulated one of the most authentic North American theologies I have been exposed to. Her project is far from complete, and I look forward to more volumes that explore other aspects of her metaphorical method and strong contextual sensibility. Her work is a testimony to the power of a theological reflection that takes seriously both authentic subjectivity and authentic faith. The same power is also present in the second theologian I have chosen to illustrate the transcendental model.

JUSTO L. GONZÁLEZ

Justo L. González was born in Cuba and served as a pastor of the United Methodist Church until he emigrated to the United States in 1957. Having completed the Ph.D. in historical theology at Yale, González has been a member of the faculties of several theological schools, including that of the Evangelical Seminary of Puerto Rico (where he was dean), Candler School of Theology at Emory University, Interdenominational Theological Center, and Columbia Theological Seminary. He has served on the Faith and Order Commission of the World Council of Churches and is a staff member of the office of the Fund for Theological Education. His large number of publications include his three-volume *A History of Christian Thought*; *Liberation Preaching: The Pulpit and the Oppressed* (with his wife Catherine); *The Theological Education of Hispanics*; *Christian Thought Revisited: Three Types of Theology*; *Faith and Wealth: A History of Early Christian Ideas on the Origin, Significance, and Use of Money*; *Mañana: Christian Theology from a Hispanic Perspective*; and *The Acts of the Apostles: The Gospel of the Spirit*.[37] There is little doubt that González is among the most important and most creative Hispanic/Latino theologians today—Protestant or Catholic.

Of all his works, González's 1990 book *Mañana* is the most self-consciously contextual (coming out of his cultural roots and social location) and theological. The 1980 volume on liberation preaching is written with a solid commitment to the content and method of liberation theology, and his book on faith and wealth in early Christianity is inspired in part by Latin Americans.[38] But *Mañana* is an attempt to articulate a *Christian Theology*, as the subtitle says, *from a Hispanic Perspective*. It is in fact a brief *summa* of systematic theology, a reflection on a number of Christian doctrines—God, Trinity, Christ, the human person, sin—from the point of view of a person who represents a religious minority within his culture and a cultural minority within his church and adopted country. In this brief sketch of González's method, I will focus on some of the ideas presented in this book.

Mañana is developed in two "movements" that, even if they are not indicated as such, divide the work into two parts. In the first part (Chapters 1-5) González talks about his Cuban-Protestant identity in particular and Hispanic identity in general. González's own minority status in Catholic Cuba gave him a deep conviction about the authority of scripture, and while his experience as a minority in the United States has changed the focus somewhat, that conviction has nevertheless remained.[39] One reason for this change in focus in regard to biblical authority has been shaped by a new sense of cultural identity as a member of a people whose lineage is composed of invaders and those invaded and who live in various situations of exile—political exiles from Cuba and El Salvador, economic exiles from

Mexico, and cultural exiles who live in a land that once belonged to their ancestors but now only recognizes them as foreigners.[40] Another reason for the change in focus is the new ecumenism that has developed in the Hispanic community since Vatican Council II[41] and the emergence of liberation theology in Latin America and in other countries around the world.[42] González argues that the only way he (and the Hispanic community) can read the scriptures is to read them "in Spanish"[43]—meaning not so much in the Spanish language as through Hispanic eyes, in a communal effort,[44] through the guilt and pain of the Hispanic past, and with the suspicion of a people who have been systematically marginalized in U.S. society.

Perhaps what is most interesting in this first section on Hispanic identity is what is missing. Other Hispanic theologians (e.g., Virgilio Elizondo, Andrés G. Guerrero, Orlando Espín)[45] focus on a number of cultural and religious practices that serve either as ways to translate the gospel or points of contact with the gospel in the Hispanic/Latino community. While some of these themes are included in González's presentation—e.g., the importance of community for Hispanics and an appreciation of the symbol of the Virgin of Guadalupe, the possibility of miracles—the identity González assigns to himself as a Cuban American and to Hispanics at large is much more defined in terms of social status and historical roots. This is no doubt due in part to his Protestant identity; but it is also, perhaps, due to a desire to avoid constructing theology on the basis of what some Hispanics refer to disparagingly as a "*piñata pastoral*,"[46] that is, constructing theology on a naive appropriation of Hispanic popular culture and religiosity.

The second part of the book (Chapters 6-11) presents theological reflections on several traditional theological themes and doctrines (on God, the Trinity, creation, theological anthropology, Christology, spirituality). González proceeds here not by starting with scripture and tradition and translating the message into Hispanic culture; nor does he start with culture and show how it dovetails with the gospel. Rather, the biblical message and theological tradition are explained *by a Hispanic person who points to the relevance of the traditional doctrines for his Hispanic/ Latino community*. González accomplishes this by bringing to the tradition all his considerable resources as historian of doctrine, faithful Christian, and authentic cultural subject.

In the chapter on Christology, for example, González tries to show how the decrees of the early ecumenical councils are not only true in general but true and relevant for Hispanics today. Nicea's emphasis on essence and substance in speaking of Jesus' identity did tend to solidify a movement of "Constantinization" of theology, by which God and Jesus began to take on characteristics that both hellenized and "imperialized" the divine: Jesus' unchanging divine nature was imaged in terms of imperial power, thus legitimizing the latter in perpetuity. Nevertheless, the definitions of the councils form a "stumbling block that no form of Constantinian theology can overcome."[47]

Orthodox Christology has successfully avoided two temptations. The first is that of gnosticism. While acknowledging the existence of evil and injustice in the world, gnostics sought salvation by trying to escape from the world into a purely spiritual state—this through the discovery of some kind of secret *gnosis* (knowledge). The Christological brand of gnosticism was termed "docetism" (from the Greek *dokein*: "to seem"). Jesus was not really human; he only seemed so. But he was God in all God's unchanging spiritual majesty, present among men and women, and promising them release from this evil world.

González points out the political implications of this gnostic/docetic position and so explains its attraction for those in power and its tempting power for those who are oppressed, whether in Constantine's empire or in twentieth-century North America:

> There is comfort in believing that whatever happens in this world has no ultimate significance, and that for that reason one is not to be too concerned about the evil one sees in the world. If the emperors and the aristocracy now live in comfort while the masses toil, or if someone owns our bodies as slaves, this is nothing to be concerned about, for in the end we shall flee from this vale of tears. If my body, or my neighbor's, is now hungry, there is little cause for concern, since bodily privations prepare the soul for its future life of freedom from the body.[48]

But the early councils, particularly that of Chalcedon, avoided this temptation of the spiritualization of Jesus and his redemption by remaining faithful to the biblical witness of Jesus' humanity: the word was made *flesh*. Jesus was not simply God; Jesus was equally a human being. And Jesus' humanity was the only way that divinity could touch men and women: what was not assumed is not redeemed. A truly Hispanic/Latino Christology needs precisely to be faithful to this tradition. It is not a Christology that takes people out of the world or promises future reward for present misery. A Hispanic/Latino Christology, like every orthodox Christology, needs to emphasize the human Jesus, who empowers men and women for responsibility toward their own selves and to others. The gnostic temptation appeals strongly to those, like Hispanics, who belong to groups who lack power. "But when Hispanics succumb to the gnostic-docetic temptation, even though we may believe we are exalting Jesus, in truth, like the earlier gnostics, we are depriving him of his greatest glory. And we are also depriving ourselves of the most far-reaching consequences of his saving work, whereby we shall be given 'all things' jointly with him."[49]

Christology's second temptation is that of Adoptionism—that Jesus was not really God. González maintains that this temptation was a temptation not for the poor and dispossessed in the early church, but for the rich and powerful. The reason was that it expressed the pride and self-sufficiency of the ruling class contained in the myth that "anyone can make it if they really try." Adoptionism is not a great temptation for Hispanics or other minority groups because they know that the myth is not true: because of the systemic nature of racism and classism, only the rare minority individual can "make it," and when that rare individual does, it is often at the price of alienation from his or her original culture and social class. And so:

The one who "makes it" must also be the expression of a reality beyond our closed reality. Jesus Christ must be more than the first among the redeemed, more than the local boy who makes good. He must also be the Redeemer, the power from outside who breaks into our closed reality and breaks its structures of oppression. He must be more than the "adopted son of God." He must be God adopting us as sons and daughters.[50]

Chalcedon's definition of Jesus' divinity and humanity—"*homoousios* with the Father as to his Godhead, and the same *homoousios* with us as to his manhood"[51]—is the only Christology acceptable to Hispanics:

The gory Hispanic Christ that so offends North Atlantic sentiments must be truly smitten, truly one of us. He must be divine, for otherwise his suffering has no power to redeem, and he must also be human, for otherwise his suffering has nothing to do with ours. And the two must be joined in such a way that his true humanity is neither destroyed nor swallowed up in his divinity.[52]

The Christology of the early councils presents the parameters within which a truly Hispanic theology needs to be worked out, but without a fresh reading of the scriptures such an understanding of Jesus will remain static. Scripture reveals Jesus as the one for others, and Jesus' humility, patience, and empowerment of others reveals the depth to which humanity is called and the breadth of divinity as the one who does the calling.

Reading González, one is not confronted at every turn with what it means to be Hispanic; nor is one reminded frequently that the Christian message has to be preserved as one speaks of God in a Hispanic/Latino context. What does become clear is that theology is done out of a deep conviction of the value of Hispanic identity as well as of the Christian tradition. González might well be an example of the praxis model as I have described and illustrated it; nevertheless, what seems even more evident is a commitment not to a particular method or model, but to being faithful to history: *his* history as a Hispanic and the history of the Christian church, which he also cherishes as his own.

9

The Countercultural Model

"Good contextualization offends." So writes Darrell Whiteman in an important article on the significance and challenges of contextualizing the church's communication of the gospel today.[1] But the gospel should only offend, Whiteman is quick to add, for the right reasons. It should not offend because it does not take a particular context seriously, or because it belittles a person's experience or a people's customs or cultures, or because it sees a particular context as totally wrong or totally corrupt. It offends, rather, because there is always something in a communication of the gospel that calls a particular human experience, a particular culture, a particular social location and historical situation to judgment. As A. G. Hogg put it decades ago, the gospel always presents a "challenging relevance" to the human situation; or as Hendrik Kraemer expressed it, the gospel offers to all peoples a "subversive fulfillment" to their human, cultural, and historical situations.[2]

What these three missiological thinkers express so succinctly points to the sixth model on which we will reflect in this book: the countercultural model. This is a model that takes context (experience, culture, social location, and social change) with utmost seriousness. It recognizes that human beings and all theological expressions only exist in historically and culturally conditioned situations. On the other hand, however, it warns that context always needs to be treated with a good deal of suspicion. If the gospel is to truly take root within a people's context, it needs to challenge and purify that context: "if it is truly the communication of the gospel," writes Lesslie Newbigin, "it will call radically into question that way of understanding embodied in the language it uses. If it is truly revelation, it will involve contradiction, and call for conversion, for a radical *metanoia*, a U-turn of the mind."[3]

Newbigin wrote these lines in the specific context of late-twentieth-century British culture, which he found to be, upon his return to Britain in 1974 after years of ministry in India,[4] "profoundly syncretistic."[5] And in fact, the countercultural model finds its most vigorous proponents today among theologians who have recognized the deeply anti-Christian nature of all contemporary western culture, whether in Europe, in North America, or in the developed parts of the southern Pacific region. But the countercultural model of doing contextual theology is hardly confined to the West. It is the model that marks the profound engagement with South African culture found in the *Kairos Document* of 1985; it is the spirit behind Pope John Paul II's 1995 encyclical *Evangelium Vitae*, which speaks about the "culture of death" rampant in contemporary society that needs to be confronted and healed by the "gospel of life"; it is operative as well in the pope's call for a "New Evangelization" and finds echoes in documents of the Federation of Asian Bishops' Conferences and those of the Latin American Bishops at their 1992 meeting at Santo Domingo.[6]

What this model realizes more than any other model is how some contexts are simply antithetical to the gospel and need to be challenged by the gospel's liberating and healing power. To refer once more to the horticultural analogy that we have used throughout this book, this model would say that the native soil of a particular context needs to be weeded and fertilized in order that the seeds can be planted. The soil itself otherwise could not support the healthy growth of the plant, and thereafter it needs continued care and vigilance.

The countercultural model draws on rich and ample sources in scripture and tradition. From the Bible it calls upon the strongly countercultural prophetic literature of the Old Testament, the ambiguous notion of "world" in the New Testament, particularly in the gospel of John; and texts such as Rom 12:2 ("do not conform yourselves to this age . . ."), 1 Cor 1:23 ("we preach Christ crucified—a stumbling block to Jews, and foolishness to the Greeks"), and 1 Peter's designation of Christians as "resident aliens" (see 1:1). From tradition the countercultural model builds on insights from, among many others, Tertullian ("what does Athens [human culture, context] have to do with Jerusalem [the gospel]?"), the Letter to Diognetus ("Christians are in the world but not of the world"), the long practice of monasticism, the powerful witness of the Anabaptist movements, and the vigorous example of Dorothy Day and Peter Maurin. In addition, more than any other model as well, it recognizes that the gospel represents an all-encompassing, radically alternate worldview that differs profoundly from human experiences of the world and the culture that humans create. Particularly in contexts that exude a "culture of death," in contexts in which the gospel seems irrelevant or easily ignored, or in those in which the gospel has become "a stained glass version" of a particular worldview,[7] this model can prove to be a powerful way by which the gospel is able to be communicated with new freshness and genuine engagement.

A SKETCH OF THE MODEL

TERMINOLOGY

A first thing to be said about the term *countercultural model* is that it is not *anti*cultural.[8] Some extreme forms of the model, for instance, in H. Richard Niebuhr's depiction of "Christ against Culture" in his classic work,[9] and some rhetorical expressions such as those of Stanley Hauerwas and William Willimon ("the world, for all its beauty, is hostile to the truth")[10] may point the model in an anticultural direction. The term, however, is intended to express the strong critical function that the model plays over against human context. It in no way regards the human context as something to be *replaced* with a purer religious one—as might, for example, some fundamentalist Christian or Islamic perspectives.[11] Rather, while practitioners of the countercultural model recognize that if the gospel is to be adequately communicated, it has to be done "in the language of those to whom it is addressed and has to be clothed in symbols which are meaningful to them"[12] and that "culture itself is not an evil,"[13] it needs to recognize nevertheless that, as a human product, "it bears the marks of the human propensity to resist and undercut the rule of the creator of the world."[14] Contextual theology is best done, they say, by an analysis of the context and by respect for it, but by allowing the gospel to take the lead in the process so that the context is shaped and formed by the reality of the gospel and not vice-versa. Context is to be given, says Lamin Sanneh, a "penultimate status," since it is "both a natural ally as well as a natural foe of the gospel."[15] As George Hunsberger puts it, the challenge of the countercultural model is "to develop approaches that navigate between the Scylla of culture bashing on the one side and the Charybdis of absorption into the culture on the other," thus attempting to avoid both shipwreck on the rocks (i.e., being simply irrelevant—offensive for the wrong reason) and getting swallowed by the sea (i.e., caving in to a false syncretism, presenting a domesticated version of the gospel).[16]

To clarify the nature of the model, alternative titles might be proposed. Since the dynamic of this model is neither to translate the gospel in terms of the context (as the translation model would do), nor to facilitate new understandings to emerge from experience, culture, social location, and social change (as in the anthropological model), nor even to discover new meanings of the gospel from a faithful exercise of praxis (the praxis model), but to truly *encounter* and *engage* the context through respectful yet critical analysis and authentic gospel proclamation in word and deed, we might speak of this model as one of *encounter* or *engagement*.[17] The fact that the model is committed to a prophetic "telling forth" of the truth in the context of and sometimes over against a "culture of death" might point to a term such as the *prophetic model*. Several practitioners of the model, as will be seen below, take inspiration from Gerhard Lohfink's description of the Christian church as a "contrast community," and so an apt title for this approach to doing contextual theology may well be the *contrast model*.[18] Finally, Stanley Hauerwas and William Willimon propose, as a "radical alternative" to an "activist" (Constantinian, established) or "conversionist" (privatized) understanding of Christianity, an understanding that is unabashedly "confessionalist."[19] Such an understanding might suggest a *confessional model* of contextual theology, confessional in that it seeks both first and foremost to confess the gospel as an alternative worldview in a hostile or indifferent culture and, at least in some cases, to confess the gospel in the context of a mortal threat to the gospel's integrity—a *status confessionis* (invoked by the Barmen Declaration in the 1930s and the *Kairos Document* in the 1980s).

Nevertheless, I still prefer the term *countercultural* to describe this model. It is a term that practitioners of the model invoke—explicitly and implicitly—to describe the kind of Christianity they propose;[20] in addition, it captures best the real contextual interaction between a dynamic, challenging gospel community and a powerful, even hostile, environment. When I propose the term counter*cultural*, however, I do have in mind a notion of *culture* in the broadest sense, one that includes everything that I have included in the term context: human experience, whether personal or social; "culture" in its secular and religious dimensions as "the sum total of ways of living built up by a group of human beings and transmitted from one generation to another";[21] a person's or group's social location; and the movement of social change in a particular situation.

PRESUPPOSITIONS OF THE COUNTERCULTURAL MODEL

A first presupposition of the countercultural model is the radical ambiguity and insufficiency of human context. There is no question of the importance of human culture, for example, for even revelation is offered to women and men in a particular cultural and historical form: "there can never be a culture-free gospel."[22] Nor is there a question that if the gospel is to be adequately and authentically communicated, it must be done with meticulous attention to all aspects of the context in which it is being proclaimed.[23]

But "true contextualization accords the gospel its rightful primacy, its power to penetrate every culture and to speak within each culture, in its own speech and symbol, the word which is both No and Yes, both judgement and grace."[24] Human context is never enough. It can form no firm basis for an authentic acceptance of Christian truth, for the gospel "calls into question all cultures, including the one in which it was originally embodied."[25] While Christians who approach people with the gospel, writes Newbigin, have to relate their presentation "to the place where they stand," they must both "state the Gospel in the language of the hearer and also . . . show his precarious foothold."[26] Newbigin finds that the "boldest and most brilliant essay" in communicating the gospel within a particular culture is the gospel of John. While John uses the language and thought-forms of Hellenistic culture—so much so that "Gnostics of all ages have thought that the book was written especially for them"—nowhere in the whole Bible do we find the radical contrast between human cultural forms and the word of God "stated with more terrible clarity."[27] For Newbigin, and I believe this is true for all who practice the countercultural model, the gospel must be communicated with both faithfulness and relevance;[28] but in order to be truly both, it needs to be experienced as something deeply contradictory to the human condition, calling it to that "U-turn" of conversion. Only then will humanity find healing and fulfillment. Left to itself, a particular context will always resist the call of the gospel, for the gospel calls humanity not simply to see its best self but to question and judge even what is best and so to come to new life.[29] It is foolishness to the Greeks; Christians live as resident aliens.

Such strong insistence upon the challenging, critical function of the gospel suggests the second presupposition of the countercultural model: the nature of revelation, or, in other words, the nature of the gospel. Once more it is Newbigin who expresses it most seminally: revelation, the heart of which is the gospel, is not essentially the "disclosure of eternal truths" but the "total fact of Christ."[30]

This notion of "total fact," however, needs unpacking. In the first place, revelation/the gospel is fact in the sense of the Latin *factum*—it is something that has been *done*. What has first been done is that God in Jesus of Nazareth has become incarnate in human history. Second, as a human being, Jesus preached the reign of God, died a horrendous death on the cross, and was raised again by God to live among us. Third, these deeds (*facta*) point to the truth (the fact!) that now, in Jesus, we have the clue to all of human and indeed cosmic history, and it is against this fact that all human experience or context is to be measured.[31]

God's revelation in Jesus Christ, therefore, has an essentially narrative quality to it. The gospel, rather than being a list of doctrines or moral principles, is conceived as a story to be told and witnessed to rather than something to be argued for abstractly. As one practitioner of the countercultural model, David Lowes-Watson, puts it, we have to image persons who proclaim the gospel not as "salespersons" but as "journalists."[32] Watson also suggests that the story has two aspects to it: it is at once the gospel *about* Jesus and the gospel *of* Jesus. On the one hand, the story is the story about one man who incarnated God's presence and through his concrete life of service, death, and resurrection brought the world to reconciliation and new life. It is through acceptance of this one man—despite the "scandal of particularity," so difficult to believe, and not only in contemporary culture[33]—that one embraces the gospel. At the same time, however, the gospel is something that engages one in the same vision as that of Jesus; it is the gospel *of* Jesus, the good news that Jesus preached. "No less at the heart of the gospel . . . is the prophetic announcement of Jesus in the synagogue at Nazareth: the promise of good news for the poor, release for captives, sight for the blind, and freedom for the oppressed (Luke 4:18-19)."[34]

It is because of this second meaning of the gospel story that the story is not complete. It is a story that is a clue to the entire story of humankind: it does not know *where* that story will end, or *how* it will end but it knows where it is going. It is because the gospel story holds the clue to the future that it can be so involved with history, so concerned with what is authentically human, so "political." Christianity is not only historical in that it is based on historical facts; it is an interpretation of history and committed to involvement in history.[35] It is precisely because the gospel is the clue to history—the lens through which history can be viewed rightly[36]—that we can say that faith in the gospel calls Christians to a genuine encounter or engagement with the human context.

As I indicated briefly above, that context, for the majority of practitioners of the countercultural model, is contemporary western culture, and the particular resistance that this contemporary context evidences is a third presupposition for the countercultural model. I have referred to the thought of Lesslie Newbigin so much in the preceding pages because he has emerged as a major spokesperson for the kind of theological dynamic that this model has developed. Upon his return to Britain in 1974, Newbigin was appalled to find his native country and indeed all of western Christianity in a "syncretistic" relationship with western, Enlightenment, and postmodern culture. Even more than secular, he said, western society had become pagan; he considered it far more resistant to the gospel than pre-Christian paganism, and he was fond of quoting a question asked by Indonesian general T. B. Simatupang, "Can the West be [re]converted?"[37] Newbigin's thought launched a movement in Britain that has begun to reflect on ways to preach the gospel both faithfully and relevantly within its strongly secularist and newly multireligious context, and similar movements followed suit under Newbigin's inspiration in the United States and New Zealand. From a slightly different perspective, theologians such as Stanley Hauerwas and William Willimon emphasized the fact that Christianity's task in North America, while certainly about the engagement of North American culture, is not thereby about the underwriting and promotion of the "values" of American democracy. Christianity's task, on the contrary, is to provide another story and an alternate community, based not on the abstract virtues of justice and freedom, but on the Christian beatitudes and the practices of Christian tradition. In contrast to an American culture of individualism and consumerism, Christians are called into a "community of character."[38]

While the model certainly has a more universal relevance—as Newbigin himself mentions from his experience in India[39]—the model as I envision it here takes its origin from the realization that Christianity in the West exists in a context that is very un-Christian in its basic spirit. Christianity has been marginalized as a private option, based on unprovable "values." This situation has its roots in the darker side of the Enlightenment, with its elevation of human reason and its canonization of the individual as the basic unit of society. With the dawn of postmodernity, individualism has been carried to the extreme. On the contrary, say the practitioners of the countercultural model, Christianity is public truth. Its major tenets, however—the historical significance of one person for all, the importance of tradition and community, the priority of the supernatural over the merely natural—all fly in the face of the basic faith (and they insist that it is faith!) of the western cultural context. Instead of an attempt to accommodate to such a situation, the times call for a clear witness to the transforming power of the Christian story.

How this is to be done is a fourth presupposition of this model. The gospel encounters or engages the human context, say the practitioners of the countercultural model, by its concretization or incarnation in the Christian community, the church. Such an encounter takes place in two ways. First, the church community itself—as a community of women and men who have allowed the gospel to critique and transform their lives—realizes itself as a "contrast community," a "parallel community," a community of "resident aliens," a "colony of heaven" where the gospel is lived out fully over against the surrounding context of materialism, individualism, consumerism, militarism, and quick gratification.[40] In this community, women and men are continually formed and converted to be wary of the seduction of the surrounding pagan context, and find as well a community of support to live a countercultural lifestyle. The countercultural model emphasizes the importance of Christian "practices"—reading the Bible (especially together), hospitality (especially to the stranger), participation in communal prayer, celebrating baptism and reconciliation, celebrating Eucharist, developing skill in Spirit-guided discernment, keeping the Sabbath—as ways to provide "meaning, orientation, and purpose" within the community and within the surrounding world.[41] Second, and this is crucial since some critics accuse those who practice this model of "sectarianism," these formed and transformed Christians live and work in the world, testifying by their lifestyle and choices that their life is lived according to the gospel and not according to the surrounding cultural atmosphere.

Newbigin is clear, even eloquent about this. He strongly affirms the priesthood of all believers and the role of leadership in the church to cultivate this priesthood among all the members. Such a priesthood, he writes, "has to be exercised in the world. It is in the ordinary secular business of the world that the sacrifices of love and obedience are to be offered to God. It is in the context of secular affairs that the mighty power released into the world through the work of Christ is to be manifested. . . . It is only in this way that the public life of the world, its accepted habits and assumptions, can be challenged by the gospel and brought under the searching light of the truth, as it has been revealed in Jesus."[42] The leadership of the church may need occasionally to speak out or express some public support for an issue or an incident (condemning terrorism, for instance, or a particular policy regarding immigration). "But such pronouncements carry weight only when they are validated by the way in which Christians are actually behaving and using their influence in public life."[43] Newbigin and those influenced by him speak of the church—and in particular the local congregation—as a "hermeneutic of the gospel." The local church is not just *in* a place or *of* a place; it finds its identity in being *for* the particular place in which it finds itself. [44]

It is this essentially centrifugal nature of the Christian community that is recognized as its missionary stance in regard to context. The church is, as Vatican II expressed it, missionary by its very nature, and this is recognized in a particular way by practitioners of the countercultural model. The Christian community, no matter where it finds itself, is always in a cross-cultural, frontier situation; it is always on the boundary between faith and unbelief. And so just as the classical foreign missionary needs to be keenly aware of and in touch with the context in which he or she works, so must all Christians today—particularly those living in the neopagan world of western society—recognize the difference between the context of the church, which is being continually transformed by the ever-challenging gospel, and the cultural context, which is held captive by the powers of the market, the military and the media. One does not join the church, however, to escape or be sheltered from these powers; one becomes a member of the church to engage them, to unmask them, and to invite women and men into this community of missionary concern for the world.[45]

Figure 8 illustrates the general dynamic of the countercultural model. A first step is to recognize the validity of the Christian story, embodied in the experience of the past within scripture and tradition, as the clue to the meaning of human and cosmic history. With this perspective of a "supernatural sociology,"[46] the Christian story is used as a lens through which to interpret, engage, unmask, and challenge the experience of the present, the context of individual and social experience, secular and/or religious culture, social location, and social change. It is important that this process is understood not as a simple, one-time operation, but as something that is ongoing, a *habitus*, and is both individual and communal. It is important to stress as well that this process of discernment and critique through the lens of the gospel (the experience of the past in scripture and tradition) is one that goes on just as much *within* the individual Christian and the Christian community as it does looking "outward" from the converted subject or the "contrast community."

Figure 8
The Countercultural Model

1. Conversion
    Acceptance of the experience of the
    past (scripture and tradition) as clue
    to the meaning of history ("supernatural
    sociology") ↘

            2. Perspective
                Using the experience of the past
                as a lens   ↘

                        3. Interpretation, critique,
                            unmasking, challenging
                                Experience of the Present
                                Experience
                                Culture
                                Social location
                                Social change

CRITIQUE OF THE COUNTERCULTURAL MODEL

While this model of contextual theology has found fresh and powerful expression in its practitioners—Lesslie Newbigin, Stanley Hauerwas, John S. Milbank, and (occasionally) Pope John Paul II and the Asian and Latin American Catholic bishops—a further source of its strength comes from its rootedness in scripture and Christian tradition. With the possible exception of the translation model, no other model discussed in this book wants to be as engaging of and relevant to the context while at the same time remaining faithful to the gospel. It recognizes that the genius of Christianity lies neither in its endorsement of the status quo nor in its cultivation of "the new and the next,"[47] but in its challenging and transforming power. With the possible exception of the praxis model, no other model discussed here recognizes the deep ambiguity and even antigospel character of context. Particularly in regard to so much of western culture, with its emphasis on individualism, unlimited choice, and "having" over "being" and its evils of school violence, unstable family life, sexual promiscuity, and unheeding destruction of the natural world, it seems that Christianity today must speak a word of radical dissent and offer an alternate way of living. Like the prophets in Israel, perhaps the greatest service Christians today can render to humanity is to be a sign of God's "No" to the world because of God's deeper word of "Yes," and to be an instrument and foretaste of what Christians believe will surely arrive as a "new heaven and a new earth."[48]

There are, however, four areas of caution that need mentioning here. First, although most practitioners of the model recognize the need to be *counter*cultural rather than *anti*cultural, the danger does persist. This was certainly a danger for missionaries in times past, and while many accusations of missionaries destroying cultures in their efforts to preach Christ are surely exaggerated, such destruction did indeed take place.[49] If such disregard for the Spirit's presence in the human context was present in the past, it is certainly a danger today. Practitioners of the countercultural model seem at times to demonize western culture, but it must be very clear that no culture is entirely corrupt or evil. Richard Mouw's wise words of caution in this regard should be carefully heeded: "Many of us have failed to take seriously the job of reflecting back upon ourselves as a Christian community in North America. Or to the extent that we have done so, we have gone about it somewhat carelessly compared to the probing we have made of other cultures. Our cross-cultural reflections on North American culture have, in fact, been rather limited, and often guided by biased sensitivities."[50] An attentive reading of a work such as Tom Beaudoin's *Virtual Faith: The Irreverent Spiritual Quest of Generation X* might be a good antidote for such careless negativity.[51]

A second caution is related to the first. While it is important to stress the "challenging relevance" of an alternative community of resident aliens as the way the contemporary context is authentically engaged, the danger of sectarianism is always present. One of the marks of the church remains its catholicity (small "c"), and it is a mark that calls the church to engagement with the whole world, not withdrawal from it. While the "sign" aspect of the church is extremely important for its missionary task in the world, the danger is that the community focuses on its own integrity, the quality of its community, the authenticity of its worship and does not move into the world. It is not enough for Christians to be an inviting milieu; Christians must "dirty their hands" in real work with real institutions in the world. Michael Baxter, on whom we will focus in the next section, makes light of Brian Hehir's reluctance for the church to be "out of the loop" in regard to the U. S. government.[52] While Baxter makes a real point, if the church is so isolated from the "powers that be," Christian action and witness may make little difference. Committed groups of Catholics, for example, such as Network, the lobbyists from the Conference of Major Superiors of Men (CMSM) and the Leadership Conference of Women Religious (LCWR), and the Center for Concern do have some impact in Washington and on U. S. foreign policy, albeit limited.

A third caution regarding the countercultural model is in regard to its relatively monocultural makeup, at least in terms of practitioners in the context of the contemporary West. With few exceptions, the practitioners are white and for the most part middle-class. This social location may point to a particular point of view that is served in their critique of contemporary western culture. From my own participation (somewhat marginally, unfortunately) in the Gospel and Our Culture Network here in the United States—a group on which we will focus in the next section as well—I know that efforts have been made to include persons of other cultures and races, but those efforts have met with small success. Even when people of other cultural and racial identities did participate, their focus was not so much on a challenge and critique of culture, but on the need for their own cultures to be valued by the wider, dominant white culture. The point is that while the countercultural model may be very appropriate for affluent, white, European contexts, other models—for example, the anthropological or transcendental models—might better be employed in contexts in which cultural and personal identity has often been threatened.

Finally, there is a danger of Christian exclusivism over against other religious ways. On the one hand, one of the great strengths of the countercultural model is its clear and courageous stand in the midst of what is often a lazy pluralism of religious belief, one that reduces religious faith to mere opinion or taste. In this regard as well, it is certainly true that advocates of the model such as Lesslie Newbigin are much more inclusivist in their understanding of the unique revela-

---

The Countercultural Model

Alternative Titles: *encounter model; engagement model; prophetic model; contrast model; confessional model*

Basis in Scripture and Tradition: *prophetic tradition; Johannine notion of "world"; Rom 12:2; 1 Cor 1:23; 1 Pet 1:1; Tertullian; Letter of Diognetus; monastic tradition; Anabaptist tradition; Dorothy Day*

Revelation: *narrative and story; the "fact" of Jesus Christ*

Scripture/Tradition: *the "clue" to the meaning of history; complete, even though human understanding of it is not; can be understood more completely through the understanding of other cultures*

Context: *radically ambiguous and resistant to the gospel; unequal to scripture/tradition*

Method: *commitment to Christian story as clue to history; use story as lens to interpret, critique, and challenge context*

Analogy: *the soil needs weeding and fertilizing so that the seeds can be planted*

Legend: *"challenging relevance" (Hogg); "subversive fulfillment" (Kraemer)*

Critique: *Positive: strong engagement of context and fidelity to gospel; relevant in western contexts*
      Negative: danger of being anticultural; danger of sectarianism; tends to be monocultural; danger of exclusivism

tion of God in Christ.[53] On the other hand, the danger is there. Particularly in a western context that is becoming more and more multireligious, a way has to be found to discover commonalities and continuities within other religious traditions rather than to emphasize the discontinuity and superiority of the "Christian fact" and the "Christian story." Jesus Christ is the clue to human history and human and cosmic well-being, and Christians believe that he is the clearest and the best clue. But just as important in our multireligious age is to acknowledge that there very well may be other clues as well.

EXAMPLES OF THE COUNTERCULTURAL MODEL

The Gospel and Our Culture Network (GOCN)

In the early 1980s, Lesslie Newbigin became involved in a planning process of the British Council of Churches to mark in some way the year 1984 of George Orwell fame. Newbigin's remarks about the need for a "missionary encounter" of the British churches with contemporary British culture prompted the council to ask him to expand his ideas. The result was *The Other Side of 1984: Questions for the Churches*, and out of this eventually came a program entitled Gospel and Culture, sponsored by the British Council of Churches, the C. S. Lewis Society, and the British and Foreign Bible Society. In the year 1984 itself, Newbigin delivered the Benjamin B. Warfield Lectures at Princeton Theological Seminary in Princeton, New Jersey, published in 1986 as *Foolishness to the Greeks: The Gospel and Western Culture*. Among the audience at Princeton was a young doctoral student, George Hunsberger, who eventually wrote a doctoral dissertation on Newbigin's thought and became personally acquainted with him.[54]

Several years later, both Newbigin and Hunsberger (who was now a professor of theology) attended a conference in the United States on the common witness of Christians in missionary work, and Newbigin challenged the group at one point to do something like the Gospel and Culture program in this country. Hunsberger took up the challenge and with a few colleagues began a Gospel and Our Culture newsletter to anchor a movement called the "Gospel and Our Culture Network" (GOCN). Through a series of conferences the movement began to take shape; a series of books was established that has so far published six volumes;[55] the newsletter began to appear with regularity; and a core group emerged.

The GOCN is marked particularly by its vision that if the gospel is to be communicated in North America today, it must be through a missionary or "missional" encounter between the Christian church and the contemporary North American context. Theological reflection in North America, members of the movement argue, has been based on the supposition that both the United States and Canada are Christian nations, that North American culture is basically Christian, and so church life and theological reflection are fairly well contextualized within this context. But this supposition is false, they say, for two reasons. First, if the church is honest, it will have to admit that it has been marginalized in the present North American context. "The day has gone," writes Hunsberger, "when the church was generally valued by the society as important to the social and moral order." And quoting Kennon Callahan, he says, "The day of the church culture is over."[56] If we are going to do theology effectively in North America today, insists Craig van Gelder, we need to accept our minority status in the face of the indifference of the contemporary context, "shake off the remaining vestiges of Christendom perspective that expects the world to take the church seriously," and refocus on "how we should now seek out the world."[57] Christian life has to be lived, and theology has to be done, by Christians not as participants but as strangers in this context. As church we have ceased being "chaplains" of the culture and have become marginalized within it.

Second, the members of GOCN have begun to recognize that perhaps the very reason the church has become irrelevant in North America is that is has ceased to have anything to say. It has, ironically, contextualized itself all too well, to the extent that it has accommodated itself to its context, rather than truly engaging it. Walter C. Hobbs expresses it graphically: "North American Christianity is in great measure a faith *twisted* by culture. Too often, we have uncritically embraced many of the taken-for-granted presumptions and priorities that characterize the dominant worldview of Western civilization instead of testing our culture's values and perspectives against the biblical standards."[58]

Donald Poterski sums up the situation of the North American church well when he notes the irony that, instead of being "in the world but not of the world," Christians today have inverted the dictum and have become "of the world but not in the world."[59] And this explains why the church today in this context needs to be missionary: it needs to be missionary to *itself*—to challenge and purify itself of the surrounding culture—so as to be missionary *to the world*. Only if Christians themselves can be countercultural and as a church be formed together into an alternative, contrast community can they have anything to say to the world. In a way, the present marginalization within the North American context is a good thing, the GOCN members say, for it helps us realize that the church *never* should be fully at home within a particular context. The church is "missionary by its very nature," as Vatican Council II described it (AG 2); it always needs to exist as a pilgrim people, a community of "resident aliens." Christians' task is not to be chaplains to society, but witnesses to the present-yet-future reign of God, collaborators through the grace of election in God's saving mission in the world.

It is precisely the further articulation of a missionary ecclesiology in the North American context that the GOCN has contributed most to a contextual theology that employs the countercultural model. While ecclesiological essays are scattered throughout the network's published volumes, and while one of the volumes offers a fine ecclesiology by one of the GOCN members (Darrell Guder), two volumes of multiple authorship perhaps best exemplify the GOCN's approach. In the volume *Missional Church* this ecclesiology is laid out theologically; in *Treasure in Clay Jars* this ecclesiology is further developed by a study of a number of congregations that seem to function as missional communities and by the subsequent drawing up of a number of "indicators" of what it means to be a missional, missionary church.

Missional Church, though edited by Darrell Guder, is the product of several years of collaboration by six scholars—Lois Barrett, Inagrace Dietterich, George Hunsberger, Alan Roxburgh, Craig van Gelder, and Guder himself—each of whom drafted a chapter in the book but allowed that chapter to be critiqued and rewritten by all the members of the group. As the authors describe the process: "We struggled with our shared assumptions and our differences, sought to define our terms, and arrived at a consensus that, we trust, will serve to stimulate more discussion of the crucial issues of a missional theology of the church."[60] When the book was published, the author's names were not attached to individual chapters.

The book's first chapter, entitled "Missional Church: From Sending to Being Sent," lays down the foundation for what follows: the church does not *have* a mission; it *is* mission. And it is mission because it gets its very identity from being chosen to collaborate with God's own mission in the world. Any reflection on the church needs to recognize its divine and human character, its visible and invisible nature, its identity as a spiritual community on the one hand and an all-too-human institution on the other. It is called to shape the context as God's sign and instrument; but it is also shaped, sometimes even misshaped, by that same context. Interacting with context, then, is an inextricable part of the church's life and mission: a missional church will always be a church that witnesses to God's transforming action in culture, always aware of its own continuing need of transformation as well.

A first task, therefore, is to understand the context, and Chapters 2 and 3 attempt to do this in terms of contemporary culture and the history of the church in North America. North American culture, in the first place, bears the imprint both of modernity, with its myths of objective scientific truth and the autonomous individual, and of postmodernity, with its extreme relativism, thirst for community, and cultural and religious pluralism. Such a culture, as Newbigin has said, is one that has relegated faith to the private sphere of values and has proved itself immensely resistant to the Christian gospel.[61] Nevertheless, this is the context in which the church exists and in which it is called to persuade the world of the truth of an alternative vision. This context is further complicated, however, by the "historical accident"[62] of both U.S. and Canadian denominationalism. While this complex situation needs to be respected, building or reforming denominations can be a distraction to the church's true task. "The current predicament of the churches in North America requires more than a mere tinkering with long-assumed notions about the identity and mission of the church."[63] A fresh basis needs to be established, and this can only be found by looking at the cultural and historical context through the lens of the Christian story. The remainder of the book tries to do this.

Chapter 4 bears the title "Missional Vocation: Called and Sent to Represent the Reign of God" and so tries to sketch out the essence of the church as God's people, chosen by God to participate in the divine mission in the world. Rather than conceiving the church as "a place where certain things happen"[64] (e.g., the gospel preached and the sacraments celebrated) or as a place that offers a variety of services (a "vendor," as the authors say),[65] contemporary ecclesiology has begun once again to think of the church as "a body of people sent on a mission."[66] That mission, however, is not the church's own; it is none other than the continuation of the mission of Jesus, under the power of God's Spirit. If one reads the scriptures, Jesus' mission was to proclaim in word and deed what he called the "reign of God," and his proclamation was an assurance that this reality, which was the fulfillment of all human hopes, was already present in his person and in those in relation to him.

What is Jesus' vision of the reign of God? It can be described in one word: *shalom*—that rich Hebrew word that means justice with peace and peace with justice, expressed as well in the words of the Lucan version of Jesus' reading of the prophet Isaiah in the synagogue at Nazareth: good news to the poor, release to the captives, sight to the blind, freedom for the oppressed (Lk 4:18). It is a vision, in the gospel of John, strongly at odds with the world, and one for which Jesus was eventually rejected, arrested, and executed. Ultimately, however, it is a vision that is vindicated in Jesus' being raised to life through the Spirit. And it is a vision that has been passed on to us, the church.

We have been called, therefore, to *represent* the reign of God—in two senses. We represent it by being a *sign and foretaste*, by living a life together that points to the divine shalom already present in germ but promised to come in full; and we represent God's reign by being an *instrument and agent*, by offering forgiveness, promoting justice, suffering, working for reconciliation. The church does this by being a vibrant community, a loyal servant, and a humble messenger. This means that "in a free world of the autonomous and decentered self . . . the churches must revive what it means to be communities of the reign of God. . . . In a secular world of privatized religious faith . . . the church must discover what it means to act faithfully on behalf of the reign of God within the public life of society," and "in a plural world of relativized perspectives and loyalties . . . the churches must learn to speak in post-Christendom accents as confident yet humble messengers of the reign of God."[67]

This engaged, countercultural witness in the name of Jesus is further explored in the following two chapters. Chapter 5 explores how the church lives "in, but not of the world" as an alternative community. "An important task of the church is to discern what are those key points at which to be different from the evil of the world,"[68] whether that be a strong community emphasis over against contemporary individualism, a community of goods in the face of North American power and consumerism, or a community of hospitality and forgiveness to those contemporary society deems unworthy of such respect. The church is called to heal society but "not to make the dominant culture run better, or to make good people who can go out and do the work of the dominant culture in beneficial ways."[69] Its task is rather to be a demonstration of God's love and power in the world, especially among those the dominant culture spurns. The church's charter is the beatitudes: not having life in control (as the culture teaches) but the blessedness of the poor in spirit; not avoidance of suffering but the blessedness of those who mourn; not revenge but meekness; not acquisitiveness but hunger and thirst for justice; not conditional love but mercy; not legal correctness but single-mindedness; not disengagement but active peacemaking; not popularity but integrity.[70]

Witnessing, say the authors, is not for the timid, and it is something that Christians must train for in the safe but challenging environment of community. Chapter 6 speaks of a number of practices that help form and transform the missional church so it, and individual Christians in it, can be credible and engaging representatives of God's countercultural reign. Such practices are not self-help techniques; they are "socially established cooperative human activities carried in traditions that form people in a way of life" or—perhaps more accurately—open up people to be formed by God's Spirit.[71] Through liturgical actions together (baptism, Eucharist, rituals of reconciliation), the discipline of listening to one another in acts of communal discernment, and being intentional about hospitality to visitors or strangers, practices both form the internal life of the community and serve to shape the church into a credible sign and instrument in the world. "Witnessing to God's creative intent for all humanity, they model and thus proclaim a different way of life to a watching world. They demonstrate how to confront division by practicing a unity that relativizes prior statifications and classifications. . . . They confront moral relativism and societal conflict through competition and power politics by engaging in open conversation and sharing wisdom."[72] Practices, in sum, both form women and men for countercultural engagement and are in themselves actions of that encounter.

Chapter 7, entitled "Missional Leadership: Equipping God's People for Mission," eschews such traditional images of church leadership as "priest" (a vessel only through whom God works), "pedagogue" (the minister in academic gown), or "professional" (managing the parish plant), as well as more contemporary images of counselor, manager, and technician. Rather, the task of leadership in a missional church—and leadership is conceived as not so much one person but a leadership team, whether clerical or lay—is no less than to equip the members of the church themselves for ministry in the world. So often ministerial leadership in the church is conceived as providing services to the church itself—liturgical celebration, counseling, gracing social events. This, however, is ministry in a church conceived along the lines of a "vendor of services." Such "services" will not be totally ignored, of course, but the main purpose of ministry in the missional church is to challenge, develop, supervise, and console women and men for their ministry in the world as witnesses to God's reign. Within the wider congregation there should exist, the authors say, a "covenanted community," a group of members particularly committed to the church's vision, a kind of "secular order" "bound together through specific practices and disciplines"—of common life, learning, and mission. While the leadership of the congregation would certainly not ignore the rest of the congregation, this is where the leadership would "focus their time, energy and thinking."[73] The concrete structure of the community, Chapter 8 insists, is something that can only be developed to serve the mission, not for its own sake. The structures of the earliest churches "were necessarily and primarily missional," and so only structures that are developed to enable the community to best carry out its mission in a specific context—and these may vary according to the context—can have any claim to be in authentic apostolic succession.[74]

A final chapter in the book speaks about the universal church as "the community of communities in mission." What is particularly important here, I believe, is the authors' construal of the four traditional "marks" of the church (under the inspiration of Charles van Engen) as qualities of the church to be conceived dynamically. However, "going one step further"[75] than van Engen, they propose to reverse the traditional order and speak of the church as proclaiming (apostolic), reconciling (catholic), sanctifying (holy), and unifying (one). The rationale for both moves (making the marks more dynamic and reversing their traditional order) allows them once again to emphasize the primary nature of the church as missionary. This is an ecclesiology from beginning to end that is inspired by the gospel call of Jesus to change one's mind—make a U-turn, in Newbigin's words— and embrace in faith the countercultural vision of the reign of God.

In 2002, three of the authors of *Missional Church*—Lois Barrett, Darrell Guder, and George Hunsberger—collaborated with four other members of the GOCN— Walter Hobbs, Linford Stutzman, Jeff van Kooten, and Dale Ziemer—to produce *Treasure in Clay Jars: Patterns of Missional Faithfulness*. This book, written in the same collaborative style as the earlier work, studied nine concrete congregations (one study was of a group of congregations in New Jersey) that had been recommended as examples of churches with a particularly missional spirit and focus. The book is a good example of a narrative theology. Out of the study of these congregations the authors distilled eight "patterns" that they believe distinguish a church that is truly a product of missional engagement of context by the gospel community. Readers of the foregoing summary of the GOCN's theologizing will not be surprised at some of these patterns, but the list goes further, I believe, particularly since it comes out of concrete communities, in articulating the GOCN ecclesiology. The patterns are (1) a sense of having been called or "elected" to be church for the world; (2) a commitment to biblical formation and discipleship; (3) a commitment to taking risks as a contrast community; (4) the cultivation of concrete traditional practices; (5) a belief that worship is more than just something for the congregation alone, that it is public witness; (6) a dependence on the Holy Spirit; (7) a centeredness on the reign of God; and (8) the development of authority according to the missional needs of the congregation, and not authority for its own sake.

No summary can fully capture the full dynamic of these two works of the Gospel and Our Culture Network. Nevertheless, I think what is emerges even in summary is the consistent way a sense of the countercultural interpretation of the gospel is used to guide the shape of the inevitable relation to the church's context—both within it and without. Such an interpretation gives the church a particularly dynamic (missional) relation to the context, besides suggesting concrete ways in which that mission can take concrete form.

MICHAEL J. BAXTER

In his 1999 book on Catholics and U. S. culture, Mark S. Massa makes the point that Dorothy Day, despite her strong and somewhat traditional Catholic identity and despite her countercultural stance over against much of what the United

States stands for, is, ironically, one of the most American Catholic thinkers the United States has produced.[76] Standing on the earliest Puritan tradition of free and independent thinking, Day was able to link up in a creative way both the deepest strands of U. S. convictions and values and the radical gospel principles anchored in the beatitudes. Dorothy Day, in other words, was a superb contextual theologian, and she did theology (although quite unconsciously, I am sure) according to what I have described as the countercultural model.

Michael J. Baxter, a priest of the Congregation of the Holy Cross and currently teaching theology at the University of Notre Dame, is a contextual theologian who follows very much in Dorothy Day's footsteps. In the 1980s, Baxter took time out from his theological studies and formation to found André House of Hospitality in Phoenix Arizona, a house run in the Catholic Worker tradition. After ordination to the priesthood, he obtained a doctorate in theology at Duke University, where he wrote a dissertation on Catholic liturgist and social ethicist Virgil Michel, OSB, under Stanley Hauerwas (with whom he also studied as a seminarian when Hauerwas taught at Notre Dame). He is a committed pacifist, has been arrested in Arizona and California for civil disobedience, and has counseled draft-registration resistors and U. S. soldiers in Germany who had declared themselves conscientious objectors in the 1991 Gulf War. He quotes with some glee the title of one of Dorothy Day's essays at the time of the Army-McCarthy hearings on un-American activities in the early fifties: "We Are Un-American; We Are Catholics."[77] He believes that "Catholics really aren't 'at home' here in the United States. Our true home is in the city of God, the heavenly Jerusalem."[78] Like Dorothy Day in her own time, therefore, I believe that Baxter is one of the most articulate practitioners of the countercultural model doing theology today. While he is definitely trying to forge a "countertradition," and much of his thought goes against the grain of "received tradition" in Catholicism today, his is a voice worth listening to, particularly as an example of the method he espouses.

Baxter's field—unlike that of so many of the theologians discussed in this book—is social ethics, and his writings (so far only a small sheaf of articles)[79] take on some of the most eminent Catholic thinkers in this area today. His thought, although strongly influenced by his former teachers John Howard Yoder and Stanley Hauerwas, has a particularly Catholic slant to it, since he is also influenced by the Catholic Worker tradition, the "supernatural sociology" of Catholic sociologist Paul Hanley Furfey, and the ethics of "Christian social reconstruction" of Benedictine Virgil Michel.

Drawing all of these influences together, Baxter develops his ideas out of two principles. The first is that, whether based on a neo-scholastic notion of the sufficiency of "nature" (as the "foundation" of "supernature") or Karl Rahner's emphasis on the "supernatural existential" of nature (i.e., that nature is always graced *as nature* and so always *in fact* more than itself), any social ethics that is built on nature with natural reason is fatally flawed. Baxter's point of view is that while there is no dichotomy between nature and supernature (or grace), it is only the latter that gives nature its dignity and wholeness. To put it another way, a truly Catholic social ethics cannot be built on a kind of "common ground" that is shared by secular values or the ethical traditions of other religions. It can only be based on the gospel story: the example of Jesus, the beatitudes, doctrines such as the Trinity and the church as the Mystical Body of Christ.

Baxter's second principle is that a social ethics needs to be constructed not as a "means" but with a view to "ends." Rather than abstracting certain commonly agreed upon principles and ignoring others in the Christian tradition so that Christians can sit at the table with the makers of public policy (thus invoking what John A. Ryan ["Rt. Rev. Msgr. New Dealer"] called the "principle of expediency"),[80] Christians need to develop an ethics that keeps before them the "new heaven and new earth" that the New Testament promises. What Christians would like society to *be* (i.e., its final and formal causes) should guide the formation of a Christian social ethics, not what Christians can *get* if they compromise with the powers that be (i.e., efficient causes). In both cases, it is the Christian "fact," the Christian story, that functions as the interpretative lens for an authentically moral society, not the values of the surrounding culture or context. As this lens is put to use, there emerges in Baxter's thought a forceful countercultural vision of what society—in particular U. S. society—can be.

Perhaps the place where Baxter brought his thought together most clearly, and linked it to some practical reflections as well, was in a workshop he gave in March, 2001, at the Los Angeles Religious Education Congress in Anaheim, California. The talk was in two parts. In a first section (after which there was a break for several questions), Baxter provided the theoretical background for his disagreement with contemporary mainstream Catholic social ethics. In a second section, he sketched out another, countercultural way of looking at social ethics.[81]

The title of Baxter's presentation is "Blowing the Dynamite of the Church: A How-To in Catholic Social Theory and Practice." The "dynamite" image he refers to is taken from an "Easy Essay" by Catholic Worker cofounder Peter Maurin. Maurin says that, for the church to be effective in its teaching, it needs to set off some of the dynamite that is inherent in its message. Unfortunately, however, members of the church have wrapped that dynamite in "nice phraseology" and have sat on the lid. Those who have done this, Baxter says, are the scholars and many of the church hierarchy who have developed the "Americanist tradition" of U.S. social ethics—an ethics that holds (Baxter says later in the talk) that there exists a fundamental harmony between Catholicism and the United States.

Baxter begins his story of the development of the Americanist tradition with a letter from James Cardinal Gibbons in 1917, written in the name of the entire U.S. Catholic hierarchy to President Woodrow Wilson just weeks after the American declaration of war. In the letter Gibbons affirms the loyalty of the Catholic people to the United States and its war effort and assures Wilson of the church's complete cooperation. It is, says Baxter, "an uncritical loyalty to the nation-state" and signifies a readiness and willingness to come to the service of the nation. Despite the fact that U. S. Catholics were Irish who disliked Britain, or Germans who had recently emigrated from their homeland, Gibbons was saying, Catholics are loyal citizens of the United States.

As a followup to the U. S. hierarchy's declaration of cooperation with the war effort, a National Catholic War Council was established to provide chaplains for the troops, religious articles for them (prayer cards, rosaries, etc.), and—especially after the war—war relief. Many dioceses in the United States established diocesan chapters of the War Council, as did many parishes. After the war, in 1921, the War Council's name was changed to the National Catholic Welfare Council, and changed to the National Catholic Welfare Conference the following year. In 1964 it was renamed the United States Catholic Conference to work with the newly formed National Conference of Catholic Bishops. (In 2001 the two conferences merged into one under the name of the United States Conference of Catholic Bishops.)

The purpose of these postwar organizations, Baxter says, was all the same: it was to participate in the drama entitled "American Catholics to the Rescue." Catholics saw themselves not only as a group that was able to "fit in" with American democracy; if the truth be told, Catholic bishops and scholars said, the spirit of Catholicism is really the founding spirit of the United States. The writings of Jefferson, Adams, and Madison were inspired with what were ultimately Catholic ideas, and could be traced back to the political theory of Aquinas, Bellarmine, and Suarez. More than any other group, Catholics were in a position, with their theory of natural-law ethics, to shape American policy according to true Christian principles. The task of the National Catholic Welfare Conference (NCWC) in the 1920s through the 1950s was to spread the wisdom of Catholic ethical thinking—especially the social teachings of the popes—to the whole nation.

A key figure in the NCWC was John A. Ryan, priest of the archdiocese of Minneapolis, professor at the Catholic University of America, and head of the conference's social-action department. Relying on Catholic natural-law theory, says Baxter, Ryan was the key shaper of what became mainstream Catholic social ethics. His was an ethics that was purely philosophical; it contained no reference to the liturgy, the sacraments, the scriptures, or the lives of the saints. It attempted— to some, successfully—to articulate the principles of Leo XIII's *Rerum Novarum* into terms that Americans could understand. Some even say that Ryan's work was instrumental in developing the policies of Roosevelt's New Deal.

In the 1950s and 1960s, Jesuit John Courtney Murray worked in the same natural-law tradition as Ryan. His great contribution was his argument that Catholics could support the notion of separation of church and state, and his thought is generally acknowledged to have been studied and used by John F. Kennedy to counter the charges that a Catholic's loyalty to the pope would hinder him from carrying out his duties as president. And with the election of Kennedy in 1960, Catholics thought that, at last, they had "arrived." Like Ryan, Murray's ideas were based not on a distinctively Catholic or Christian claim, but on the generalities and shared assumptions of natural law. Politics, he argued, does not deal with ends, but with means, and so specific religious beliefs are to be kept out of the political realm. The Sermon on the Mount has nothing to do with politics—or even with morality. Murray and Ryan have been hailed as two of the best exemplars of a truly American theology.[82]

It is in this tradition of "Americanism" that the letters of the U. S. bishops on peace (*The Challenge of Peace* [1983]) and the economy (*Economic Justice for All* [1986]) need to be seen. *The Challenge of Peace*, for example, has an introductory section on the importance of faith and a long section on biblical and church teachings on peace. But the body of the document uses natural-law reasoning to discuss issues for the consideration of Pentagon policy makers. *Economic Justice for All* is much the same. The idea of the letters was to pose issues for discussion in terms that all parties could understand and debate, but, Baxter says, the effect was practically nil. One person Baxter talked to who had worked at the Pentagon in the early 1980s said that the letter was never discussed by the policy makers there. And on another front, with the Roe v. Wade decision, the war in El Salvador in the 1980s, and increased pressure for the legality of assisted suicide, what was becoming clear was that, rather than a harmony between Catholicism and U. S. government and culture, there really exists a tension. While the social ethics of Ryan and Murray may have helped Catholics to "arrive" in the mainstream, Baxter asks, "now that we've made it into the mainstream, is this where we want to be?"

His answer, not surprisingly, is no, and an alternative, more countercultural approach to social ethics is developed in the second part of his workshop. Baxter's vision is based on the conviction that an authentic social ethics can never rely on the state—we have to "unthink the necessity of the state" and recognize with Dorothy Day that the state is always the tool of the ruling classes to keep in place an unjust economic and political system. It is the gospel that needs to be proclaimed, says Baxter, not America. Christians owe allegiance to God; they are, in the words of 1 Peter, "resident aliens," and they must "live lives that reflect another city." A Catholic social ethics, says Baxter, should perhaps take as its motto Gandhi's dictum that "non-cooperation with evil is a moral duty." Imagine, says Baxter, a social ethics based on noncooperation with evil!

Such an alternative, countercultural social ethics has, he says, two advantages. In the first place, it creates a distance between Christians and loyalty to the state, allowing them to develop a critical perspective. Thus Dorothy Day's declaration of passivism during World War II (we will quote the beatitudes, she said, we will quote St. Francis and the teaching of the popes) gave her an ability to denounce the United States' use of the atomic bomb in 1945 and to be actively against nuclear armaments throughout the Cold War. It is the same distance that allowed the Catholic Worker movement to condemn "the largest air assault in the history of the world" during the Gulf War—when the U. S. bishops, only three years after the publication of *The Challenge of Peace*, had very little voice and very little clout despite their claim to be "in the loop" at the Pentagon. If the bishops had written that the United States is a war-making nation, that it worships a warrior God, then people might at least have known that the Catholic Church had taken a stand. A critical distance from the state would also free Christians, in the name of the gospels, to condemn and work against legislation that legalizes the killing of the unborn, the killing of killers with the death penalty, and the assisted suicide of the terminally ill, the seriously impaired, and those who have become burdensome because of age or illness.

A second advantage to this counterproposal, Baxter says, is that it is a social ethics not reserved to the experts, but rather one that can be practiced by ordinary Christians. Foundational to all of the four concrete actions he proposes is the formation of a community "to sustain life in Christ." Only in a vital "alternative community," as members of the GOCN would say, can Christians find the inspiration, the formation, the challenge, and the support to live out a more radical lifestyle.

First among the actions that committed Christians might do to live out a Christian social ethics is to care for the homeless. Baxter quotes Peter Maurin: "parish homes, not parish domes." Christians need to construct communities that give hospitality to homeless people. Every diocese should have a shelter for the homeless; every parish and, in Peter Maurin's vision, every house should have a "Christ room." A second action that can be taken is one that commits Christian communities to care for the elderly. An important development would be an increase in parishes that offer parish-based nursing care. In the third place, Baxter calls for support for the family farm, and fourth and finally, he calls for the faithful keeping of the Sabbath. If we do not keep the Sabbath, Baxter remarks characteristically, we lose sight of our end.

Although he possesses wide experience working for justice in the countercultural, Catholic Worker style, Baxter is relatively new to the academic scene. He is in demand as a speaker, however; one of his courses at Notre Dame, called "A Faith to Die For," is quite popular among students at this bastion of relatively wealthy and conservative Catholic youth; and he has a reputation as an excellent teacher. His writing so far has taken on some of the most revered proponents of what he calls the Americanist tradition—Charles Curran, the Himes brothers, John Tracy Ellis, and Jay Dolan, to name a few. United States contextual theology can look forward to much more development of his challenging, sometimes disturbing, countercultural perspective.

Conclusion:
Is One Model Better Than Another?

Is one model of contextual theology better than the others? Is there one way of taking account of the experience of the past and the experience of the present that is more adequate than another? The answer to these questions might be both yes and no.

On the one hand, each one of these models is a valid one, and so none can claim hegemony. Each, as I have tried to point out in my critiques, has a number of distinct advantages, and each has representatives who do the model justice. From one point of view, it would be wrong to say that the anthropological model presents more possibilities for contextualization than, say, the praxis model. There was a time when contextual theologians argued over whether one way of doing theology was the only way, but this kind of discussion has been recognized as futile.[1] Every person involved in doing theology needs to be aware of the range of methodological options available. There needs to be a healthy pluralism.

In addition, as I pointed out in Chapter 3, it is important to recognize that the models I have outlined are *inclusive* in nature—there is no need to commit oneself to any one model to the exclusion of one or more of the others. We have seen, for instance, how Justo L. González might be described as employing the transcendental model. What is also evident, however, is that González is greatly influenced by the theology of liberation and is convinced that theology needs to be done as critical reflection on praxis. And while I have characterized José de Mesa as a practitioner of the synthetic model, the thoughtful reader will notice a marked predilection in his thought for theologizing out of Filipino cultural forms. While I disagree with Doug Priest that my distinction of models is reductionistic, I would agree wholeheartedly with his point: "It is not contradictory to hold a high value of both Gospel and culture, nor is it wrong to take one's theological agenda from various sources: society at large; the current world scene as expressed in both the economic and political realms; the Biblical data; or the guidance of the Spirit."[2]

On the other hand, certain models can function more adequately within certain sets of circumstances. It seems to me that the praxis model might be better employed in a situation that calls for radical social change or creative pastoral action than, say, the translation model, which might tend to be content with the status quo. It is not surprising, therefore, that the translation model is the one preferred by someone like Pope John Paul II, whose duty it is to safeguard the integrity of doctrinal expression. And in a situation of primary evangelization, translating one's own understanding of the gospel into the language and customs of another culture may be the only option open until indigenous Christians are able to reflectively construct their own local theology, perhaps by employing the transcendental model as they accept insights from missionaries on the one hand and disagree with them in certain cases, only to find their own way of expressing faith or acting on its consequences.

Robert Schreiter reflects in the introduction to his collection of contemporary African Christologies that, "for too long, embracing Christ and his message meant rejection of African cultural values. Africans were taught that their ancient ways were deficient or even evil and had to be set aside if they hoped to become Christian."[3] In a such a situation, it seems to me, a preference for the anthropological model would be highly appropriate. On the other hand, in a culture such as that of the Philippines, where despite significant cultural depreciation there has been constant cross-fertilization for centuries, a more inclusive and synthetic approach such as José de Mesa's might be the only way of capturing the complexity of Filipino Christian identity. I myself have found that in situations of multicultural diversity the transcendental model can be employed with considerable effectiveness. In a theology course in which there can be students from six or seven cultural groups, the best tactic might be for the teacher to articulate as clearly as possible his or her own theology, with the expectation that the similarities and differences that the students discover in their own experience will provoke them to do their own theologizing as well.[4] Finally, I believe strongly that in a situation such as that of contemporary Europe, Australia, New Zealand, and North America, only a theology that engages the secular context critically can be one that faithfully presents and lives out the gospel.

The move to understand all theology as contextual is also a move to recognize the complex reality of theological pluralism. In times past we could confidently speak of the unity of theology, and theological students from Manila, Chicago, São Paolo, and Accra all studied the same theology out of pretty much the same books—Ott or Tanquerey or van Noort were all cut from the same theological cloth. The question of the best model of contextual theology is an appropriate one, but within today's world of radical plurality and ambiguity the best answer to the question can only be: "It depends on the context."

SYNTHETIC TABLES OF THE SIX MODELS

The Translation Model

Alternative Titles: *accommodation; adaptation*
Basis in Scripture and Tradition: *Acts 14:15-17; Acts 17:2-31; Cyril and
  Methodius; Ricci; de Nobili; John XXIII at opening of Vatican II*
Revelation: *tends to be interpreted as propositional, content-oriented*
Scripture/Tradition: *supracontextual; complete*
Context: *basically good and trustworthy*
Method: *kernel/husk; know the context so as to effectively* insert *the gospel*
Analogy: *bring seeds, plant in native ground*
Legend: *"putting the gospel into" (Bruce Fleming)*
Critique: *Positive: takes Christian message seriously; recognizes contextual
        ambiguity; can be used by participants and nonparticipants in a
        culture*
      *Negative: naive notions of culture and gospel; propositional notion
        of revelation*

The Anthropological Model

Alternative Titles: *indigenization; ethnographic model*
Basis in Scripture and Tradition: *Mt 15:21-28; Mk 7:24-30; Jn 3:16; move-
  ment of Acts; Justin Martyr—"seeds of the word"; GS, S 44; AG 11; CT 53*
Revelation: *tends to be understood as "personal presence"*
Scripture/Tradition: *culturally conditioned; like all human expressions, in-
  complete*
Context: *basically good and trustworthy; equal to scripture and tradition*
Method: *know the culture to "pull the gospel out of it"*
Analogy: *seeds are already in the ground; just need to be watered to sprout*
Legend: *"take off your shoes" (Max Warren)*
Critique: *Positive: takes context seriously; provides fresh perspectives of
        Christianity; starts with where people are*
      Negative: prey to cultural romanticism

The Praxis Model

Alternative Titles: *situational theology; theology of the signs of the times; liberation model*

Basis in Scripture and Tradition: *prophetic tradition; Jas 1:22; Irenaeus; Karl Barth*

Revelation: *envisioned as God at work in the world, calling men and women as partners*

Scripture/Tradition: *culturally conditioned, like all human expressions; incomplete*

Context: *basically good and trustworthy but can be distorted; should be approached with some suspicion; can be equal to scripture and tradition*

Method: *practice/reflection/practice—in unending spiral*

Analogy: *garden needs to be constantly weeded; the work never ends; practice makes one a better gardener*

Legend: *"to know Christ is to follow him" (Alfred Hennelly)*

Critique: *Positive: strong epistemological basis; provides an "alternate vision"; influence on theology*
Negative: critiqued for close connection with Marxism

The Synthetic Model

Alternative Titles: *dialogical model; analogical model*

Basis in Scripture and Tradition: *formation of the Bible; development of doctrine; EN 64*

Revelation: *elements of all three previous models*

Scripture/Tradition: *culturally conditioned; incomplete*

Context: *ambiguous and incomplete; needs the "other" for completion*

Method: *conversation with all partners*

Analogy: *cross-pollination*

Legend: *"between the lines" (Horacio de la Costa)*

Critique: *Positive: attitude of dialogue; emphasis on ongoing process; witness to universality; easy to   dialogue with other churches*
Negative: danger of "selling out"; might seem "wishy-washy"

The Transcendental Model

Alternative Title: *subjective model*
Basis in Scripture and Tradition: *Mk 2:21-22*
Revelation: *tends to be understood as personal presence, encountered in subjective (personal, communal) experience*
Scripture/Tradition: *culturally conditioned; incomplete*
Context: *good and trustworthy; individual experience is clue to wider experience; individual experience is conditioned by the radical communal nature of humanity*
Method: *sympathy and antipathy*
Analogy: *if I cultivate my garden, another will be inspired to cultivate his or hers*
Legend: *"the most personal is the most general" (Carl Rogers)*
Critique: *Positive: emphasizes theology as activity; recognizes contextual nature of all theology*
　　　　Negative: too abstract; false claim to universality; too ideal to be practical

The Countercultural Model

Alternative Titles: *encounter model; engagement model; prophetic model; contrast model; confessional model*
Basis in Scripture and Tradition: *prophetic tradition; Johannine notion of "world"; Rom 12:2; 1 Cor 1:23; 1 Pet 1:1; Tertullian; Letter of Diognetus; monastic tradition; Anabaptist tradition; Dorothy Day*
Revelation: *narrative and story; the "fact" of Jesus Christ*
Scripture/Tradition: *the "clue" to the meaning of history; complete, even though human understanding of it is not; can be understood more completely through the understanding of other cultures*
Context: *radically ambiguous and resistant to the gospel; unequal to scripture/tradition*
Method: *commitment to Christian story as clue to history; use story as lens to interpret, critique, and challenge context*
Analogy: *the soil needs weeding and fertilizing so that the seeds can be planted*
Legend: *"challenging relevance" (Hogg); "subversive fulfillment" (Kraemer)*
Critique: *Positive: strong engagement of context and fidelity to gospel; relevant in western contexts*
　　　　Negative: danger of being anticultural; danger of sectarianism; tends to be monocultural; danger of exclusivism

Notes

INTRODUCTION

[1]Stephen B. Bevans, "Becoming a Filipino Theologian," *Ilocos Review*, 5, 1/2 (January-December, 1973): 208-214; "The Subject as Indigenous Theologian," *Philippine Priests' Forum*, 7, 2 (June, 1975): 51-56.

[2]Stephen B. Bevans, "Five Approaches to the Indigenization of Theology," in *The Kingdom of the Word*, Philippine SVD Festschrift (Manila: Catholic Trade School, 1976), 112-137.

[3]Stephen B. Bevans, "Models of Contextual Theology," *Missiology: An International Review*, 13, 2 (April, 1985): 185-202.

1. CONTEXTUAL THEOLOGY AS A THEOLOGICAL IMPERATIVE

[1]The term *Third World* is admittedly a controversial one. W. J. Grimm points out that while the term originally had a positive meaning, analogous to the emerging power of the Third Estate during the French Revolution, its meaning has subsequently shifted: "it no longer referred to the aspirations of nations hoping to develop independent governments and economies. It became a term of comparison. The third world was now defined in terms of the first." See W. J. Grimm, "The 'Third' World," *America* (May 5, 1990): 449. Because of this, Grimm suggests that the term be abandoned. On the other hand, the Ecumenical Association of Third World Theologians (EATWOT)—a group that would be very sensitive to any term that would demean their cultures—uses the term quite unapologetically. See K. C. Abraham, ed., *Third World Theologies: Commonalities and Convergences* (Maryknoll, NY: Orbis Books, 1990); and V. Fabella, "Third World," in V. Fabella and R. S. Sugirtharajah, eds., *Dictionary of Third World Theologies* (Maryknoll, NY: Orbis Books, 2000), 202. It is because these theologians use the term that I have chosen to use it here.

[2]Parts of this section follow very closely a section of my essay "Living between Gospel and Context: Models for a Missional Church in North America," in Craig van Gelder, ed., *Confident Witness—Changing World: Rediscovering the Gospel in North America* (Grand Rapids: Eerdmans, 1999), 141-154.

[3]My use of the term *loci theologici* reflects the traditional Roman Catholic usage, especially developed by Melchior Cano in his *De Locis Theologicis* (Salamanca, 1563). See Jared Wicks, "Luoghi theologici," in *Dizionario di theologia fondamentale* (Assisi: Editrice Citadella, 1990), 645-647; and J. Thornhill, "Loci Theologici," in *New Catholic Encyclopedia*, vol. 8 (New York: McGraw-Hill, 1967), 950. *Loci* in some Protestant circles is used to designate the various classical themes of theology, e.g., God, Trinity, Christ, grace, etc. This use is based on Melanchthon's work *Loci Communes Rerum Theologicarum* (1521), revised as *Loci Praecipui Theologici* in 1559. For a contemporary example of this use of *locus* or *loci*,

see Carl Braaten and Robert Jenson, eds., *Christian Dogmatics* (Philadelphia: Fortress Press, 1984), v-xv and xix.

[4]Karl Rahner uses this phrase in several of his essays. See, for example, "The Hermeneutics of Eschatological Assertions," in *Theological Investigations*, vol. 4 (Baltimore: Helicon Press, and London: Darton, Longman and Todd, 1966), 324.

[5]This phrase is one used often by Bernard Lonergan. See, for instance, *Insight: A Study in Human Understanding* (New York: Philosophical Library, 1957), 251-252; and *Method in Theology* (London: Darton, Longman and Todd, 1972), 263. Lonergan's underlying epistemology might be referred to as a "critical realism." For a discussion of the importance of a shift from "naive realism" or "naive idealism" to critical realism, see Paul Hiebert, "Epistemological Foundations for Science and Theology," *TSF Bulletin* (March-April, 1985): 5-10; "The Missiological Implications of an Epistemological Shift," *TSF Bulletin* (May-June, 1985): 12-18; and *Missiological Implications of Epistemological Shifts: Affirming Truth in a Modern/Postmodern World* (Harrisburg, PA: Trinity Press International, 1999).

[6]Charles H. Kraft, *Christianity in Culture* (Maryknoll, NY: Orbis Books, 1979), 300.

[7]See Lonergan, *Method in Theology*, 28, 76-77, 238.

[8]José M. de Mesa, *Inculturation as Pilgrimage*, First Annual Louis J. Luzbetak, SVD, Lecture on Mission and Culture (Chicago: CCGM Publications, 2001), 14.

[9]Anthony J. Gittins, *Reading the Clouds: Mission Spirituality for New Times* (Liguori, MO: Liguori Publications, 1999), xi.

[10]Ian G. Barbour, *Myths, Models, and Paradigms: A Comparative Study in Science and Religion* (New York: Harper and Row, 1974), 120-121. See Peter Berger and Thomas Luckmann, *The Social Construction of Reality: A Treatise on the Sociology of Knowledge* (New York: Doubleday, 1967); and Anthony J. Gittins, *Gifts and Strangers: Meeting the Challenge of Inculturation* (Mahwah, NJ: Paulist Press, 1989), 1-28. See also J. B. Miller, "The Emerging Postmodern World," in F. B. Burnham, ed., *Postmodern Theology: Christian Faith in a Pluralist World* (San Francisco: Harper and Row, 1989), 11. For a striking illustration of the "social construction of reality," see Mircea Eliade, *No Souvenirs: Journal, 1957-1969* (San Francisco: Harper and Row, 1977), 213-214.

[11]Kraft, *Christianity in Culture*, 296.

[12]See Karl Rahner, "The Hermeneutics of Eschatological Assertions," in *Theological Investigations*, vol. 4, 324; and Jeffery Hopper, *Understanding Modern Theology II: Reinterpreting Christian Faith for Changing Worlds* (Philadelphia: Fortress Press, 1987), 4-31.

[13]Douglas John Hall, *Professing the Faith: Christian Theology in a North American Context* (Minneapolis, MN: Fortress Press, 1993), 34-36; Rosemary Radford Ruether, *Sexism and God-Talk: Toward a Feminist Theology* (Boston: Beacon Press, 1993), 12-16.

[14]Hall, *Professing the Faith*, 33.

[15]Ibid.

[16]Clifford Geertz, *The Interpretation of Cultures* (New York: Basic Books, 1973), 89, as quoted in Gerald A. Arbuckle, *Earthing the Gospel: An Inculturation Handbook for the Pastoral Worker* (Maryknoll, NY: Orbis Books, 1990), 28. Geertz presents here what Robert J. Schreiter has called an "integrated" concept of culture. In this understanding, culture is the "glue" that gives coherence to a particular worldview. Also operative today are what Schrieter names as "globalized" concepts of culture. In this understanding of culture, one's worldview or meaning structure is not so much inherited as it is *constructed*, often in the context of a power struggle between a dominant group and an oppressed subaltern group. This latter understanding of culture will be dealt with under the rubrics of "social location"

and "social change" below. See Robert J. Schreiter, *The New Catholicity: Theology between the Global and the Local* (Maryknoll, NY: Orbis Books, 1997), 46-61.

[17]See: Federation of Asian Bishops' Conferences, "Evangelization in Modern Day Asia," in G. B. Rosales and C. G. Arévalo, eds., *For All the Peoples of Asia: Federation of Asian Bishops' Conferences Documents from 1970-1991* (Maryknoll, NY: Orbis Books; Quezon City: Claretian Publications, 1992), 11-25. See also Stephen Bevans, "Inculturation of Theology in Asia (the Federation of Asian Bishops' Conferences, 1970-1995)," *Studia Missionalia*, 45 (1996): 1-23.

[18]For example, José Miguez Bonino, "Social Location," in Fabella and Sugirtharaja, *Dictionary of Third World Theologies*, 187.

[19]See Malcolm Waters, *Globalization* (London and New York: Routledge, 1995).

[20]Benjamin R. Barber, *Jihad vs. McWorld* (New York: Times Books, 1995), 17.

[21]Schreiter, *The New Catholicity*, 74-78; see also Virgil P. Elizondo, *The Future Is Mestizo: Life Where Cultures Meet* (New York: Meyer-Stone, 1988); Jung Young Lee, *Marginality: The Key to Multicultural Theology* (Minneapolis, MN: Fortress Press, 1995), 55-70; Peter C. Phan, "Asian Catholics in the United States: Challenges and Opportunities for the Church," *Mission Studies*, XVI-2, 32 (1999): 151-174.

[22]Douglas John Hall, *Thinking the Faith: Christian Theology in a North American Context* (Minneapolis, MN: Augsburg, 1989), 21.

[23]Stephen Sykes, *The Identity of Christianity* (London: SPCK, 1984), 23. The entire argument is laid out on pp. 11-34. See also Stephen Bevans and Roger Schroeder, "Missionary by Its Very Nature: A Reading of the Acts of the Apostles," in Heribert Bettscheider, ed., *Reflecting Mission, Practicing Mission*, vol. I (Nettetal, Germany: Steyler Verlag, 2001), 3-36, especially note 127 on p. 36.

[24]On the strong contextual nature of early Christian theology, see David J. Bosch, *Transforming Mission: Paradigm Shifts in Theology of Mission* (Maryknoll, NY: Orbis Books, 1991), 190-213; see also Justo L. González, *Christian Thought Revisited: Three Types of Theology*, revised edition (Maryknoll, NY: Orbis Books, 1999); Andrew F. Walls, "Old Athens and New Jerusalem: Some Signposts for Christian Scholarship in the Early History of Mission Studies," *International Bulletin of Missionary Research*, 21, 4 (1997): 146-153; and Dale T. Irvin and Scott W. Sunquist, *History of the World Christian Movement, vol. I: Earliest Christianity to 1453* (Maryknoll, NY: Orbis Books, 2001), 47-153.

[25]See John Courtney Murray, *The Problem of God, Yesterday and Today* (New Haven and London: Yale University Press, 1964), 45-53; and Bernard J. F. Lonergan, *The Way to Nicea: The Dialectical Development of Trinitarian Theology* (London: Darton, Longman and Todd, 1976), 136-137.

[26]V. Fabella, "Christology from an Asian Woman's Perspective," in V. Fabella and S. Ai Lee Park, eds., *We Dare to Dream: Doing Theology as Asian Women* (Maryknoll, NY: Orbis Books, 1989), 9.

[27]Henri de Lubac, *Corpus Mysticum: L'eucharistie et l'Eglise au Moyen Age*, second edition (Paris: Aubier, 1949). On the Teutonic influence on Christianianity, see James C. Russell, *The Germanization of Early Medieval Christianity: A Sociohistorical Approach to Religious Transformation* (New York and Oxford: Oxford University Press, 1994); and Andrew F. Walls, "Culture and Coherence in Christian History," in *The Missionary Movement in Christian History: Studies in the Transmission of Faith* (Maryknoll, NY: Orbis Books, 1996), 16-25.

[28]For an example of how context affected theologies of ministry, see Thomas F. O'Meara, *Theology of Ministry*, completely revised edition (Mahwah, NJ: Paulist Press, 1999), 111-129.

[29]See Brian Gerrish, "Continuity and Change: Friedrich Schleiermacher on the Task of Theology," in *Tradition and the Modern World: Reformed Theology in the Nineteenth Century* (Chicago: University of Chicago Press, 1978), 13-48; and *A Prince of the Church: Schleiermacher and the Beginnings of Modern Theology* (Philadelphia: Fortress Press, 1984); on the Catholic Tübingen school, see Thomas F. O'Meara, *Romantic Idealism and Roman Catholicism: Schelling and the Theologians* (Notre Dame, IN: University of Notre Dame Press, 1982).

[30]Paul Tillich, *Systematic Theology*, vol. I (Chicago: University of Chicago Press, and New York: Harper and Row, 1967), 60.

[31]See David Tracy, *Blessed Rage for Order: The New Pluralism in Theology* (New York: Seabury, 1975), 27; Hall, *Thinking the Faith*, 355.

[32]See Francis George, "Ecclesiological Presuppositions in Inculturating the Faith: Three Examples from Mission History," *Neue Zeitschrift für Missionswissenschaft*, 45 (1989/4): 256-264.

[33]For much of this section I am indebted to my colleague Robert Schreiter's *Constructing Local Theologies* (Maryknoll, NY: Orbis Books, 1985), 1-5. See also Peter Schineller, *A Handbook on Inculturation* (Mahwah, NJ: Paulist Press, 1990), 5-13.

[34]See Francis Schüssler Fiorenza, "Systematic Theology: Task and Methods," in Francis Schüssler Fiorenza and John Galvin, eds., *Systematic Theology: Roman Catholic Perspectives*, vol. 1 (Minneapolis, MN: Fortress Press, 1991), 35-65; and J. J. Mueller, *What Are They Saying about Theological Method?* (Mahwah, NJ: Paulist Press, 1984).

[35]See J. W. McClendon, *Biography as Theology: How Life Stories Can Remake Today's Theology* (Nashville: Abingdon Press, 1974); Peter C. Phan and Jung Young Lee, eds., *Journeys at the Margin: Toward an Autobiographical Theology in American-Asian Perspective* (Collegeville, MN: Liturgical Press, 1999); Stanley Hauerwas and L. G. Jones, eds., *Why Narrative? Readings in Narrative Theology* (Grand Rapids: Eerdmans, 1989); Robert A. Krieg, *Story-Shaped Christology: The Role of Narrative in Identifying Jesus Christ* (Mahwah, NJ: Paulist Press, 1988); W. W. Everett and T. J. Bachmeyer, *Disciplines in Transformation: A Guide to Theology and the Behavioral Sciences* (Lanham, MD: University Press of America, 1979); Arbuckle, *Earthing the Gospel*, 5; Louis J. Luzbetak, *The Church and Cultures: New Perspectives in Missiological Anthropology* (Maryknoll, NY: Orbis Books, 1989); Robert J. Schreiter, "Anthropology and Faith: Challenges to Missiology," *Missiology: An International Review*, XIX, 3 (July, 1991): 283-294.

[36]So I heard Panikkar say in a lecture he gave at the University of Notre Dame in 1983.

[37]To Thi Anh, *Cultural Values East and West: Conflict or Harmony?* (Manila: East Asian Pastoral Institute, 1975); Jung Young Lee, *The Trinity in Asian Perspective* (Nashville: Abingdon Press, 1996).

[38]Schreiter, *Constructing Local Theologies*, 2.

[39]See, for example, Thomas Bamat and Jean-Paul Wiest, eds., *Popular Catholicism in a World Church: Seven Case Studies in Inculturation* (Maryknoll, NY: Orbis Books, 1999); Leonardo N. Mercado, *Doing Filipino Theology* (Manila: Divine Word Publications, 1997); Anthony J. Gittins, *Mende Religion*, Studia Instituti Anthropos 41 (Nettetal, Germany: Steyler Verlag, 1987); Stuart C. Bate, *Inculturation and Healing* (Pietermaritzburg, South Africa: Cluster Publications, 1995).

[40]James Cone, *A Black Theology of Liberation*, second edition (Maryknoll, NY: Orbis Books, 1986); and *Speaking the Truth: Ecumenism, Liberation, and Black Theology* (Grand Rapids: Eerdmans, 1986).

[41]José Rizal, *The Subversive* (*El Filibusterismo*), L. M. Guerrero, trans. (Bloomington,

IN: Indiana University Press, 1962), 54. The *Fili*, as it is called by Filipinos, was first published in 1891.

[42]Lonergan, *Method in Theology*, xi. This is also the notion of culture operative in the document on inculturation prepared by the Roman Catholic International Theological Commission in 1988. The document can be found in *Irish Theological Quarterly*, 55, 2 (1989): 142-161; and in James A. Scherer and Stephen B. Bevans, eds., *New Directions in Mission and Evangelization 1: Basic Documents 1974-1991* (Maryknoll, NY: Orbis Books, 1992), 154-161.

[43]Lonergan, *Method in Theology*, xi. Alward Shorter makes the same points in his *Toward a Theology of Inculturation* (Maryknoll, NY: Orbis Books, 1988), 17-30.

[44]Shorter deals extensively with the implications of the incarnation for contextual theology in *Toward a Theology of Inculturation*, 75-88.

[45]René Padilla, "The Contextualization of the Gospel," in C. H. Kraft and T. N. Wisley, eds., *Readings in Dynamic Indigeneity* (Pasadena: William Carey Library, 1979), 286.

[46]Edward Schillebeeckx, *Christ the Sacrament of the Encounter with God* (New York: Sheed and Ward, 1963). The whole question of the uniqueness or finality of Christ, of course, has been the subject of hot debate in theological circles in the last several years; for example, Paul F. Knitter, *No Other Name? A Critical Survey of Christian Attitudes toward the World Religions* (Maryknoll, NY: Orbis Books, 1985); Paul F. Knitter and John Hick, eds., *The Myth of Christian Uniqueness: Towards a Pluralistic Theology of Religions* (Maryknoll, NY: Orbis Books, 1987); Gavin D'Costa, ed., *Christian Uniqueness Reconsidered: The Myth of a Pluralistic Theology of Religion* (Maryknoll, NY: Orbis Books, 1990); Bosch, *Transforming Mission*, 474-489; Jacques Dupuis, *Toward a Christian Theology of Religious Pluralism* (Maryknoll, NY: Orbis Books, 1997); S. Mark Heim, *Salvations: Truth and Difference in Religion* (Maryknoll, NY: Orbis Books, 1995). Pope John Paul II's 1990 encyclical *Redemptoris Missio* set out to clarify these issues and spoke of Jesus as the "only Savior" (the title of chapter 1). In 2000, the Congregation for the Doctrine of the Faith issued "Dominus Iesus," which also tried to clarify the church's position in this regard. See William R. Burrows, ed., *Redemption and Dialogue: Reading* Redemptoris Missio *and* Dialogue and Proclamation (Maryknoll, NY: Orbis Books, 1993), and "Dominus Iesus," http://www.vatican.va/roman_curia/ . . . doc_20000806_dominus-iesus_en.html.

[47]See Karl Rahner, "How to Receive a Sacrament and Mean It," *Theology Digest*, 19, 3 (August, 1971): 227-234. See also John Oman, *Grace and Personality* (Cambridge: Cambridge University Press, 1917), 177-178. Oman's ideas of sacrament at the turn of the twentieth century are remarkably close to Rahner's.

[48]Carroll Stuhlmueller and Donald Senior, *The Biblical Foundations for Mission* (Maryknoll, NY: Orbis Books, 1983), 9-35.

[49]José M. de Mesa and Lode Wostyn, *Doing Theology: Basic Realities and Processes* (Manila: Maryhill School of Theology, 1982), 80. For an example of a pre-Vatican II approach to revelation, cf. A. Tanquerey, *A Manual of Dogmatic Theology*, J. J. Byrnes, trans. (New York: Desclee, 1959), 22-34.

[50]See Karl Rahner, *Foundations of Christian Faith* (New York: Seabury, 1978), 120.

[51]Karl Rahner, "The Development of Dogma," in *Theological Investigations*, vol. 1 (Baltimore: Helicon Press, 1961), 49: "It is because the definitive Reality which resolves history proper is already here that Revelation is 'closed.' Closed, because open to the concealed presence of divine plenitude in Christ. Nothing new remains to be said, not as though there were not still much to say, but because everything has been said, everything

given in the Son of Love, in whom God and the world have become one, for ever without confusion, but for ever undivided."

[52]Avery Dulles, *The Reshaping of Catholicism: Current Challenges in the Theology of the Church* (San Francisco: Harper and Row, 1988), 71.

[53]Walls, *The Missionary Movement in Christian History*, xvii.

[54]Schreiter believes that our own era is one in which the catholicity of the church will receive special emphasis, given the dynamics of globalization and the issues of identity that it brings forth so urgently. See *The New Catholicity*, 116-133.

[55]John Thompson, "Modern Trinitarian Perspectives," *Scottish Journal of Theology*, 44 (1991): 349-365; and K. Blaser, "La remise en valeur du dogme trinitaire dans la théologie actuelle," *Etudes de Théologie et Religion*, 61, 3 (1986); Catherine M. LaCugna, *God for Us* (San Francisco: Harper/Collins, 1991).

[56]For a more detailed treatment of this trinitarian basis for contextual theology (or inculturation), see Stephen Bevans, "Inculturation and SVD Mission: Theological Foundations," *Verbum SVD*, 42, 3 (2001): 259-281.

[57]Paul VI, *Evangelii Nuntiandi*, Apostolic Exhortation on Evangelization in the Modern World (Washington, DC: United States Catholic Conference, 1976), 20. See Shorter, *Toward a Theology of Inculturation*, 215-219.

2. ISSUES IN CONTEXTUAL THEOLOGY

[1]See Krikor Haleblian, "The Problem of Contextualization," *Missiology: An International Review*, XI, 1 (January, 1983): 95-111; Robert J. Schreiter, *Constructing Local Theologies* (Maryknoll, NY: Orbis Books, 1985), 16-20; "Issues Facing Contextual Theology Today," *Verbum SVD*, 21, 3/4 (1980): 267-278; "Local Theologies in the Local Church: Issues and Methods," *Proceedings of the Catholic Theological Association of America*, 1981, 96-112; Harvie Conn, *Eternal Word and Changing Worlds: Theology, Anthropology, and Mission in Trialogue* (Grand Rapids: Zondervan, 1984), 162-205; Max Stackhouse, *Apologia: Contextualization, Globalization, and Mission in Theological Education* (Grand Rapids: Eerdmans, 1988).

[2]José M. de Mesa and Lode Wostyn, *Doing Theology: Basic Realities and Processes* (Manila: Maryhill School of Theology, 1982), 14-18.

[3]See Walter J. Ong, *Orality and Literacy: The Technologizing of the Word* (London: Methuen, 1982); and Anthony J. Gittins, *Gifts and Strangers: Meeting the Challenge of Inculturation* (Mahwah, NJ: Paulist Press, 1989), 56-83; Anthony J. Gittins, *Ministry at the Margins: Strategies and Spirituality for Mission* (Maryknoll, NY: Orbis Books, 2002), 81-100. Ana María Pineda, "Evangelization of the 'New World': A New World Perspective," *Missiology: An International Review*, 20, 2 (April, 1992): 151-161.

[4]From a vast literature, see in particular Volker Küster, *The Many Faces of Jesus Christ* (Maryknoll, NY: Orbis Books, 2001); Ron O'Grady, ed., *Christ for All People: Celebrating a World of Christian Art* (Maryknoll, NY: Orbis Books, 2001); Thomas F. Matthews, *The Clash of Gods: A Reinterpretation of Early Christian Art*, revised edition (Princeton, NJ: Princeton University Press, 1999); Edward Foley, "Art," in Karl Müller et al., eds., *Dictionary of Mission: Theology, History, Perspectives* (Maryknoll, NY: Orbis Books, 1997), 33-38; Mark J. Hatcher, "Poetry, Singing, and Contextualization," *Missiology: An International Review*, XXIX, 4 (October, 2001): 475-487.

[5]See Joseph G. Healey, "Constructing a Mission Theology Using African Proverbs and Sayings," *African Christian Studies* (June, 1988): 71-85; "Proverbs and Sayings—a Window into the African Christian World View," in *Communicatio Socialis Yearbook*, 7

(1988)—also in *Service*, 3 (1988): 1-35; *Kuishi Injili* (Peramiho: Benedictine Publications, 1982); Stan Nussbaum, ed., *African Proverbs: Collections, Studies, Bibliographies*, version 1.01 for Windows, CD #3, 20:21 Library—Mission and Evangelism Resources on CD (Colorado Springs, CO: Global Mapping International, 1996).

[6]See Schreiter, *Constructing Local Theologies*, 78. See also Olin P. Moyd, *The Sacred Art: Preaching and Theology in the African American Tradition* (Valley Forge, PA: Judson Press, 1995).

[7]George Proksch, "The Gospel in Indian Dress," in John T. Boberg, ed., *The Word in the World* (Techny, IL: Divine Word Missionaries, 1975), 58-62.

[8]N. B. Bejo, "Komiks and Movies in the Philippines," *Diwa: Studies in Philosophy and Theology*, XIII, 2 (November, 1988): 121-135; Roger Hooker, *The Quest of Ajneya: A Christian Theological Appraisal of the Search for Meaning in His Three Hindi Novels* (Delhi: Motilal Banarsidass, 1998); Tom Beaudoin, *Virtual Faith: The Irreverent Spiritual Quest of Generation X* (San Francisco: Jossey-Bass, 1998).

[9]Peter Schineller, "Inculturation and Modernity," *Sedos Bulletin*, 2 (February 15, 1988): 47.

[10]Leonardo N. Mercado, "Notes on Christ and Local Community in Philippine Context," *Verbum SVD*, 21, 3/4 (1980): 303; *Elements of Filipino Theology* (Tacloban: Divine Word University, 1975), 13.

[11]Haleblian, "The Problem of Contextualization": 99.

[12]There have been a number of works that have dealt with this question of the people being the real theologians. See Samuel Amirtham and John S. Pobee, eds., *Theology by the People: Reflections on Doing Theology in Community* (Geneva: World Council of Churches, 1986); Robert J. Schreiter, "La Communauté—Theologien," *Spiritus*, XXVII, 107 (May, 1987): 147-154; John Shea, "Theology at the Grassroots," *Church*, 2, 1 (Spring, 1986): 3-7; Patrick Kalilombe, "Doing Theology at the Grassroots: A Challenge for Professional Theologians," *African Ecclesial Review*, 27, 3 (June, 1985): 148-161; 27, 4 (August, 1985): 225-237; Howard W. Stone and James O. Duke, *How to Think Theologically* (Minneapolis, MN: Fortress Press, 1996); Richard J. Mouw, *Consulting the Faithful: What Christian Intellectuals Can Learn from Popular Religion* (Grand Rapids: Eerdmans, 1994); Mary Ann Hinsdale, Helen M. Lewis, and S. Maxine Waller, *It Comes from the People: Community Development and Local Theology* (Philadelphia: Temple University Press, 1995); Clemens Sedmak, *Doing Local Theology* (Maryknoll, NY: Orbis Books, 2002).

[13]Ralph Waldo Emerson, "Self Reliance," in W. Blair, T. Hornberger, R. Stewart, and J. Miller, Jr., eds., *The Literature of the United States*, vol. 1, third edition (Glenview, IL: Scott, Foresman and Co., 1971), 1103.

[14]We often hear how African Americans and other groups are "voiceless," but as my colleague Jamie Phelps likes to say, African Americans are *not* voiceless. They have lots to say and are skilled in saying it—it's just that people do not listen!

[15]See Gittins, *Gifts and Strangers,* 111-138; Stephen Bevans, "Seeing Mission through Images," *Missiology: An International Review*, 19, 1 (January, 1991): 51-53.

[16]See P. Adler, "The Transitional Experience," *Journal of Humanistic Psychology*, 15, 4 (Fall, 1975): 13-23; and Mary Catherine Bateson, "Insight in a Bicultural Context," *Philippine Studies*, 16 (1968): 605-621.

[17]See Stephen Bevans, "Becoming a Filipino Theologian," *Ilocos Review*, 5, 1/2 (January-December, 1973): 207-214; and "Singing the Lord's Song in a Foreign Land: The Foreigner as Theology Teacher," *South East Asia Journal of Theology*, 17, 2 (1976): 49-62.

[18]James Cone, "A Theological Challenge to the American Catholic Church," in *Speaking the Truth* (Grand Rapids: Eerdmans, 1986), 57.

[19]Stephen Bevans, "Letting Go and Speaking Out: A Spirituality of Inculturation," in Stephen Bevans, Eleanor Doidge, and Robert J. Schreiter, eds., *The Healing Circle: Essays in Cross-Cultural Mission* (Chicago: CCGM Publications, 2000), 133-146.

[20]See Karl Rahner, "Anonymous Christians," in *Theological Investigations*, vol. 6 (Baltimore: Helicon Press, 1969), 393-394; *Foundations of Christian Faith* (New York: Seabury, 1978), 123-124; 126-133.

[21]See Karl Rahner, "How to Receive a Sacrament and Mean It," *Theology Digest*, 19, 3 (August, 1971): 227-234.

[22]Karl Rahner, "Anonymous Christians," 390-398; "Anonymous Christianity and the Missionary Task of the Church," in *Theological Investigations*, vol. 11 (New York: Seabury, 1974), 161-178; "Observations on the Problem of the 'Anonymous Christians,' " in *Theological Investigations*, vol. 14 (New York: Seabury, 1976), 280-294; "On the Importance of Non-Christian Religions for Salvation," in *Theological Investigations*, vol. 18 (New York: Crossroad, 1983), 288-295.

[23]Raimon Panikkar, *The Unknown Christ of Hinduism: Towards an Ecumenical Christophany* (Maryknoll, NY: Orbis Books, 1981).

[24]See David Tracy, *The Analogical Imagination: Christian Theology and the Culture of Pluralism* (New York: Crossroad, 1981); "The Uneasy Alliance Reconceived: Catholic Theological Method, Modernity, and Postmodernity," *Theological Studies*, 50, 3 (September, 1989): 548-570.

[25]John Oman, *Grace and Personality* (Cambridge: Cambridge University Press, 1917), 225.

[26]Søren Kierkegaard, *Papirer, 1849*, P. A. Heiberg, ed., 1924. Kierkegaard goes on to say: "This means . . . that humanity is capable of nothing, it is God who gives everything. . . ." See also *The Sickness unto Death* (Garden City, NY: Doubleday Anchor Books, 1954). Kierkegaard says that one of the key elements of "despair" is a lack of acknowledgment of one's finitude in the face of God's infinity—this is the essence of sin. "As a sinner man is separated from God by a yawning qualitative abyss. And obviously God is separated from man by the same yawning qualitative abyss when He forgives sins" (p. 253).

[27]Karl Barth, "Foreword" to *Church Dogmatics, I,1, The Doctrine of the Word of God*, G. T. Thomson, trans. (Edinburgh: T and T Clark, 1936, 1960), x.

[28]Tracy, *The Analogical Imagination*, 405-445.

[29]Conn, *Eternal Word and Changing Worlds*, 176-184. But see also J. D. Gort, H. M. Vroom, R. Fernhout, and A. Wessels, eds., *Dialogue and Syncretism: An Interdisciplinary Approach* (Grand Rapids: Eerdmans, 1989); Louis J. Luzbetak, *The Church and Cultures: New Perspectives in Missiological Anthropology* (Maryknoll, NY: Orbis Books, 1989), 360-373; Carl F. Starkloff, "The Problem of Syncretism in the Search for Inculturation," *Mission*, 1, 1 (1994): 75-94; Schreiter, *Constructing Local Theologies*, 144-158; and *The New Catholicity: Theology between the Global and the Local* (Maryknoll, NY: Orbis Books), 62-83. Works such as these take a more positive approach to syncretism and place less emphasis on possible distortions in an encounter between religion and culture than on the cultural changes that result. As Luzbetak points out (p. 369): "A syncretism-free Church is an eschatological hope, not a reality. A positive attitude is called for also because syncretism often indicates human needs and demands responses to true human values, such as a tribe's appreciation of its traditions and ancestors. Finally, syncretism can also provide important clues to a mission strategy. Syncretism may thus be a bridge and an accelerator in the acculturative process from unchristian to Christian ways and beliefs." Several authors have pointed out that often what is judged as *syncretism* in the eyes of those who hold religious authority and power might be judged as authentic *inculturation* in the eyes of the ordinary

people. See Manuel M. Marzal et al., eds., *The Indian Face of God in Latin America* (Maryknoll, NY: Orbis Books, 1996).

[30]Paul VI, *Evangelii Nuntiandi* (Washington, DC: U. S. Catholic Conference, 1976), 65.

[31]Sacred Congregation for the Doctrine of the Faith, *Instruction on Certain Aspects of the "Theology of Liberation"* (Washington, DC: U. S. Catholic Conference, 1984). The document is also printed as an appendix in Roger Haight, *An Alternative Vision: An Interpretation of Liberation Theology* (Mahwah, NJ: Paulist Press, 1985), 269-291.

[32]See David Tracy, *Blessed Rage for Order: The New Pluralism in Theology* (New York: Crossroad, 1976); and *Plurality and Ambiguity: Hermeneutics, Religion, Hope* (San Francisco: Harper and Row, 1987).

[33]De Mesa and Wostyn, *Doing Theology*, 86.

[34]I owe the idea of a "basic religious proposal" to my friend Timothy R. Stinnett. See his "The Logic of 'Decisiveness' and Religious Dialogue," unpublished manuscript.

[35]See Mark L. Taylor, *God Is Love: A Study in the Theology of Karl Rahner* (Atlanta: Scholars Press, 1986).

[36]Schreiter, *Constructing Local Theologies*, 117-121.

[37]Ibid., 119.

[38]Michael H. Taylor, "People at Work," in Amirtham and Pobee, *Theology by the People*, 124.

[39]See Conn, *Eternal Word and Changing Worlds*, 224-260; and Francis George, "The Process of Inculturation: Steps, Rules, Problems," *Kerygma*, 22, 1 (1988): 93-113.

[40]See José M. de Mesa, *In Solidarity with the Culture: Studies in Theological Re-rooting*, Maryhill Studies 4 (Quezon City: Maryhill School of Theology, 1987), especially 1-42; and *Inculturation as Pilgrimage*, First Annual Louis J. Luzbetak, SVD, Lecture on Mission and Culture (Chicago: CCGM Publications, 2001).

[41]Ibid., 30-32.

[42]John S. Pobee, *Toward an African Theology* (Nashville: Abingdon, 1979), 44.

[43]Chang Tarya, "Korean Christmas Crib," *Inculturation*, 2, 1 (Spring, 1987): 39, as quoted in Sean Dwan, "Theological Notes on Inculturation," *Inculturation*, 3, 1 (Spring, 1988): 32.

[44]See SVD Working Group, "Secularization, Dialogue, and Inculturation: Mission towards the Millennium and Beyond," *Sedos Bulletin*, 23, 8 (September 15, 1991): 240-246; William Jenkinson and Helene O'Sullivan, eds., *Trends in Mission: Toward the Third Millennium* (Maryknoll, NY: Orbis Books, 1991), 118-166; Michael Amaladoss, "Modernity: The Indian Experience," in *Making All Things New: Dialogue, Pluralism, and Evangelization in Asia* (Maryknoll, NY: Orbis Books, 1990), 131-141.

[45]Theological Education Fund, *Ministry in Context: The Third Mandate Programme of the Theological Education Fund (1970-1977)* (Bromley, Kent: New Life Press, 1972); see also Shoke Coe, "Contextualizing Theology," in Gerald H. Anderson and Thomas F. Stransky, eds., *Mission Trends No. 3: Third World Theologies* (New York: Paulist Press, and Grand Rapids: Eerdmans, 1976), 19-24; and William P. Russell, *Contextualization: Origins, Meaning, and Implications* (Rome: Pontificia Studiorum Universitas a S. Thoma Aquinate in Urbe, 1995).

[46]Aylward Shorter, *Toward a Theology of Inculturation* (Maryknoll, NY: Orbis Books, 1988), 10-11; Peter Schineller, *A Handbook on Inculturation* (Mahwah, NJ: Paulist Press, 1990), 14-27; Gerald Arbuckle, *Earthing the Gospel* (Maryknoll, NY: Orbis Books, 1990). Shorter prefers the term *inculturation*, but it seems to me that his usage implies a model rather than a general term. Inculturation for him is the *insertion* of faith *into* culture. As he himself admits, *contextualization* is a wider term. Arbuckle speaks of *contextualization* as more

superficial than *inculturation*, and as allied to the idea of adaptation. He does not seem to be familiar with the standard definition given by the Theological Education Fund in 1972, although he cites it from a secondary source (see Arbuckle, p. 21).

[47]*FABC Newsletter*, April, 1979.

[48]Ibid.

3. THE NOTION AND USE OF MODELS

[1]Peter Schineller, "Christ and the Church: A Spectrum of Views," *Theological Studies*, 37, 4 (December, 1976): 545-566. This article also appears in a book version of the issue: Walter Burghardt and William Thompson, eds., *Why the Church?* (Ramsey, NJ: Paulist Press, 1977), 3-22.

[2]Thomas F. O'Meara, "Philosophical Models in Ecclesiology," *Theological Studies*, 38, 1 (March, 1978): 3-21.

[3]David Tracy, *Blessed Rage for Order: The New Pluralism in Theology* (New York: Seabury, 1975), 22-42; and Sallie McFague, *Models of God: Theology for an Ecological, Nuclear Age* (Philadelphia: Fortress Press, 1987). See Raymond Collins, *Models of Theological Reflection* (Lanham, MD: University Press of America, 1984); John F. O'Grady, *Models of Jesus* (Garden City, NY: Doubleday, 1981); David J. Hesselgrave and Edward Rommen, *Contextualization: Meanings, Methods, and Models* (Grand Rapids: Baker, 1989). Gerald Arbuckle presents four models of culture in *Earthing the Gospel* (Maryknoll, NY: Orbis Books, 1990), 44-61.

[4]Avery Dulles, *Models of the Church* (Garden City, NY: Doubleday Image Books, 1978). The hardcover edition was published in 1974.

[5]Avery Dulles, *Models of Revelation* (New York: Doubleday, 1983).

[6]H. Richard Niebuhr, *Christ and Culture* (New York: Harper Torchbooks, 1975), xii.

[7]Ian G. Barbour, *Myths, Models, and Paradigms: A Comparative Study in Science and Religion* (New York: Harper and Row, 1974); Ian T. Ramsey, *Models and Mystery* (London: Oxford University Press, 1964); Max Black, *Models and Metaphors* (Ithaca, NY: Cornell University Press, 1962), especially 219-242.

[8]See Dulles, *Models of the Church*, 28ff.

[9]Paul Ricoeur, *The Symbolism of Evil* (Boston: Beacon Press, 1967), 347-357.

[10]Barbour, *Myths, Models, and Paradigms*, 29-30. Max Black speaks of scale models, analogue models, and mathematical models before settling on theoretical models, which he explains ultimately in terms of archetypes; see *Models and Metaphors*, 239-243. Ramsey equates analogue models with disclosure models, but his use of the term *disclosure model* seems closer to Black's use of *theoretical model*; *Models and Mystery*, 9-11. See also M. Hesse, "Models and Analogy in Science," in P. Edwards, ed., *The Encyclopedia of Philosophy*, vol. 5 (New York: Macmillan Co. and Free Press, 1967), 354-359.

[11]Barbour, *Myths, Models, and Paradigms*, 6.

[12]Dulles, *Models of Revelation*, 30.

[13]Barbour, *Myths, Models, and Paradigms*, 7.

[14]Sallie McFague, *Metaphorical Theology: Models of God in Religious Language* (Philadelphia: Fortress, 1982), 74-75.

[15]Barbour, *Myths, Models, and Paradigms*, 29-48.

[16]Schineller, "Christ and the Church": 3.

[17]See McFague, *Metaphorical Theology*, 81; and Thomas Kuhn, *The Structure of Scientific Revolutions* (Chicago: University of Chicago Press, 1970), 144-159.

[18]Barbour, *Myths, Models, and Paradigms*, 7.

[19]This concern, Black points out, was the basis for P. Duhem's critique of the use of models. Black, *Models and Metaphors*, 233-235; and Ramsey, *Models and Mystery*, 18-19.

[20]Niels Bohr, *Atomic Theory and the Description of Nature* (Cambridge: Cambridge University Press, 1934), 96. Quoted in Barbour, *Myths, Models, and Paradigms*, 75.

[21]M. Hesse in D. Bohm, et al., *Quanta and Reality* (New York: World Publishing Company, 1964), 57. Quoted in Barbour, *Myths, Models, and Paradigms*, 75.

[22]Dulles, *Models of the Church*, 32.

[23]Dulles, *Models of Revelation*, 34-35.

[24]Francis Crick, paraphrased in G. Johnson, "Two Sides to Every Science Story," *New York Times Book Review* (April 9, 1989): 41.

[25]Another helpful map is found in Hesselgrave and Rommen, *Contextualization*, 148, 151, and 157. The reader will notice, however, that the authors work with exclusive and not complementary models of contextualization.

[26]Darrell Whiteman, "Contextualization: The Theory, the Gap, the Challenge," *International Bulletin of Missionary Research*, 21, 1 (1997): 3.

[27]I would disagree, therefore, with the critique of Doug Priest in his *Doing Theology with the Maasai* (Pasadena, CA: William Carey Library, 1990), who says that these models are reductionistic.

4. THE TRANSLATION MODEL

[1]Robert J. Schreiter, *Constructing Local Theologies* (Maryknoll, NY: Orbis Books, 1985), 7.

[2]See Mark R. Francis, "Adaptation, Liturgical," in *New Dictionary of Sacramental Worship* (Collegeville, MN: Michael Glazier/Liturgical Press, 1990), 14-25. Francis's understanding of "adaptation," however, is quite nuanced. A careful reading of the documents of Vatican II, especially that of the Constitution on the Liturgy, 37, "will reveal that the term 'adaptation' when applied to the liturgy variously refers to concepts borrowed from the social sciences such as 'localization,' 'acculturation,' 'contextualization,' 'indigenization,' and 'inculturation,' as well as the more theological expression 'incarnation.' " In his *Liturgy in a Multicultural Community* (Collegeville, MN: Liturgical Press, 1991), Francis is quite clear that a mere *translation* of liturgy into cultural forms is inadequate (pp. 16-17). See also Mark Francis's latest work, *Shape a Circle Ever Wider: Liturgical Inculturation in the United States* (Chicago: Liturgical Training Publications, 2000).

[3]Pope John Paul II, *Redemptoris Missio* (RM) (Washington, DC: United States Catholic Conference, 1991), 25.

[4]Daniel von Allmen, "The Birth of Theology," in C. Kraft and T. Wisley, eds., *Readings in Dynamic Indigeneity* (Pasadena: William Carey Library, 1979), 33-35.

[5]Charles H. Kraft, *Christianity in Culture: A Study in Dynamic Biblical Theologizing in Cross-Cultural Perspective* (Maryknoll, NY: Orbis Books, 1979), 295-296.

[6]Ibid., 264.

[7]Ibid., 265.

[8]Ibid., 269ff.

[9]Eugene A. Nida and Charles R. Taber, *The Theory and Practice of Translation* (Leiden: Brill, 1969), 24. Quoted in Kraft, *Christianity in Culture*, 271.

[10]N. O. Osborn, "Examples from the Ilokano Popular Version Bible," *Ilocos Review*, 14 (1982): 28-29. Citing Nida and Taber, Kraft gives several examples of dynamic equivalent translations of the Greek *soma* (body), *sarx* (flesh), and *dikaioo* (justify). See Kraft, *Christianity in Culture*, 266-67.

[11]Kraft, *Christianity in Culture*, 297. Kraft's emphasis.

[12]See Krikor Haleblian, "The Problem of Contextualization," *Missiology: An International Review*, XI, 1 (January, 1983): 101-102.

[13]Ibid., 101.

[14]Max Stackhouse, *Apologia: Contextualization, Globalization, and Mission in Theological Education* (Grand Rapids: Eerdmans, 1988), 182.

[15]Ibid., 170; see 170-182.

[16]Robert McAfee Brown, "The Rootedness of All Theology: Context Affects Content," *Christianity in Crisis*, 37 (July 18, 1977): 170-174.

[17]Bruce Fleming, *Contextualization of Theology: An Evangelical Assessment* (Pasadena: William Carey Library, 1980), 66.

[18]Morris A. Inch, *Doing Theology across Cultures* (Grand Rapids: Baker, 1982); and *Making the Good News Relevant* (Nashville: Thomas Nelson, 1986).

[19]Byang Kato, quoted in Fleming, *Contextualization of Theology*, 62.

[20]"Culture must always be tested and judged by Scripture. ... The Gospel does not presuppose the superiority of any culture to another, but evaluates all cultures according to its own criteria of truth and righteousness and insists on moral absolutes in every culture." *The Lausanne Covenant*, 10, in Gerald H. Anderson and Thomas F. Stransky, eds., *Mission Trends No. 2: Evangelization* (New York: Paulist Press, and Grand Rapids: Eerdmans, 1975), 245. "We must understand the context in order to address it, but the context must not be allowed to distort the Gospel." *Manila Manifesto,* 10, in *Proclaim Christ until He Comes* (Lausanne Conference on World Evangelism, 1989), 35. Both of these documents can also be found in James A. Scherer and Stephen B. Bevans, eds., *New Directions in Mission and Evangelization 1: Basic Statements 1974-1991* (Maryknoll, NY: Orbis Books, 1992).

[21]"Pope John's Opening Speech to the Council," in W. M. Abbot, ed., *The Documents of Vatican II* (New York: Herder and Herder/Association Press, 1966), 715.

[22]Charles Kraft, for example, tries to speak of revelation in other terms, and his position has been criticized strongly by other evangelicals. See Kraft, *Christianity in Culture*, 178-187; and D. Hesselgrave and E. Rommen, *Contextualization: Meanings, Methods, and Models* (Grand Rapids: Baker Book House, 1989), 59-69.

[23]So the wonderfully expressive title of Harvie Conn. See *Eternal Word and Changing Worlds: Theology, Anthropology, and Mission in Trialogue* (Grand Rapids: Zondervan, 1984).

[24]Schreiter, *Constructing Local Theologies*, 8.

[25]See, for instance, Eugene Hillman, *Polygamy Reconsidered: African Plural Marriages and the Christian Churches* (Maryknoll, NY: Orbis Books, 1975).

[26]Jeffrey Hopper, *Understanding Modern Theology II: Reinterpreting Christian Faith for Changing Worlds* (Philadelphia: Fortress, 1987), 25.

[27]Haleblian, "The Problem of Contextualization": 102.

[28]Sallie McFague, *Models of God: Theology for an Ecological, Nuclear Age* (Philadelphia: Fortress, 1987), 30.

[29]Vinay Samuel and Chris Sugden, eds., *Sharing Jesus in the Two Thirds World* (Grand Rapids: Eerdmans, 1983); Bong Rin Ro and R. Eschenauer, eds., *The Bible and Theology in Asian Contexts: An Evangelical Perspective on Asian Theology* (Taichung, Taiwan: Asia Theological Association, 1984); Louis J. Luzbetak, *The Church and Cultures: New Perspectives in Missiological Anthropology* (Maryknoll, NY: Orbis Books, 1988), 79. Luzbetak refers here to his position in the earlier (1963) version of his book.

[30]David J. Hesselgrave, "Counselling: Good Faith Not Enough," *Evangelical Missions Quarterly*, 21, 2 (April, 1985): 186-188; "Culture-Sensitive Counselling and the Christian

Mission," *International Bulletin of Missionary Research*, 10, 3 (July, 1986): 109-113; "Christian Communication and Religious Pluralism: Capitalizing on Differences," *Missiology: An International Review*, XVIII, 2 (April, 1990): 131-138.

[31]David J. Hesselgrave, ed., *Theology and Mission* (Grand Rapids: Baker, 1978); *Dynamic Religious Movements: Case Studies in Growing Religious Movements in Various Cultures* (Grand Rapids: Baker, 1978).

[32]David J. Hesselgrave, *Communicating Christ Cross-Culturally: An Introduction to Missionary Communication* (Grand Rapids: Zondervan, 1978); *Planting Churches Cross-Culturally: A Guide for Home and Foreign Missions* (Grand Rapids: Baker, 1980); *Counseling Cross-Culturally: An Introduction to Theory and Practice for Christians* (Grand Rapids: Baker, 1984).

[33]Hesselgrave and Rommen, *Contextualization*.

[34]"Contextualization . . . is not simply nice. It is necessary" (Hesselgrave, *Communicating Christ Cross-Culturally*, 85); "contextualization is more than a neologism, it is a necessity" (Hesselgrave and Rommen, *Contextualization*, xi).

[35]Hesselgrave, *Communicating Christ Cross-Culturally*, 85; *Planting Churches Cross-Culturally*, 207; Hesselgrave and Rommen, *Contextualization*, 3-26.

[36]Hesselgrave, *Communicating Christ Cross-Culturally*, 69.

[37]Ibid., 19-21; Hesselgrave and Rommen, *Contextualization*, 1.

[38]Hesselgrave, *Communicating Christ Cross-Culturally*, 29.

[39]Hesselgrave, *Planting Churches Cross-Culturally*, 208.

[40]Hesselgrave, *Communicating Christ Cross-Culturally*, 29, 44.

[41]Hesselgrave, *Planting Churches Cross-Culturally*, 202.

[42]Ibid., 208-209; the quotation is from Bruce Nicholls, "Theological Education and Evangelization," in J. D. Douglas, ed., *Let the World Hear His Voice* (Minneapolis, MN: World Wide Publications, 1975). In reference to the ideas immediately preceding the quotation, see Hesselgrave, *Counseling Cross-Culturally*, 173-174, 227-233.

[43]Hesselgrave, *Communicating Christ Cross-Culturally*, 86. For Hesselgrave's whole development, see 67-86. The reference to E. Nida is *Message and Mission: The Communication of Christian Faith* (New York: Harper and Row, 1960), 46-48. The three-culture model is used again in *Counseling Cross-Culturally*, 176. Here Hesselgrave describes the situation of a U. S. American counseling a Vietnamese refugee: "Our counsellor friend must have an understanding of at least three very different views of what humankind and the world really are—the Christian (biblical), the naturalistic (Western secular), and the Hindu-Buddhistic (Vietnamese version). Without a thoroughgoing and biblical theology, his secular training may influence him to offer counseling that is deficient or even heretical from a Christian point of view. Without an understanding of Vietnamese Buddhism, his counselling may be ineffective from a practical point of view." This idea appears again in Hesselgrave and Rommen, *Contextualization*, 200.

[44]Hesselgrave and Rommen, *Contextualization*, 198.

[45]What I have summarized here is found developed in Hesselgrave, *Communicating Christ Cross-Culturally*, 130-196.

[46]Ibid., 76-77 (the examples are from E. Nida, *God's Word in Human Language* [New York: Harper and Row, 1952], 45-46); Hesselgrave, *Planting Churches Cross-Culturally*, 207-208; *Counseling Cross-Culturally*, 176-177. See the title of Part 4 of Hesselgrave and Rommen, *Contextualization*: "Authentic and Relevant Contextualization: Some Proposals," 197-257.

[47]Hesselgrave and Rommen, *Contextualization*, 222-227.

[48]Ibid., 222.

[49]See ibid., 223-224. Eight reasons are given in all; see 224.

[50]Ibid., 227.

[51]Ibid., 228-237. The quotation is from 228. See Bruce J. Nicholls, *Contextualization: A Theology of Gospel and Culture* (Downers Grove, IL: Inter-Varsity, 1979), 54.

[52]Hesselgrave and Rommen, *Contextualization*, 230. Niles's word is *kamma*.

[53]Ibid., 233.

[54]Ibid., 235.

[55]The letters "DS" followed by a number or numbers refer to the collection of official Roman documents edited originally by H. Denzinger ("D") in the nineteenth century, and edited and revised in the 1960s by A. Schönmetzer ("S"): *Enchiridion Symbolorum Definitionum et Declarationum de Rebus Fidei et Morum* (Barcelona, Freiburg, Rome: Herder, 1976). I am referring to the numbering of the thirty-sixth edition.

[56]See Aylward Shorter, *Toward a Theology of Inculturation* (Maryknoll, NY: Orbis Books, 1988), 164-236; Hervé Carrier, *Gospel Message and Human Cultures: From Leo XIII to John Paul II* (Pittsburgh: Duquesne University Press, 1989), 14-28; Francis, *Liturgy in a Multicultural Community*, 13-14.

[57]Paul VI, *Evangelii Nuntiandi* (EN), 20. See also J. Snijders, "*Evangelii Nuntiandi*: The Movement of Minds," *Clergy Review*, 62: 170-175.

[58]Shorter, *Toward a Theology of Inculturation*, 223.

[59]See Karol Wojtyla, *The Acting Person*, A. Potocki, trans. (Dordrecht, Holland; Boston; London: D. Reidel, 1979); see also R. Modras, "A Man of Contradictions? The Early Writings of Karol Wojtyla," in Hans Küng and Leonard Swidler, eds., *The Church in Anguish: Has the Vatican Betrayed Vatican II?* (San Francisco: Harper and Row, 1986), 39-51.

[60]The number of documents and discourses in which the pope deals with the question of culture—especially the dialogue between faith and culture—are too numerous to list here. I will cite a number of them in this brief summary of the pope's approach to contextualization, but there are many, many more. Several of the pope's writings are seminal, however, and should be mentioned: *Catechesi Tradendae* (CT 1979), 53; *Slavorum Apostoli* (SA 1985), 9-11, 18-20; and RM 52-54. For the relevant sections of these texts, see Scherer and Bevans, *New Directions 1*. For other citations of texts, see Carrier, *Gospel Message and Human Cultures*, 75-133; and Shorter, *Toward a Theology of Inculturation*, 222-38. Since 1992, when the first edition of this book was published, the pope has continued to speak and write about the interaction of faith and culture and about the role of experience in the theological process. See, for example, his encyclicals *Evangelium Vitae* (Washington, DC: United States Catholic Conference, 1995) and *Fides et Ratio* (http://www.vatican.va/holy_father/...c 15101998 fides-et-ratio-en.shtml.

[61]*L'Osservatore Romano*, June 28, 1982: 1-8, quoted in Shorter, *Toward a Theology of Inculturation*, 230.

[62]Carrier, *Gospel Message and Human Culture*, ix; see John Paul II, "Faith and Culture," *Origins*, 18, 3 (June 2, 1988), 5: 36; RM 52. See also Francis George, *Inculturation and Ecclesial Communion: Culture and Church in the Teaching of Pope John Paul II* (Rome: Urbaniana University Press, 1990).

[63]"Faith and Culture," 6: 36.

[64]Shorter, *Toward a Theology of Inculturation*, 223; 230-231. This is borne out in John Paul's 1995 encyclical *Evangelium Vitae*, in which he distinguished between the "Gospel of life" and the "culture of death." Here the pope employs what I call the countercultural model of contextual theologizing (see Chapter 9) rather than the translation model, which I am illustrating here.

[65]See, for instance, CT 53.

[66]Dennis Doyle, "Inculturation and the Interpretation of Vatican II in Recent Papal Documents." This is a talk given at the 1991 Annual Convention of the College Theology Society in Chicago.

[67]RM 52, quoting the Final Document of the Extraordinary Synod of 1985, II, D, 4.

[68]RM 52.

[69]John Paul II, "Pope John Paul II on 'African Theology,' " *African Ecclesial Review*, 25, 5 (October, 1983): 317. On the idea of a supracultural, supracontextual, unchanging gospel message, see "Faith and Culture," 6: 36; "Carry the Authentic Gospel to African Culture," *The Pope Speaks*, 25, 4 (1980): 299.

[70]"Pope John Paul II on 'African Theology' ": 317.

[71]"Universality and Diversity," speech at a general audience on September 27, 1989, *The Pope Speaks*, 35, 1 (1990): 44.

[72]RM 54.

[73]"Carry the Authentic Gospel to the African Culture": 301; see RM 54.

[74]John Paul II, "Faith and Culture Elevate Work," address to participants of the first national congress of the Ecclesial Movement of Cultural Commitment, January 16, 1982, *The Pope Speaks*, 27, 2 (1982): 157.

[75]"Carry the Authentic Gospel to the African Culture": 300.

[76]Ibid.

[77]John Paul II, "Father Matteo Ricci: Bridge to China," address delivered by the pope to participants of the concluding session of the International Ricci Studies Congress, October 25, 1982, *The Pope Speaks*, 28, 2 (1983): 101.

[78]Ibid.: 99.

[79]Ibid.: 100.

[80]Ibid.: 101.

[81]Ibid.: 100.

[82]SA 11.

[83]Ibid.

[84]Ibid., 16.

[85]Ibid., 13.

[86]Shorter, *Toward a Theology of Inculturation*, 232.

[87]Ibid., 233.

5. THE ANTHROPOLOGICAL MODEL

[1]See M. Eugene Boring's interpretation of Mt 15:21-28 in *The New Interpreter's Bible*. Although he does not fully accept Sharon Ringe's feminist interpretation of the passage, he nevertheless reflects that "the story invites readers to place themselves in the role of the other, to struggle not only with God but also with our own perceptions of the other, and pronounces such enduring struggle to be of great faith" (Leander Keck et al., eds., *The New Interpreter's Bible*, vol. 8, New Testament articles, Matthew, Mark [Nashville: Abingdon Press, 1995], 338). In the same volume, in her commentary on Mk 7:24-30, Pheme Perkins suggests that "this passage also reminds pastors, teachers, and others in positions of authority how to lose an argument. When Jesus recognizes that the woman's argument is stronger than his own, he grants her petition" (ibid., 611). Perkins also points out that the passage should challenge us to reflect on how we regard and treat persons from other ethnic or religious backgrounds.

[2]See Justin Martyr, *I Apology*, 46:1-4; *II Apology*, 7 (8): 1-4, 10:1-3, 13:3-4. Clement of Alexandria, *Stromata*, I, 19, 91-94. See also Kwame Bediako, *Theology and Identity: The*

Impact of Culture upon Christian Thought in the Second Century and Modern Africa (Oxford: Regnum Books, 1992), 41-48; and Andrew F. Walls, "Old Athens and New Jerusalem: Some Signposts for Christian Scholarship in the Early History of Mission Studies," *International Bulletin of Missionary Research*, 21, 4 (October, 1997): 148-149.

[3]*Ad Gentes* (AG) 11. This and other church documents tend to be cautious in their treatment of the interaction between faith and culture (see, for example, AG 3 and Paul VI's *Evangelii Nuntiandi*, 20 and 53). Nevertheless, the passage quoted points to the fact that God's grace is present *already* in other religions and cultures, and this has strong implications for theological method. Rather than culture being a malleable *vehicle* for a never-changing and supracultural message, the anthropological model is based on the fact that culture and other religious ways are already expressions of God's loving and healing presence. Rather than the gospel coming in to transform a culture, these documents witness to the role of the gospel as *illuminating what is already there*.

[4]"Final Report of CWME Orthodox Advisory Group, Boston 1990," 11. In James A. Scherer and Stephen B. Bevans, eds., *New Directions in Mission and Evangelization 1: Basic Statements 1974-1991* (Maryknoll, NY: Orbis Books, 1992), 244.

[5]Robert J. Schreiter, *Constructing Local Theologies* (Maryknoll, NY: Orbis Books, 1985), 13-15.

[6]Aylward Shorter, *Toward a Theology of Inculturation* (Maryknoll, NY: Orbis Books, 1988). See especially the discussion of terms on pp. 3-16. See also Simon Smith, "The Future of Mission," remarks addressed to Entraide Missionaire Congress, Montreal, September 11, 1983, *African Ecclesial Review*, 27, 2 (April, 1985): 72-79.

[7]This passage appears in Warren's preface to the seven books in the Christian Presence Series (London: SCM Press, 1959-1966), which included books by Kenneth Cragg, George Appleton, Raymond Hammer, John V. Taylor, William Stewart, Martin Jarrett-Kerr, and Peter Schneider. Each book in the series "began with a general introduction . . . at the end of which was a comment on that particular volume" (Graham Kings, *Christianity Connected: Hindus, Muslims and the World in the Letters of Max Warren and Roger Hooker* [Utrecht, The Netherlands: Boekencentrum, 2002], 123). See, for example, the preface to John V. Taylor, *The Primal Vision* (London: SCM Press, 1963), 10.

[8]Robert T. Rush, "From Pearl Merchant to Treasure Hunter: The Missionary Yesterday and Today," *Catholic Mind* (September, 1978): 6-10. See Stephen Bevans, "Seeing Mission through Images," *Missiology: An International Review*, 19, 1 (January, 1991): 45-57.

[9]Rush, "From Pearl Merchant to Treasure Hunter": 8.

[10]This is basically the idea of Karl Rahner regarding "anonymous Christianity." It is perhaps stated more radically, however, in Raimon Pannikar's revised edition of *The Unknown Christ of Hinduism* (Maryknoll, NY: Orbis Books, 1981).

[11]See Stephen Bevans, "Reaching for Fidelity: Roman Catholic Theology Today," in Thomas McComiskey and John Woodbridge, eds., *Doing Theology in Today's World* (Grand Rapids: Zondervan, 1989), 312-338.

[12]Smith, "The Future of Mission": 73.

[13]Ibid.

[14]Ibid.

[15]Robert McAfee Brown, "The Rootedness of All Theology: Context Affects Content," *Christianity and Crisis*, 37 (July 18, 1977): 170-174.

[16]Leonardo N. Mercado, *Elements of Filipino Theology* (Tacloban City: Divine Word University Publications, 1975), 15.

[17]Ibid., 12; see also Leonardo N. Mercado, "Notes on Christ and Local Community in Philippine Context," *Verbum SVD*, 21, 3/4 (1980): 305; and *Doing Filipino Theology*

(Manila: Divine Word Publications, 1997), 8

[18]Mercado, *Elements of Filipino Theology*, 13.

[19]Leonardo N. Mercado, "Filipino Thought," *Philippine Studies*, 20, 2 (1972): 210-211.

[20]Ibid.: 54-58; cf. Mercado, *Elements of Filipino Philosophy*, Chapter 5.

[21]Mercado, "Notes on Christ": 303-315.

[22]See Rosemary Radford Ruether, *Sexism and God-Talk: Toward a Feminist Theology*, tenth anniversary edition (Boston: Beacon Press, 1993), 12-46.

[23]Mercado, "Filipino Thought": 207-211.

[24]Dionisio M. Miranda, *Loob: The Filipino Within* (Manila: Divine Word Publications, 1989); see also his *Pagkamakatao* (Manila: Divine Word Publications, 1987); although I would not classify him within this model (see chapter 7), José de Mesa also provides an analysis of the meaning of *loob* in his *In Solidarity with the Culture: Studies in Theological Re-rooting*, Maryhill Studies 4 (Quezon City: Maryhill School of Theology, 1987), 43-74; and *Inculturation as Pilgrimage*, First Annual Louis J. Luzbetak, SVD, Lecture on Mission and Culture (Chicago: CCGM Publications, 2001).

[25]"East Asian Bishops' Conferences, Major Seminaries Meeting, Conclusions and Recommendations," published in the Hong Kong *Sunday Examiner*, 20 December, 1974: 9. Quoted in Mercado, *Elements of Filipino Theology*, 7.

[26]Schreiter, *Constructing Local Theologies*, 93-94.

[27]Jon P. Kirby, SVD, "The Non-conversion of the Anufo of Northern Ghana," *Mission Studies*, II, 2 (1985): 24. See also Jon P. Kirby and Vincent Boi-Nai, "Ghana: Popular Catholicism in Ghana," in Thomas Bamat and Jean-Paul Wiest, eds., *Popular Catholicism in a World Church: Seven Case Studies in Inculturation* (Maryknoll, NY: Orbis Books, 1999), 119-156.

[28]Schreiter, *Constructing Local Theologies*, 14.

[29]Mercado, *Elements of Filipino Theology*, 15.

[30]An example of this is Mercado's article: "Notes on Christ" and his more recent *Doing Filipino Theology*.

[31]Shorter, *Toward a Theology of Inculturation*, 6-8.

[32]See Stephen Bevans, "A Local Theology in a World Church: Some U. S. Contributions to Systematic Theology," *New Theology Review*, 1, 1 (February, 1988): 72-92. The thesis of this article is that a sense of global consciousness and dialogue is what makes U. S. American theology a truly contextual theology. See also Stephen Bevans, "Partner and Prophet: The Church and Globalization," in Heribert Bettscheider, ed., *Reflecting Mission, Practicing Mission* (Nettetal, Germany: Steyler Verlag, 2001), 91-110; and Robert J. Schreiter, *The New Catholicity: Theology between the Global and the Local* (Maryknoll, NY: Orbis Books, 1997).

[33]James H. Cone, *Black Theology and Black Power* (San Francisco: Harper and Row, 1969; twentieth anniversary edition, 1989); *A Black Theology of Liberation* (New York: Lippincott, 1970; second edition, Marykoll, NY: Orbis Books, 1986; twentieth anniversary edition, Maryknoll, NY: Orbis Books, 1990). Among James Cone's other works are *The Spirituals and the Blues* (New York: Seabury, 1972); *God of the Oppressed* (New York: Seabury, 1975); *My Soul Looks Back* (Maryknoll, NY: Orbis Books, 1986); and *Malcolm and Martin and America: A Dream or a Nightmare?* (Maryknoll, NY: Orbis Books, 1991).

[34]Cecil Cone, *The Identity Crisis in Black Theology* (Nashville: AMEC, 1975), 18. The idea that black religion is the only appropriate point of departure for the construction of a black theology is Cecil Cone's thesis in the book, originally written as his doctoral disseration at Emory University in Atlanta, Georgia.

[35]Ibid., 32. Cone refers to C. H. Johnson, *God Struck Me Dead: Religious Conversion*

Experiences and Autobiographies of Ex-Slaves (Philadelphia: Pilgrim Press, 1969), vii-viii. See also Dwight N. Hopkins, *Down, Up, and Over: Slave Religion and Black Theology* (Minneapolis, MN: Fortress Press, 2000).

[36]Robert E. Hood, "Karl Barth's Christological Basis for the State and Political Praxis," *Scottish Journal of Theology*, 33, 3 (1980): 223-238; "Role of Black Religion in Political Change: The Haitian Revolution and Voodoo," *Journal of the Interdenominational Theological Center*, 9, 1 (Fall, 1981): 45-69; "From a Headstart to a Deadstart: The Historical Bases for Black Indifference toward the Episcopal Church 1800-1860," *Historical Magazine of the Protestant Episcopal Church*, 51 (1982): 269-296; "Can the Prayer Book Be Comprehensive for All Cultures?" *Anglican Theological Review*, 66, 3 (July, 1984): 269-282; "A Theological Framework for an Afro-Anglican Communion," *Journal of Religious Thought*, 44 (Summer-Fall, 1987): 61-63; "Does the Episcopal Church Have Social Teachings?" *Anglican Theological Review*, 70 (January, 1988): 62-68.

[37]Robert E. Hood, *Contemporary Political Orders and Christ: Karl Barth's Christology and Political Praxis* (Allison Park, PA: Pickwick Publications, 1985); *Must God Remain Greek? Afro Cultures and God-Talk* (Minneapolis: Fortress, 1990); *Begrimed and Black: Christian Traditions on Blacks and Blackness* (Minneapolis, MN: Fortress Press, 1994).

[38]Hood, "A Theological Framework for an Afro-Anglican Communion": 61.

[39]Ibid.: 62.

[40]Ibid.: 63.

[41]Hood, *Must God Remain Greek?* 250.

[42]Hood, "Can the Prayer Book Be Comprehensive for All Cultures?"; "Role of Black Religion in Political Change"; and *Must God Remain Greek?* 245-253.

[43]Hood, *Must God Remain Greek?* 184.

[44]Ibid., 186.

[45]Ibid., 188.

[46]Ibid.

[47]Ibid. Hood also develops this argument, at greater length, in his article "Role of Black Religion in Political Change": 63-69.

[48]Hood, *Must God Remain Greek?* 191.

[49]Ibid., 197-98.

[50]Ibid., 199.

[51]Ibid., 201-202.

[52]Vincent J. Donovan, *Christianity Rediscovered* (Chicago: Fides/Claretian, 1978; second edition, Maryknoll, NY: Orbis Books, 1982).

[53]Vincent J. Donovan, *The Church in the Midst of Creation* (Maryknoll, NY: Orbis Books, 1982). Donovan's articles include "The Naked Gospel: Stamping Out Ready-to-Wear Christianity" (interview), *U. S. Catholic*, 46, 6 (June, 1981): 24-31; "The Vatican II Church: Who Says the West Is Better?" *U. S. Catholic*, 46, 9 (September, 1981): 34-35; "Response to Reflections on *Christianity Rediscovered,*" *Missiology: An International Review*, 18, 3 (July, 1990): 276-278; "Response to Avery Dulles," in Stephen Bevans and Roger Schroeder, eds., *Word Remembered, Word Proclaimed: Selected Papers from Symposia Celebrating the SVD Centennial in North America* (Nettetal, Germany: Steyler Verlag, 1997), 38-43.

[54]Donovan, *Christianity Rediscovered*, vii; *The Church in the Midst of Creation*, 26.

[55]Donovan, *Christianity Rediscovered*, 30. Cf. Titus Pressler, "*Christianity Rediscovered*: A Reflection on Vincent Donovan's Contribution to Missiology," *Missiology: An International Review*, 18, 3 (July, 1990): 272.

[56]Donovan, *The Church in the Midst of Creation*, 85.

[57]See ibid., 127; Donovan, "The Naked Gospel": 26.

[58]Donovan, *The Church in the Midst of Creation*, 143; see another more Christianly explicit formulation of the message on 144.

[59]Donovan, "The Naked Gospel": 26; "The Vatican III Church": 35; *The Church in the Midst of Creation*, 119.

[60]Donovan, *Christianity Rediscovered*, 58. A little further on, Donovan elaborates: "Goodness and kindness and holiness and grace and divine presence and creative power and salvation were here before I got here. Even the fuller understanding of God's revelation to man, of the gospel, of the salvific act that had been accomplished once and for all for the human race was here before I got here. My role as a herald of that gospel, as a messenger of the news of what had already happened in the world, as the person whose task it was to point to 'the one who had stood in their midst whom they did not recognize' was only a small part of the mission of God to the world" (63-64).

[61]Donovan, *The Church in the Midst of Creation*, 96.

[62]Ibid., 119.

[63]Donovan, "The Naked Gospel": 26.

[64]See Donovan, *Christianity Rediscovered*, 41-64.

[65]Ibid., 30-31.

[66]See ibid., 119-128.

[67]Ibid., 125.

[68]Ibid., 127. Donovan admits that there was the possibility that the people would have rejected bread and wine as the eucharistic elements in favor of, perhaps, meat and honey beer. As it happened, however, the people showed no reluctance in accepting the elements common to the whole church. This, as he said some years ago at a lecture that I attended, was deliberate on the people's part. It gave them a sense of connection with the wider, catholic church.

[69]In the first edition of this book, I raised the question in the text whether the story was fictional or factual. In a subsequent conversation, Fr. Donovan assured me that the story was true, although the people in the story remained anonymous.

[70]Donovan, *The Church in the Midst of Creation*, 146.

[71]Ibid., 148.

[72]Ibid., 149-50.

6. THE PRAXIS MODEL

[1]Virginia Fabella, ed., *Asia's Struggle for Full Humanity* (Maryknoll, NY: Orbis Books, 1980), 4.

[2]See James D. Whitehead and Evelyn Eaton Whitehead, *Method in Ministry: Theological Reflection and Christian Ministry*, revised edition (Kansas City: Sheed and Ward, 1995); Don S. Browning, *A Fundamental Practical Theology: Descriptive and Strategic Proposals* (Minneapolis, MN: Augsburg Fortress, 1991); Randy L. Maddox, "The Recovery of Theology as a Practical Discipline," *Theological Studies*, 51, 4 (December, 1990): 650-672; James N. Poling and Donald E. Miller, *Foundations for a Practical Theology of Ministry* (Nashville: Abingdon Press, 1985); Thomas H. Groome, *Sharing Faith: A Comprehensive Approach to Religious Education and Pastoral Ministry—the Way of Shared Praxis* (San Francisco: HarperCollins, 1991); Carol Lakey Hess, "Becoming Mid-wives to Justice: A Feminist Approach to Practical Theology," in Denise Ackermann and Riet Bons-Storm, eds., *Liberating Faith Practice: Feminist Practical Theologies in Context* (Leuven, Belgium: Peeters, 1998), 51-74; J. B. Banawiratma and Tom Jacobs, "Doing Theology with

Local Resources: An Indonesian Experiment," *East Asian Pastoral Review*, 1 (1989): 51-72.

[3]Justo L. González, *Christian Thought Revisited: Three Types of Theology*, second edition (Maryknoll, NY: Orbis Books, 1999), 125-145. González distinguishes Irenaeus's approach from the more legalistic approach of Tertullian and the more abstract and academic approach of Origen, both of whom serve as models for the more classical approach to theology.

[4]See D. Forrester, "Praxis," in A. Richardson and J. Bowden, eds., *A New Dictionary of Christian Theology* (London: SCM, 1983), 457; Matthew Lamb, "Praxis," in J. A. Komonchak, M. Collins, and D. Lane, eds., *New Dictionary of Theology* (Wilmington, DE: Michael Glazier, 1987), 784-787; Philip Berryman, *Liberation Theology* (Oak Park, IL: Meyer, Stone, 1987), 86; Max Stackhouse, *Apologia: Contextualization, Globalization, and Mission in Theological Education* (Grand Rapids: Eerdmans, 1988), 84-105; João B. Libânio, "Praxis," in V. Fabella and R. Sugirtharajah, eds., *Dictionary of Third World Theologies* (Maryknoll, NY: Orbis Books, 2000), 172.

[5]Jon Sobrino, "El conocimiento teológico en la teología europea y latinoamericana," in *Liberación y cautiverio: Debates en torno al método de la teología en América Latina* (Mexico City: Comité Organizador, 1975), 177-207. An English summary of this important article is given in Alfred T. Hennelly, "Theological Method: The Southern Exposure," *Theological Studies*, 38, 4 (December, 1977): 718-725.

[6]John Oman, *Grace and Personality* (Cambridge: Cambridge University Press, 1917), 4.

[7]Karl Marx, *Theses on Feuerbach*, 11, in L. D. Easton and K. H. Guddat, eds. and trans., *Writings of the Young Marx on Philosophy and Society* (Garden City, NY: Doubleday Anchor Books, 1967), 402.

[8]Sobrino, "El conocimiento," 93, quoted in Hennelly, "Theological Method": 721.

[9]José Miguez Bonino, *Doing Theology in a Revolutionary Situation* (Philadelphia: Fortress Press, 1975), 72.

[10]Berryman, *Liberation Theology*, 86. For a profound discussion of praxis, see Douglas John Hall, *Thinking the Faith: Christian Theology in a North American Context* (Minneapolis, MN: Augsburg, 1989), 20-21.

[11]For example, Robert J. Schreiter, *Constructing Local Theologies* (Maryknoll, NY: Orbis Books, 1985), 15.

[12]See Browning, *A Fundamental Practical Theology*; Whitehead and Whitehead, *Method in Ministry*; Maddox, "The Recovery of Theology."

[13]Gustavo Gutiérrez, *A Theology of Liberation* (Maryknoll, NY: Orbis Books, 1973), 15. See Juan Luis Segundo, *The Liberation of Theology* (Maryknoll, NY: Orbis Books, 1976): "The one and only thing that can maintain the liberative character of any theology is not its content but its methodology" (39). See also Samuel Rayan, "Third World Theology: Where Do We Go from Here?" in Leonardo Boff and Virgilio Elizondo, eds., *Theologies of the Third World: Convergences and Differences* (*Concilium* 199 [5/1988]) (Edinburgh: T and T Clark, 1988): "We believe that our greatest gain is the articulation of our methodology" (129).

[14]Ecumenical Dialogue of Third World Theologians, Dar es Salaam, Tanzania, August 5-12, 1976, "Final Statement," in Sergio Torres and Virginia Fabella, eds., *The Emergent Gospel* (Maryknoll, NY: Orbis Books, 1978), 269.

[15]Leonardo Boff, "What Are Third World Theologies?" in Boff and Elizondo, *Theologies of the Third World*, 10.

[16]See Schreiter, *Constructing Local Theologies*, 15.

[17]Ada María Isasi-Díaz, "The Task of Hispanic Women's Liberation Theology—

Mujeristas: Who We Are and What We Are About," in Ursula King, ed., *Feminist Theology from the Third World: A Reader* (Maryknoll, NY: Orbis Books, 1994), 90-91.

[18]On this see Pedro Trigo, "Teología de la liberación y cultura," *Iglesia Viva*, 116-117 (March-June, 1985): 121-134; Diego Irrarázaval, "Mission in Latin America: Inculturated Liberation," *Missiology: An International Review*, 20, 2 (April, 1992): 221-239; and *Inculturation* (Maryknoll, NY: Orbis Books, 2000); Paulo Suess, "Evangelization and Inculturation: Concepts, Options, Perspectives," in James A. Scherer and Stephen B. Bevans, eds., *New Directions in Mission and Evangelization 3: Faith and Culture* (Maryknoll, NY: Orbis Books, 1999), 159-174.

[19]"Final Statement," Dar es Salaam, 270.

[20]See Schreiter, *The New Catholicity: Theology between the Global and the Local* (Maryknoll, NY: Orbis Books, 1997); and Katherine Tanner, *Theories of Culture: A New Agenda for Theology* (Minneapolis: Fortress, 1997).

[21]On this see Robert N. Bellah et al., *Habits of the Heart: Individualism and Commitment in American Life* (New York: Harper and Row, 1986); and *The Good Society* (New York: Alfred A. Knopf, 1991). See also Donald P. Gelpi, ed., *Beyond Individualism: Toward a Retrieval of Moral Discourse in America* (Notre Dame, IN: University of Notre Dame Press, 1989).

[22]"Final Statement," Dar es Salaam, 270.

[23]Sobrino, "El conocimiento," 207, quoted in Hennelly, "Theological Method": 724.

[24]Boff, "What Are Third World Theologies?" 10; Rayan, "Third World Theologies," 129.

[25]Berryman, *Liberation Theology*, 85.

[26]Rayan, "Third World Theology," 129, quoting Gutiérrez, *Theology of Liberation*, 8.

[27]Gustavo Gutiérrez, *On Job: God-Talk and the Suffering of the Innocent* (Maryknoll, NY: Orbis Books, 1987), xiii.

[28]See the quotation from Isasi-Díaz above.

[29]See Lamb, "Praxis," 796.

[30]Clodovis Boff, *Feet-on-the-Ground Theology: A Brazilian Journey* (Maryknoll, NY: Orbis Books, 1987). See Susan Brooks Thistlethwaite and Mary Potter Engel, eds., *Lift Every Voice: Constructing Theologies from the Underside* (San Francisco: Harper and Row, 1990), 1-9.

[31]Boff, "What Are Third World Theologies?" 12.

[32]Roger Haight, *An Alternative Vision: An Interpretation of Liberation Theology* (Mahwah, NJ: Paulist Press, 1985).

[33]See, for instance, Yves Congar's influence by the Young Christian Workers in the introduction to *Dialogue between Christians* (Westminster, MD: Newman Press, 1964); and J. Puyo, *Une vie pour la vérité* (Paris: Editions du Centurion, 1975).

[34]D. Ferm, *Third World Liberation Theologies: An Introductory Survey* (Maryknoll, NY: Orbis Books, 1986), 1. See Schreiter, *Constructing Local Theologies*, 15; and Alan Neely, "Liberation Theology and the Poor: A Second Look," *Missiology: An International Review*, XVII, 4 (October, 1989): 387-404.

[35]See King, *Feminist Theology from the Third World*; Rosemary Radford Ruether, *Women and Redemption* (Minneapolis, MN: Fortress Press, 1998); Lynn Japinga, *Feminism and Christianity: An Essential Guide* (Nashville: Abingdon Press, 1999); and Ann Clifford, *Introducing Feminist Theology* (Maryknoll, NY: Orbis Books, 2001).

[36]See Boff and Elizondo, *Theologies of the Third World*; Thistlethwaite and Engel, *Lift Every Voice*; Gregory Baum, "The Impact of Marxist Ideas on Christian Theology," in Gregory Baum, ed., *The Twentieth Century: A Theological Overview* (Maryknoll, NY: Orbis Books, 1999), 173-185; Michael Amaladoss, *Life in Freedom: Liberation Theologies from*

Asia (Maryknoll, NY: Orbis Books, 1997).

[37]This is one of the criticisms leveled by the 1984 "Instruction on Certain Aspects of the Theology of Liberation," issued by the Sacred Congregation for the Doctrine of the Faith. A copy of this document is found in an appendix to Haight's *An Alternative Vision*.

[38]See, for instance, John P. Meier, "The Bible as Source for Theology," in the *Proceedings of the Catholic Theological Society of America*, 1988, 1-14.

[39]Schreiter, *Constructing Local Theologies*, 15. The critique of liberation theology's neglect of popular religiosity, however, is aimed mostly at early published attempts. See, for example, Irrarázaval, *Inculturation*, and Suess, "Evangelization and Inculturation."

[40]See Neely, "Liberation Theology"; Juan Luis Segundo, *Theology and the Church: A Response to Cardinal Ratzinger and a Warning to the Whole Church* (Minneapolis, MN: Seabury-Winston, 1985); and Stackhouse, *Apologia*, 84-105.

[41]Leonardo Boff, *Jesus Christ Liberator: A Critical Christology for Our Time* (Maryknoll, NY: Orbis Books, 1978); *Liberating Grace* (Maryknoll, NY: Orbis Books, 1979); *Trinity and Society* (Maryknoll, NY: Orbis Books, 1988); See my review of *Trinity and Society* in *New Theology Review*, 2, 3 (August, 1989): 104-105.

[42]Boff, *Jesus Christ Liberator*, 46-47; *Liberating Grace*, 79.

[43]Leonardo Boff, *Ecclesiogenesis: The Base Communities Reinvent the Church* (Maryknoll, NY: Orbis Books, 1986); *Church: Charism and Power—Liberation Theology and the Institutional Church* (New York: Crossroad, 1985). In this latter book, see the essays "Models and Pastoral Practices of the Church," 1-11; "Theological Tendencies and Pastoral Practices," 12-21; "The Base Ecclesial Community: A Brief Sketch," 125-130; and "Underlying Ecclesiologies of the Base Ecclesial Communities," 131-137.

[44]Douglas John Hall, *Lighten Our Darkness: Toward an Indigenous Theology of the Cross* (Philadelphia: Westminster, 1976); *Has the Church a Future?* (Philadelphia: Westminster, 1980); *The Steward: A Biblical Symbol Come of Age* (New York: Friendship Press, 1982); *The Stewardship of Life in the Kingdom of Death* (Grand Rapids: Eerdmans, 1985/1988); *Imaging God: Dominion as Stewardship* (New York: Friendship Press, and Grand Rapids: Eerdmans, 1986); *God and Human Suffering: An Exercise in the Theology of the Cross* (Minneapolis, MN: Augsburg, 1986); *Thinking the Faith / Professing the Faith / Confessing the Faith: Christian Theology in a North American Context* (Minneapolis, MN: Augsburg/Fortress, 1989, 1993, 1996).

[45]Hall, *Lighten Our Darkness*, 203.

[46]Ibid., 204.

[47]Hall, *The Steward*, 1-2.

[48]Ibid.

[49]Ibid., 9.

[50]Ibid., 10.

[51]Ibid., 28.

[52]Ibid., 53.

[53]Hall, *The Stewardship of Life in the Kingdom of Death*, xii.

[54]Hall, *Imaging God*; and *God and Human Suffering*.

[55]Hall, *Thinking the Faith*, 13. "*Thinking* faith, as Buri insists, is the only kind of faith that can be taken seriously in today's world" (66).

[56]Ibid., 19.

[57]Ibid., 21.

[58]"*Vivendo, immo moriendo et damnando fit theologus, non intelligendo, legendo aut speculando*" (WA 5.162.28), quoted by Hall in *Thinking the Faith*, 237-238.

[59]Ibid., 238.

[60]Ibid., 172-176.

[61]The term *prophetic realism* is my own, but it captures the sense of Hall's explanation of a third alternative; see, ibid., 176-177. The quotation is from C. F. von Weizsaecker; see ibid., 177, note 34.

[62]Ibid., 140; see 134-141.

[63]Ibid., 201.

[64]Ibid., 197-235.

[65]Virginia Fabella and Mercy Amba Oduyoye, eds., *With Passion and Compassion: Third World Women Doing Theology* (Maryknoll, NY: Orbis Books, 1988).

[66]Ibid., ix-x. See also K. C. Abraham, *Third World Theologies: Commonalities and Convergences* (Maryknoll, NY: Orbis Books, 1990), especially 143-146.

[67]Letty M. Russell, Kwok Pui-lan, Ada María Isasi-Díaz, and Katie Geneva Cannon, eds., *Inheriting Our Mothers' Gardens: Feminist Theology in Third World Perspective* (Philadelphia: Westminster, 1988).

[68]Elsa Tamez, ed., *Through Her Eyes: Women's Theology from Latin America* (Maryknoll, NY: Orbis Books, 1989). The original Spanish version of the book is *El rostro femenino de la teología* (Costa Rica: Departamento Ecuménico de Investigaciones, 1986).

[69]Virginia Fabella and Sun Ai Lee Park, *We Dare to Dream: Doing Theology as Asian Women* (Maryknoll, NY: Orbis Books, 1990).

[70]Virginia Fabella, "Christology from an Asian Perspective," ibid., 10.

[71]Ibid., 5.

[72]Ibid., 6.

[73]Ibid., 9.

[74]Yong Ting Jin, "New Ways of Being Church. II. A Protestant Perspective," ibid., 44-51.

[75]Ibid., 44.

[76]Ibid., 46-47.

[77]Ibid., 47.

[78]Mary John Mananzan, "Redefining Religious Commitment in the Philippine Context," ibid., 101.

[79]Ibid., 113.

[80]Ibid., 108-109.

[81]For example, Robert J. Schreiter, "Signs of the Times: The Future of Religious Life in the United States," *New Theology Review*, 3, 1 (February, 1990): 74-86; Gerald A. Arbuckle, *Out of Chaos: Refounding Religious Congregations* (Mahwah, NJ: Paulist Press, 1988); Sandra M. Schneiders, *Finding the Treasure: Locating Catholic Religious Life in a New Ecclesial and Cultural Context* (Mahwah, NJ: Paulist Press, 2000); and *Selling All: Commitment, Consecrated Celibacy, and Community in Religious Life* (Mahwah, NJ: Paulist Press, 2001); Edênio Valle, SVD, "Mission for the Twenty-First Century in Latin America: A View from the Perspective of the Missionary Religious Life," in Stephen Bevans, SVD, and Roger Schroeder, SVD, eds., *Mission for the 21st Century* (Chicago: CCGM Publications, 2001).

7. THE SYNTHETIC MODEL

[1]Horacio de la Costa, "A Commencement of Teaching," in *The Background of Nationalism and Other Essays* (Manila: Solidaridad, 1965), 70.

[2]This is particularly true of the Old Testament, or Hebrew Scriptures. See Donald Senior and Carroll Stuhlmueller, *Biblical Foundations for Mission* (Maryknoll, NY: Orbis Books, 1983).

[3]This word is used with precision by Aylward Shorter. See *Toward a Theology of Inculturation* (Maryknoll, NY: Orbis Books, 1988), 12.

[4]Paul VI, *Evangelii Nuntiandi* (Washington, DC: U. S. Catholic Conference, 1976), 64. See Shorter, *Toward a Theology of Inculturation*, 206-221, to see Paul VI's whole teaching. Paul VI, like John Paul II after him, feels more comfortable in a translation model. Still, there are glimmers of a deeper understanding in Paul VI's writings, as indeed there are glimmers in John Paul II.

[5]David Tracy, *The Analogical Imagination* (New York: Crossroad, 1981). The following paragraph, the penultimate of the book, expresses Tracy's, and the synthetic model's, purpose quite succinctly: "We understand one another, if at all, only through analogy. Who you are I know only by knowing what event, what focal meaning, you actually live by. And that I know only if I too have sensed some analogous guide in my own life. If we converse, it is likely we will both be changed as we focus upon the subject matter itself—the fundamental questions and the classical responses in our tradition. The analogical imagination seems and is a very small thing. And yet it does suffice" (454-455).

[6]Shorter, *Toward a Theology of Inculturation*, 11. For the concept of "interculturation," see ibid., 13-16. As I understand it, Shorter sees these two terms as roughly the same. See also Robert J. Schreiter, *The New Catholicity: Theology between the Global and the Local* (Maryknoll, NY: Orbis Books, 1997), 46-61. Schreiter here speaks of "intercultural theology."

[7]Leonardo N. Mercado, *Elements of Filipino Theology* (Tacloban: Divine Word University Publications, 1975), 15.

[8]To Thi Anh, *Cultural Values East and West: Conflict or Harmony?* (Manila: East Asian Pastoral Institute, 1975).

[9]Mercado, *Elements of Filipino Theology*, 233.

[10]David Tracy, *Plurality and Ambiguity: Hermeneutics, Religion, Hope* (New York: Harper and Row, 1987), 16.

[11]Shorter, *Toward a Theology of Inculturation*, 247. The book Shorter refers to is *Ma foi d'africain* (Paris, 1985), which appeared in English as *My Faith as an African* (Maryknoll, NY: Orbis Books, 1993).

[12]Shorter, *Toward a Theology of Inculturation*, 247.

[13]See Robert J. Schreiter, *Constructing Local Theologies* (Maryknoll, NY: Orbis Books, 1985), 26-28.

[14]Shorter, *Toward a Theology of Inculturation*, 254.

[15]Ibid., 256.

[16]Krikor Haleblian, "The Problem of Contextualization," *Missiology: An International Review*, XI, 1 (January, 1983):106-108; Stephen Bevans, "Models of Contextual Theology," *Missiology: An International Review*, XIII, 2 (April, 1985): 196-198.

[17]Schreiter, *Constructing Local Theologies*, 22-38, especially the illustration on p. 25.

[18]This is an idea that Shorter, *Toward a Theology of Inculturation*, opposes throughout his book. See, for instance, his treatment of it on pp. 18-20.

[19]Tracy, *Plurality and Ambiguity*, 18.

[20]Ibid., 19.

[21]Shorter, *Toward a Theology of Inculturation*, 6.

[22]Schreiter, *Constructing Local Theologies*, 10.

[23]David J. Hesselgrave and Edward Rommen, *Contextualization: Meanings, Methods,*

and Models (Grand Rapids: Baker Book House, 1989), 79.

[24]C. G. Arévalo, review of Kosuke Koyama, *Mt. Fuji and Mt. Sinai: A Critique of Idols*, *International Bulletin of Missionary Research*, 10, 3 (July, 1986): 141. See also Dale T. Irvin and Akintunde Akinade, eds., *The Agitated Mind of God: The Theology of Kosuke Koyama* (Maryknoll, NY: Orbis Books, 1996).

[25]Kosuke Koyama, *Waterbuffalo Theology* (London: SCM, and Maryknoll, NY: Orbis Books, 1974; twenty-fifth anniversary edition, 1999); *No Handle on the Cross: An Asian Meditation on the Crucified Mind* (London: SCM, 1976, and Maryknoll, NY: Orbis Books, 1977); *50 Meditations* (Belfast: Christian Journals Limited, 1975, and Maryknoll, NY: Orbis Books, 1979); *Three Mile an Hour God: Biblical Reflections* (London: SCM, 1979, and Maryknoll, NY: Orbis Books, 1980). Koyama's second book makes an effort to systematize the idea of the "crucified mind," but it is clear that it is still a collection of essays. Several of these books have appeared at different times and under different titles in other parts of the world.

[26]The British and U.S. editions have different subtitles: Kosuke Koyama, *Mt. Fuji and Mt. Sinai: A Pilgrimage in Theology* (London: SCM, 1985); *Mt. Fuji and Mt. Sinai: A Critique of Idols* (Maryknoll, NY: Orbis Books, 1985).

[27]Gerald H. Anderson and Thomas F. Stransky, eds., *Mission Trends*, nos. 1-3 (Grand Rapids: Eerdmans, and Ramsey, NJ: Paulist Press, 1974, 1975, 1976); Gerald H. Anderson, ed., *Asian Voices in Christian Theology* (Maryknoll, NY: Orbis Books, 1976); Douglas J. Elwood, ed., *Asian Christian Theology: Emerging Themes* (Philadelphia: Westminster, 1980); Kosuke Koyama, "Ecumenical and World Christianity Center, Union Theological Seminary, New York City," *Theological Education* (Spring, 1986): 132-137; "Tribal Gods or Universal God," *Missionalia*, 10, 3 (November, 1982): 106-112; "The Asian Approach to Christ," *Missiology: An International Review*, XII, 4 (October, 1984): 435-447; *Christian Century*, 106: 347, 379, 411, 442, 467, 651.

[28]Koyama, *50 Meditations*, 16.

[29]Koyama, *Waterbuffalo Theology*, 9; this is one of the main ideas of *Mt. Fuji and Mt. Sinai* as well.

[30]Koyama, *Waterbuffalo Theology*, 24; 209-224. This is the basic theme that runs throughout *No Handle on the Cross*.

[31]Koyama, *Three Mile an Hour God*, 3-7; *50 Meditations*, 9-10; *Waterbuffalo Theology*, 133-160; "The Asian Approach to Christ": 438-441.

[32]Koyama, *Waterbuffalo Theology*, viii.

[33]Hesselgrave and Rommen, *Contextualization*, 96.

[34]Ibid., 141.

[35]Kosuke Koyama, *Theology in Contact* (Madras: Christian Literature Society, 1975), 67-68. Quoted in Elwood, *Asian Christian Theology*, 27.

[36]Koyama, *Mt. Fuji and Mt. Sinai*, 212.

[37]Koyama, *Waterbuffalo Theology*, 74. Hesselgrave and Rommen, *Contextualization*, 176, criticize Koyama, however, for what they consider a mistranslation of the German *Anfectung*, which literally means "contestation" or, in theological language, "temptation."

[38]Koyama, *Waterbuffalo Theology*, 74.

[39]For example, in a reference to the Traja people in Central Celebes, who are described as having an entirely Dutch Christianity, complete with the Heidelberg Catechism and Luther's Larger Catechism, Koyama remarks: "I was not sorry to see them there, but I am puzzled why and how they could have remained intact, in their original forms, in lands of such tremendous spiritual and cultural wealth. Wasn't there any need to adjust them or at least to change expressions in a fundamental way? In truth there ought to be a Traja-berg

Catechism instead of the Heidelberg Catechism and a Batak Catechism instead of Luther's Catechism" (*No Handle on the Cross*, 34). Notice the words "adjust" and "change expressions." See also *50 Meditations*, 7-11; *Mt. Fuji and Mt. Sinai*, 53 and 56.

[40]Koyama, *Waterbuffalo Theology*, 133-160.

[41]Ibid., 27-42.

[42]Ibid., 41.

[43]Arévalo, review of *Mt. Fuji and Mt. Sinai*, 141.

[44]Koyama, *Mt. Fuji and Mt. Sinai*, 7.

[45]Koyama, "The Asian Approach to Christ": 445-447.

[46]Several contextual factors might contribute toward such conservative or liberal uses of the same model. In the first place, Koyama comes from the more "dialectical" tradition of Protestantism; de Mesa comes from the more "analogical" tradition of Catholicism. Second, while Koyama is constructing his theology in the context of non-Christian Thailand and Japan, de Mesa speaks out of the overwhelmingly Christian/Catholic world of the Philippines. What seems to be common in both, however, and why I identify them both as practitioners of the synthetic model, is that each is aware of other concerns. On the one hand, Koyama is aware of the goodness of culture and of God's revealing presence within it; on the other, as will be clear in the following summary of de Mesa's thought, some aspects of culture are seen as definitely ambiguous and need to come under the judgment of the gospel. One might, to use David Hesselgrave's and Edward Rommen's classification, speak of Koyama and de Mesa as employing neo-orthodox and neo-liberal methods respectively (see Hesselgrave and Rommen, *Contextualization*, 151-157).

[47]Dr. de Mesa was the first lecturer in the annual series of the Louis J. Luzbetak, SVD, Lectures on Mission and Culture at Catholic Theological Union, Chicago, in the spring of 2000, and so I can personally testify to his engaging speaking style, mild manner, and depth of thought. See *Inculturation as Pilgrimage*, the First Annual Louis J. Luzbetak, SVD, Lecture on Mission and Culture (Chicago: CCGM Publications, 2001). He has contributed to journals such as *Witness*, *UST Journal of Theology*, and *East Asian Pastoral Review*, and his article "Doing Theology as Inculturation in the Asian Context" appears in James A. Scherer and Stephen B. Bevans, eds., *New Directions in Mission and Evangelization 3: Faith and Culture* (Maryknoll, NY: Orbis Books, 1999), 117-133. He has published the following books: *And God Said, "Bahala Na!": The Theme of Providence in the Lowland Filipino Context*, Maryhill Studies 2 (Quezon City: Maryhill School of Theology, 1979); *Isang Maiksing Katesismo Para Sa Mga Bata: A Study in Indigenous Catechesis* (Quezon City: CSP Bookshop, 1984); *In Solidarity with the Culture: Studies in Theological Re-rooting*, Maryhill Studies 4 (Quezon City: Maryhill School of Theology, 1987). With L. Wostyn: *Doing Theology: Basic Realities and Processes* (Manila: Wellspring Books, 1982); *Doing Christology: The Re-appropriation of a Tradition* (Quezon City: Claretian Publications, 1989).

[48](1) There is a way of experiencing reality that leads us to ideological suspicion; (2) application of our ideological suspicion to the whole ideological superstructure in general and to theology in particular; (3) a new way of experiencing theological reality that leads to exegetical suspicion that prevailing interpretation of the Bible has not taken into account important pieces of data; (4) we have a new hermeneutic, i. e., our new way of interpreting the fountainhead of our faith (scripture) with new elements at our disposal. See De Mesa and Wostyn, *Doing Theology*, 71-79.

[49]See ibid., 5-6; the quotation is from 215.

[50]De Mesa, *In Solidarity with the Culture*, 4. This is the essay that appears in Scherer and Bevans, *New Directions 3*.

[51]De Mesa, *In Solidarity with the Culture*, 12-13.

[52]Ibid., 167-168.

[53]Ibid., 102-146.

[54]Ibid., 103. De Mesa identifies the quotation as coming from Frank Lynch, "Catholicism," in *Area Handbook on the Philippines*, II (1956), 662-673.

[55]De Mesa, *In Solidarity with the Culture*, 110.

[56]Ibid., 125.

[57]Ibid., 128.

[58]Ibid., 130.

[59]Ibid., 10.

[60]It is very likely that these cartoons are de Mesa's main contribution to Filipino theology. In a culture in which cartoons and comic books provide most of the reading material, a less linear and textual theological approach may be more relevant than works written with sensitivity to the culture. Comic books and cartoons appeal to subjects of more "oral" cultures, which many Filipino theologians claim Filipinos are.

[61]De Mesa and Wostyn, *Doing Christology*, 5-6.

8. THE TRANSCENDENTAL MODEL

[1]Bernard J. F. Lonergan, *Insight: A Study of Human Understanding* (New York: Philosophical Library, 1957), 396.

[2]See Otto Muck, *The Transcendental Method* (New York: Herder and Herder, 1968).

[3]Bernard J. F. Lonergan, *Method in Theology* (New York: Herder and Herder, 1972), 292.

[4]See Matthew Lamb, "The Notion of the Transcultural in Bernard Lonergan's Theology," unpublished manuscript of a talk given in a Lonergan seminar at the annual convention of the American Academy of Religion, November 19, 1988, p. 10.

[5]Ibid., 15. Given what I have said above, the "I" could just as easily be substituted by a "we."

[6]Bernard J. F. Lonergan, "Lectures on Religious Studies and Theology. Second Lecture: Religious Knowledge," in *A Third Collection* (Mahwah, NJ: Paulist Press, 1985), 129-144. See especially 144.

[7]Carl Rogers, *On Becoming a Person: A Therapist's View of Psychotherapy* (Boston: Houghton Mifflin Company, 1961), 25.

[8]Bernard J. F. Lonergan, "Theology in Its New Context," in L. K. Shook, ed., *Theology of Renewal*, vol. 1, *Renewal of Religious Thought* (Montreal: Palm Publishers, 1968), 45.

[9]See Lonergan, *Insight*, 736; and Lamb, "The Notion of the Transcultural," 17.

[10]See Thomas Gilby, "Theology," in P. K. Meagher, T. C. O'Brien, C. M. Aherne, eds., *Encyclopedic Dictionary of Religion* (Washington, D.C.: Corpus Publications, 1979), "O-Z," 3498. Gilby makes the point that the real master of theology is one who respects not only the faith of simple people who have not been formally trained in theology but also their ability to theologize. As an example, he cites Cajetan, who thought that his washerwoman was not only a better Christian than he but also a better theologian!

[11]Lonergan, *Method in Theology*, 53.

[12]Lonergan, *Insight*, 577-578, 580-581, 586-587; *Method in Theology*, 293.

[13]Tracy, *The Achievement of Bernard Lonergan* (New York: Herder and Herder, 1970), 80. In his essay "Theology in Its New Context," Lonergan speaks of how contemporary theology has undergone a shift from being a deductive to an empirical science. What this means is that "where before the step from premises to conclusions was brief, simple, and

certain, today the steps from data to interpretation are long, arduous, and, at best, probable. An empirical science does not demonstrate. It accumulates information, develops understanding" (38). One of Lonergan's more eminent and creative disciples, John S. Dunne, often speaks of the importance of moving from a search for certitude to a search for understanding. On this see especially Jon Nilson, "Doing Theology by Heart: John S. Dunne's Theological Method," *Theological Studies*, 48 (1987): 71.

[14]See Herbert Anderson, "Seeing the Other Whole," *Mission Studies* 14, 1-2, 27-28 (1997): 40-63; see also Edward Poitras, "The Self of Mission," in the same issue: 22-39.

[15]When a translation of one of my earlier formulations of the various models was published in *Theologie der Gegenwart*, 28 Jg., 3 (1985): 135-47, the transcendental model was not included—with no explanation. I suspect, however, the omission was because the model was not seen as accessible or as practical as the others. Ironically, I have had several persons from the Third World tell me that, of all the models, this was the model they most preferred.

[16]That there may be different ways of knowing is suggested by the title of the book by M. F. Blenky, B. M. Clinchy, N. R. Goldberg, and J. M. Tarule: *Women's Ways of Knowing: The Development of Self, Voice, and Mind* (New York: Basic Books, 1986). Interestingly, however, the way that these authors describe *women's* ways of knowing comes very close to the way transcendental philosophers such as Lonergan describe the way *all people* come to knowledge. Perhaps the conversion needed is toward a more personal, intuitive notion of knowing and truth rather than a conversion toward different ways of knowing for men and women—and/or other cultures. Nevertheless, this model is criticized by several quarters, including a criticism from my friend and colleague Robert Schreiter (see Robert J. Schreiter, "A Semiotic-Linguistic Theory of Tradition: Identity and Communication amid Cultural Difference," in Barbara Schoppelreich and Siegfried Wiedenhofer, eds., *Zur Logik religiöser Traditionen* [Frankfurt: IKO, 1998], 93, quoting Hans Kessler, "Partikularität und Universalität Jesu Christi: Zur Hermeneutik und Kriteriologie kontextueller Christologie," in Raymund Schwager, ed., *Relativierung der Wahrheit? Kontextuelle Christologie auf dem Prüfstand* [Freiburg: Herder, 1998], 116).

[17]Followers of Lonergan would deny this objection in the strongest way possible. See Lamb, "The Notion of the Transcultural"; and Robert M. Doran, "Theological Grounds for a World-Cultural Humanity," in Matthew L. Lamb, ed., *Creativity and Method: Essays in Honor of Bernard Lonergan* (Milwaukee: Marquette University Press, 1981), 105-122.

[18]Robert N. Bellah, Richard Madsen, William M. Sullivan, Ann Swidler, and Stephen Tipton, *Habits of the Heart: Individualism and Commitment in American Life* (New York: Harper and Row, 1985).

[19]John R. Stacer, "The Hope of a World Citizen: Beyond National Individualism," in Donald Gelpi, ed., *Beyond Individualism: Toward a Retrieval of Moral Discourse in America* (Notre Dame: University of Notre Dame Press, 1989), 214. Stacer's essay, focused on the thought of William Ernest Hocking, is part of the second book published by the John Courtney Murray Group, a group of scholars whose project is the construction of an inculturated North American theology. While Lonergan's work is acknowledged by the group, their inspiration comes more from the thought of Josiah Royce and Charles Sanders Peirce, who stress the social dimension of human existence.

[20]Sallie McFague, *Speaking in Parables: A Study in Metaphor and Theology* (Philadelphia: Fortress Press, 1975); *Metaphorical Theology: Models of God in Religious Language* (Philadelphia: Fortress Press, 1982; second printing, with an additional preface, 1985); *Models of God: Theology for an Ecological, Nuclear Age* (Philadelphia: Fortress Press, 1987); *The Body of God: An Ecological Theology* (Minneapolis, MN: Fortress Press, 1993);

Super, Natural Christians: How We Should Love Nature (Minneapolis, MN: Fortress Press, 1997); *Life Abundant: Rethinking Theology and Economy for a Planet in Peril* (Minneapolis, MN: Fortress Press, 2000).

[21]McFague, *Speaking in Parables*, 1.

[22]Ibid., 94.

[23]Ibid., 4-5; 15-17; McFague, *Metaphorical Theology*, 42-54.

[24]McFague, *Metaphorical Theology*, 13.

[25]McFague, *Models of God*, 35.

[26]McFague, *Speaking in Parables*, 2.

[27]McFague, *Metaphorical Theology*, 23.

[28]Ibid. The distinction between metaphor and model is a bit blurred in McFague's subsequent *Models of God*. See 31-40.

[29]McFague, *Metaphorical Theology*, 23.

[30]Ibid., vii.

[31]McFague, *Models of God*, xiv. For a critique of this stance from a liberation theology perspective, see Susan Brooks Thistlethwaite, "'I Am Become Death': God in the Nuclear Age," in Susan Brooks Thistlethwaite and Mary Potter Engel, eds., *Lift Every Voice: Constructing Christian Theologies from the Underside* (San Francisco: Harper and Row, 1990), 102.

[32]McFague, *Metaphorical Theology*, x; *Models of God*, x.

[33]McFague, *Models of God*, x. For further reflection on the notion of "postmodern," see Hans Küng, *Theology for the Third Millennium: An Ecumenical View* (New York: Doubleday, 1988); David J. Bosch, *Transforming Mission: Paradigm Shifts in Theology of Mission* (Maryknoll, NY: Orbis Books, 1991), 349-362; Terrence Tilley, *Postmodern Theologies: The Challenge of Religious Diversity* (Maryknoll, NY: Orbis Books, 1995); and Michael J. Scanlon, "The Postmodern Debate," in Gregory Baum, ed., *The Twentieth Century: A Theological Overview* (Maryknoll, NY: Orbis Books, 1999), 228-237.

[34]McFague, *Metaphorical Theology*, xii.

[35]Ibid., 174. McFague's reference is to E. McLaughlin, "'Christ My Mother': Feminine Naming and Metaphors in Medieval Spirituality," *St. Luke's Journal of Theology*, 18 (1975): 374.

[36]McFague, *Metaphorical Theology*, 179. I personally am not sure of McFague's designation of "friend" as a metaphor. Given the metaphor's "is-is not" quality, could God *not* be a friend? See my review of McFague, *Models of God* in *New Theology Review*, 1, 2 (May, 1988): 103.

[37]Justo L. González, *A History of Christian Thought*, 3 vols. (Nashville: Abingdon Press, 1970, 1971, 1975); with Catherine G. González, *Liberation Preaching: The Pulpit and the Oppressed* (Nashville: Abingdon Press, 1980); *The Theological Education of Hispanics* (Atlanta: FTE, 1988); *Christian Thought Revisited: Three Types of Theology* (Nashville: Abingdon Press, 1989; second edition, Maryknoll, NY: Orbis Books, 1999); *Faith and Wealth: A History of Early Christian Ideas on the Origin, Significance, and Use of Money* (San Francisco: Harper and Row, 1990); *Mañana: Christian Theology from a Hispanic Perspective* (Nashville: Abingdon Press, 1990); *The Acts of the Apostles: The Gospel of the Spirit* (Maryknoll, NY: Orbis Books, 2001).

[38]González, *Faith and Wealth*, vii: "a few years ago I would not even have thought of writing a book such as this. Yet now I am convinced that the issues with which it deals are not only fundamental to an understanding of early Christian theology but are also among the most urgent theological issues of our day. My first word of gratitude must go to those who have led me to this conviction. Unfortunately, in most cases I do not know their names, for

they are legion: a Mexican woman sharing her pain and her hope with other Christians in a dilapidated building; a Colombian young man risking his life daily by speaking the truth over the radio; an Afro-American student challenging me on the relevance of my field of studies, and many, many more."

[39]Ibid., 22-26.

[40]Ibid., 31-42.

[41]Ibid., 26-28, 55-74.

[42]Ibid., 63-66. González might be characterized as a "liberation theologian," and his method employs many of the resources of what I have called the "praxis model." In the introduction to *Faith and Wealth,* presumably written about the same time as *Mañana,* González acknowledges that the development of liberation theology has been the most important factor leading him to a new awareness of the centrality of liberation in Christian theology (*Faith and Wealth*, xii).

[43]González, *Mañana*, 75-87.

[44]González calls Hispanic theology "Fuenteovejuna theology," after the play by Lope de Vega in which the entire town of Fuenteovejuna in fifteenth-century Spain persists in taking responsibility for the murder of its tyrannical ruler, Don Fernán Gómez (see *Mañana*, 28-30). Other Hispanic theologians would speak of Hispanic theology as *teología de conjunto*, or a doing theology together. See Arturo Bañuelas, "U.S. Hispanic Theology," *Missiology: An International Review*, 20, 2 (April, 1992): 275-300.

[45]See Virgilio Elizondo, *Mestizaje: The Dialectic of Cultural Birth and the Gospel* (San Antonio: Mexican American Cultural Center, 1978); and *Christianity and Culture: An Introduction to Pastoral Theology and Ministry for the Bicultural Community* (Huntington, IN: Our Sunday Vistor, 1975); Andrés G. Guerrero, *A Chicano Theology* (Maryknoll, NY: Orbis Books, 1987); Orlando O. Espín, *The Faith of the People: Theological Reflections on Popular Catholicism* (Maryknoll, NY: Orbis Books, 1997).

[46]Although he acknowledges that it is not his invention, I first heard this phrase from my friend and colleague Gary Riebe-Estrella. Riebe-Estrella also cautions that a Hispanic theology is more than "processions and enchiladas."

[47]González, *Mañana*, 140.

[48]Ibid., 141.

[49]Ibid., 143.

[50]Ibid., 145.

[51]Ibid., 150, quoting R. V. Sellers, *The Council of Chalcedon* (London: SPCK, 1953), 210-211.

[52]González, *Mañana*, 149.

9. THE COUNTERCULTURAL MODEL

[1]Darrell Whiteman, "Contextualization: The Theory, the Gap, the Challenge," *International Bulletin of Missionary Research*, 21, 1 (January, 1997): 2.

[2]Quoted in Michael W. Goheen, *"As the Father Has Sent Me, I Am Sending You": J. E. Lesslie Newbigin's Missionary Ecclesiology* (Zoetermeer, Netherlands: Boekencentrum Publishing House, 2001), 357. The quotations are from Alfred G. Hogg, *The Christian Message to the Hindu: Being the Duff Missionary Lectures for Nineteen Forty Five on the Challenge of the Gospel in India* (London: SCM Press, 1945), 9-26; and Hendrik Kraemer, "Continuity and Discontinuity," in *The Authority of Faith: The Madras Series,* vol. 1 (New York, London: International Missionary Council, 1939), 4.

[3]Lesslie Newbigin, *Foolishness to the Greeks: The Gospel and Western Culture*

(London: SPCK, 1986), 5-6. See Goheen, *As the Father Has Sent Me,* 372-376.

[4]Newbigin was in many ways ways an inspiration behind the contemporary form of the countercultural model. After studying at Westminster College, Cambridge, he became a missionary in India in 1936, helped bring about the establishment of the Church of South India, and, at the inauguration of that church in 1947, was ordained one of the first bishops of that church. He subsequently became the chairperson of the International Missionary Council, and upon its integration with the World Council of Churches in 1961, he became the director of the WCC's Division of World Mission and Evangelism. In 1964 he returned to India to become bishop of Madras, and retired in 1974 to England, where he taught at the Selly Oaks Colleges, pastored a parish in Birmingham, and became the leading spirit behind the Gospel and Our Culture Movement in Britain. He died in 1998. For more on Newbigin, see Goheen, *As the Father Has Sent Me*; George R. Hunsberger, *Bearing the Witness of the Spirit: Lesslie Newbigin's Theology of Cultural Plurality* (Grand Rapids: Eerdmans, 1998); and Geoffrey Wainwright, *Lesslie Newbigin: A Theological Life* (Oxford and New York: Oxford University Press, 2000).

[5]Newbigin, quoted in Hunsberger, *Bearing the Witness of the Spirit,* 263; see also Wainwright, *Lesslie Newbigin,* 383-384. Here, of course, the term "syncretistic" is strongly negative, referring to the fact that the church had been coopted by the contemporary western culture of modernity and postmodernity.

[6]*The Kairos Document: Challenge to the Church,* second edition (Braamfontein, South Africa: Skotaville Publishers, 1986); Pope John Paul II, *Evangelium Vitae* (Washington, DC: United States Catholic Conference, 1995); Federation of Asian Bishops' Conferences, "Christian Discipleship in Asia Today: A Service to Life," in Franz-Josef Eilers, ed., *For All the Peoples of Asia, Vol. 2, Federation of Asian Bishops' Documents from 1992 to 1996* (Manila: Claretian Publications, 1997); Latin American Conference of Bishops, "Conclusions," Fourth General Conference of Latin American Bishops, in Alfred T. Hennelly, ed., *Santo Domingo and Beyond* (Maryknoll, NY: Orbis Books, 1993); on the "New Evangelization," see Avery Dulles, "The New Evangelization: Challenge for Religious Missionary Institutes," in Stephen Bevans, SVD, and Roger Schroeder, SVD, eds., *Word Remembered, Word Proclaimed: Selected Papers from Symposia Celebrating the SVD Centennial in North America* (Nettetal, Germany: Steyler Verlag, 1997), 17-31.

[7]See Douglas John Hall, "Ecclesia Crucis: The Theologic of Christian Awkwardness," in George R. Hunsberger and Craig van Gelder, eds., *The Church between Gospel and Culture: The Emerging Mission in North America* (Grand Rapids: Eerdmans, 1996), 199.

[8]Some all too easily, to my mind, equate *countercultural* with a totally negative, "anticultural" stance. A cartoon from the January 2, 1995, *Chicago Tribune,* for example, appearing after the Republican triumph of the "Agenda for America" and the emergence of Newt Gingrich as its champion, shows Michelangelo's *David* in a first frame with the caption: "culture." This is followed by a second frame of a demolished *David* in a second frame, flanked by a somber, axe-wielding Gingrich with the caption "counter-culture." Goheen argues convincingly that Newbigin's position, while highly critical of culture, is not at base *anti*cultural (see Goheen, *As the Father Has Sent Me,* 330-370, for the full argument). George Hunsberger also registers hesitation at the designation "countercultural" for the work of the Gospel and Our Culture Network (GOCN), and always insists that the GOCN is not about "culture bashing." In what follows, I hope it is clear that I heartily agree with him.

[9]H. Richard Niebuhr, *Christ and Culture* (New York: Harper Torchbooks, 1975).

[10]Stanley Hauerwas and William Willimon, *Resident Aliens: Life in the Christian Colony* (Nashville: Abingdon Press, 1989), 47.

[11]See Andrew Sullivan, "This *Is* a Religious War," *New York Times Magazine* (October 7, 2001): 44-47, 52-53.

[12]Lesslie Newbigin, *The Gospel in a Pluralist Society* (Geneva: WCC Publications, and Grand Rapids: Eerdmans, 1989), 141.

[13]Hunsberger, *Bearing the Witness of the Spirit*, 154.

[14]Ibid.

[15]Quoted in Paul Russ Satari, " 'Translatability' in the Missional Approach of Lamin Sanneh," in Hunsberger and van Gelder, *The Church between Gospel and Culture*, 274. From Lamin Sanneh, *Translating the Message: The Missionary Impact on Culture* (Maryknoll, NY: Orbis Books, 1989), 4-5.

[16]George R. Hunsberger, "The Newbigin Gauntlet: Developing a Domestic Missiology for North America," in Hunsberger and van Gelder, *The Church between Gospel and Culture*, 7.

[17]For example, see the introduction to Hunsberger and van Gelder, *The Church between Gospel and Culture*, xvii.

[18]See Gerhard Lohfink, *Jesus and Community: The Social Dimension of Christian Faith*, John Galvin, trans. (Philadelphia: Fortress Press, 1984).

[19]Hauerwas and Willimon, *Resident Aliens*, 44-49.

[20]For example, the exact term is used in ibid.; and in Michael J. Baxter, "Blowing the Dynamite of the Church: A How-To in Catholic Social Theory and Practice," Los Angeles 2001 Religious Education Congress, Convention Seminar Cassettes; James V. Brownson, "Hearing the Gospel Again, for the First Time," in Craig van Gelder, ed., *Confident Witness—Changing World: Rediscovering the Gospel in North America* (Grand Rapids: Eerdmans, 1999), 135-140; Lois Y. Barrett, ed., *Treasure in Clay Jars: Patterns in Missional Faithfulness* (Grand Rapids: Eerdmans, forthcoming). The idea is strongly alluded to, for example, in Newbigin, *Foolishness to the Greeks*, 4 (note the title!); and Darrell L. Guder, ed., *Missional Church: A Vision for the Sending of the Church in North America* (Grand Rapids: Eerdmans, 1998), 109.

[21]This is Newbigin's definition, taken from the *Random House Dictionary*. See Hunsberger, *Bearing the Witness of the Spirit*, 13.

[22]Newbigin, *Foolishness to the Greeks*, 4.

[23]See van Gelder, *Confident Witness—Changing World*, 1; and Barrett, *Treasure in Clay Jars*, 30.

[24]Newbigin, *The Gospel in a Pluralist Society*, 152; see also 195.

[25]Newbigin, *Foolishness to the Greeks*, 4.

[26]Lesslie Newbigin, "The Duty and Authority of the Church to Preach the Gospel," quoted in Wainwright, *Lesslie Newbigin*, 340.

[27]Newbigin, *Foolishness to the Greeks*, 53; quoted in Goheen, *As the Father Has Sent Me*, 338.

[28]See Goheen, *As the Father Has Sent Me*, 337.

[29]See Wainwright, *Lesslie Newbigin*, 35. Here Wainwright is discussing a student paper of Newbigin's that has recourse to both the Protestant Reformers and the theology of Karl Barth. See also Guder, *Missional Church*, ed., 68-69: "It is most critical for the church to develop a confessional understanding of all that God intends for his church, and for the church within this understanding to define itself over against a fallen world."

[30]Hunsberger, *Bearing the Witness of the Spirit*, 195, 33.

[31]These ideas occur over and over again in Newbigin's writings. See, for example, Wainwright, *Lesslie Newbigin*, 384, 387; Newbigin, *The Gospel in a Pluralist Society*, 103-115; Hunsberger, *Bearing the Witness of the Spirit*, 115-123.

[32]David Lowes Watson, "Christ All in All: The Recovery of the Gospel for Evangelism in the United States," in Hunsberger and van Gelder, *The Church between Gospel and Culture*, 197.

[33]See Hunsberger, *Bearing the Witness of the Spirit*, 77-78; Wainwright, *Lesslie Newbigin*, 61.

[34]Watson, "Christ All in All," 189.

[35]Newbigin, *The Gospel in a Pluralist Society*, 13; Hunsberger, *Bearing the Witness of the Spirit*, 125-138; Michael J. Baxter, "Writing History in a World without Ends: An Evangelical Catholic Critique of United States Catholic History," *Pro Ecclesia*, 5 (Fall, 1996): 440-469.

[36]See Wainwright, *Lesslie Newbigin*, 390.

[37]See ibid., 383, 14; Newbigin, *Foolishness to the Greeks*, 20.

[38]Hauerwas and Willimon, *Resident Aliens*, 32; Stanley Hauerwas, *A Community of Character: Toward a Constructive Christian Social Ethic* (Notre Dame, IN: University of Notre Dame Press, 1981).

[39]See Goheen, *As the Father Has Sent Me*, 336-337.

[40]The term "contrast community" is that used by Lohfink, as cited above; the term "parallel community" is developed in Mary Jo Leddy, "The People of God as a Hermeneutic of the Gospel," in van Gelder, *Confident Witness—Changing World*, 303-313; the terms "resident aliens" and "colony of heaven" are from Hauerwas and Willimon, *Resident Aliens*.

[41]Inagrace Dietterich, "Missional Community: Cultivating Communities of the Holy Spirit," in Guder, *Missional Church*, 154. See also Craig Dykstra, "Reconceiving Practice," in Barbara Wheeler and Edward Farley, eds., *Shifting Boundaries: Contextual Approaches to the Structure of Theological Education* (Philadelphia: Westminster/John Knox, 1991), 35-41; Michael J. Baxter, "Reintroducing Virgil Michel: Towards a Counter-tradition of Catholic Social Ethics in the United States," *Communio*, 24 (Fall, 1997): 527-528.

[42]Newbigin, *The Gospel in a Pluralist Society*, 230.

[43]Ibid.

[44]Ibid., 222-233; Wainwright, *Lesslie Newbigin*, 75.

[45]See Darrell L. Guder, *The Continuing Conversion of the Church* (Grand Rapids: Eerdmans, 2000); Craig van Gelder, *The Essence of the Church: A Community Created by the Spirit* (Grand Rapids: Baker Book Company, 2000); Goheen, *As the Father Has Sent Me*, 165-227; Barrett, *Treasure in Clay Jars*. Although I would not exactly call his book an exercise in the countercultural model, one of the main "indicators" that Paul Wilkes gives for an "excellent Catholic parish" is that a parish sees itself as a "missionary outpost," because Catholicism has always recognized that there is something countercultural about it. See Paul Wilkes, *Excellent Catholic Parishes* (Mahwah, NJ: Paulist Press, 2001), 157-158.

[46]The phrase is that of the Catholic sociologist Paul Hanley Furfey, adopted by Michael J. Baxter. See Baxter, "Writing a History in a World without Ends.": 463.

[47]Alan J. Roxburgh, "The Church in a Postmodern Context" in van Gelder, *Confident Witness—Changing World*, 242.

[48]The words "sign, instrument and foretaste" are a favorite description of Newbigin's for the church. See, for example, Goheen, *As the Father Has Sent Me*, 172-175, for a fine summary.

[49]For a powerful defense of missionaries and their preservation of cultures (often in spite of themselves!), see Lamin Sanneh, *Translating the Message*, and *West African Christianity: The Religious Impact* (Maryknoll, NY: Orbis Books, 1983). For a more accusatory perspective, see George Tinker, *Missionary Conquest: The Gospel and Native American Cultural Genocide* (Minneapolis, MN: Fortress Press, 1993); and Jeannette Rodriguez,

"Response to Stephen Bevans," in *Proceedings of the Catholic Theological Society of America*, 2001, 43-48.

[50]Richard J. Mouw, "The Missionary Location of the North American Churches," in van Gelder, *Confident Witness—Changing World*, 6-7.

[51]Tom Beaudoin, *Virtual Faith: The Irreverent Spiritual Quest of Generation X* (San Francisco: Jossey-Bass, 1998). Beaudoin's perspective is that, beyond what seems very negative in contemporary culture, particularly popular youth culture, there are many strands of religious meaning. The book's preface opens up with the memorable line "My most recent religious experience happened at the closing performance of [the Broadway musical] *Rent*" (p. xiii).

[52]Baxter, "Blowing the Dynamite of the Church."

[53]Hunsberger, *Bearing the Witness of the Spirit*, 204-225.

[54]Lesslie Newbigin, *The Other Side of 1984: Questions for the Churches* (London: British Council of Churches; Geneva: WCC Publications, 1984); Newbigin, *Foolishness to the Greeks*. Hunsberger's dissertation was published as *Bearing the Witness of the Spirit: Lesslie Newbigin's Theology of Cultural Plurality* (as cited above). See the opening pages of this book for a personal account of the origins of the Gospel and Culture movement and Hunsberger's acquaintance with Newbigin.

[55]All the books have been cited so far in this chapter. They are *The Church between Gospel and Culture: The Emerging Mission in North America* (1996); *Missional Church: A Vision for the Church in North America* (1998); *Bearing the Witness of the Spirit: Lesslie Newbigin's Theology of Cultural Plurality* (1998); *Confident Witness—Changing World: Rediscovering the Gospel in North America* (1999); *The Continuing Conversion of the Church* (2000); and *Treasure in Clay Jars: Patterns of Missional Faithfulness* (2002).

[56]Hunsberger, "The Newbigin Gauntlet," 17, quoting Kennon L. Callahan, *Effective Church Leadership* (San Francisco: Harper and Row, 1990), 13.

[57]Craig van Gelder, "Defining the Center—Finding the Boundaries: The Challenge of Re-visioning the Church in North America for the Twenty-First Century," in Hunsberger and van Gelder, *The Church between Gospel and Culture*, 43.

[58]Walter C. Hobbs, "Faith Twisted by Culture: Syncretism in North American Christianity," in van Gelder, *Confident Witness—Changing World*, 96-97.

[59]Donald C. Poterski, *Reinventing Evangelism: New Strategies for Presenting Christ in Today's World* (Downers Grove, IL: InterVarsity Press, 1989), 28; quoted in Hunsberger and van Gelder, introduction to *The Church between Gospel and Culture*, xv.

[60]Guder, *Missional Church*, 8.

[61]Ibid., 25, referring to Newbigin's *Foolishness to the Greeks*.

[62]Guder, *Missional Church*, 63.

[63]Ibid., 77.

[64]Ibid., 79

[65]Ibid., 83-85.

[66]Ibid., 81.

[67]Ibid., 108-109.

[68]Ibid., 127.

[69]Ibid., 135.

[70]Ibid., 137-140.

[71]Ibid., 153.

[72]Ibid., 182.

[73]Ibid., 208.

[74]Ibid., 226.

[75]Ibid., 255. The reference is to Charles van Engen, *God's Missionary People: Rethinking the Purpose of the Local Church* (Grand Rapids: Baker Book Company, 1991), 66-70.

[76]Mark S. Massa, *Catholics and American Culture: Fulton Sheen, Dorothy Day, and the Notre Dame Football Team* (New York: Crossroad, 1999), 109-111.

[77]Quoted in Baxter, "Writing History in a World without Ends": 466. I say Baxter quotes Day's title "with glee" because on the audiotape "Blowing the Dynamite of the Church" he adds the aside: "Isn't that great!"

[78]"In the World but Not of the World: The Editors Interview Father Michael Baxter, C.S.C.," *U. S. Catholic*, 66, 8 (August, 2001): 27.

[79]I would like to thank Joel Shorn of *U.S. Catholic* for helping me gather Baxter's writings and for providing me with the tape of Baxter's presentation "Blowing the Dynamite of the Church."

[80]Baxter, "Reintroducing Virgil Michel": 519.

[81]All references to what follows are from the tape of the workshop, as previously cited. It is available from Convention Seminar Cassettes, 4685 Runway Street, Unit N, Simi Valley, CA 93063. It is workshop 601.

[82]This last remark is not Baxter's but my own. On this see John A. Coleman, *An American Strategic Theology* (New York, Ramsey, NJ: Paulist Press, 1982), 71-107.

CONCLUSION

[1]See K. C. Abraham, "An Asian Perspective on the Oaxtepec Conference," in K. C. Abraham, ed., *Third World Theologies: Commonalities and Divergences* (Maryknoll, NY: Orbis Books, 1990), 181-182.

[2]Doug Priest, *Doing Theology with the Maasai* (Pasadena: William Carey Library, 1990), 160.

[3]Robert J. Schreiter, "Introduction: Jesus Christ in Africa Today," in Robert J. Schreiter, ed., *Faces of Jesus in Africa* (Maryknoll, NY: Orbis Books, 1991), viii.

[4]See Stephen Bevans, "Contextual Theology from a First World Perspective," *Diwa: Studies in Philosophy and Theology*, 13, 2 (November, 1988): 69-87; "Singing the Lord's Song in a Foreign Land: The Foreigner as Theology Teacher," *South East Asia Journal of Theology*, 17, 2 (1976): 49-62. What I have found particularly effective is the use of experiences from my own life. Such experiences tend to evoke similar experiences from the students and help them to do their own theologizing out of their own experiences.

Index